The New York Times

IT'S CROSSWORD TIME!

First published in the United States by St. Martin's Griffin,
an imprint of St. Martin's Publishing Group

THE NEW YORK TIMES IT'S CROSSWORD TIME!
Copyright © 2022 by The New York Times Company.
All rights reserved. Printed in the United States of America. For information,
address St. Martin's Publishing Group, 120 Broadway, New York, NY 10271.

www.stmartins.com

All of the puzzles that appear in this work were originally published
in *The New York Times* from January 6, 2008, to December 28, 2008;
from June 5, 2011, to December 4, 2011; or from March 7, 2021,
to July 25, 2021. Copyright © 2008, 2011, 2021 by
The New York Times Company. All rights reserved.
Reprinted by permission.

ISBN 978-1-250-83173-6

Our books may be purchased in bulk for promotional, educational, or business use.
Please contact your local bookseller or the Macmillan Corporate and Premium
Sales Department at 1-800-221-7945, extension 5442, or by email at
MacmillanSpecialMarkets@macmillan.com.

First Edition: 2022

10 9 8 7 6 5 4 3 2

The New York Times

IT'S CROSSWORD TIME!
100 Sunday Crossword Puzzles

Edited by Will Shortz

ST. MARTIN'S GRIFFIN
NEW YORK

1   TAKE TWO

ACROSS

1 After the fact, as a justification
8 Co-star of "Golden Girls"
17 Knock over, so to speak
20 Quaker fare
21 Go poof
22 Drop the ball
23 ILLUS_RA_ORS
25 What a third wheel might see, in brief
26 Setting for most of "Life of Pi"
27 Tests the weight of
28 One of the Greats?
30 Oscars of the sporting world
33 Good sign for an angel
34 Intl. org. headquartered in Geneva
37 Some bad sentences
39 ACC_L_RATOR
44 Grapple, in dialect
47 Exercise too much, say
48 A as in Arles
49 LUXUR_ _ACHT
54 "_ Agnus Dei" (Mass phrase)
55 Peak in Turkey mentioned in both the "Iliad" and the "Aeneid"
56 Runner Sebastian who once held the world record for the mile
57 What you might get from a trailer
59 Sport played at British boarding schools
60 Post production?
64 _ mater, membrane surrounding the brain
65 Popular 90-min. show
66 ENDANGER_EN_
70 Man's name that coincidentally is Latin for "honey"
73 Word with small or fish
74 Weak
75 What may result in a handshake
76 Help to one's destination
82 The Blue Jays, on scoreboards
83 Comeback to a challenge of authority
84 Bitter
85 CONFIG_ _ATION
90 Actor Somerhalder
91 Most in the style of comedian Steven Wright
92 Unfocused
93 POI_T OF _IEW
100 Go all out
101 French fashion inits.
102 "Kinda sorta"
103 Pan-cook, in a way
107 Supermodel Bündchen
109 Pepé _ (cartoon skunk)
111 Drop off
112 Admit (to)
113 _OTIC_
120 Hit the weed?
121 Have guests over
122 Guest, e.g.
123 Place full of guests
124 Start of a seasonal request
125 Some kitchen utensils

DOWN

1 Entourage
2 Hall's partner in pop
3 Part of a thong
4 "OK, you can stop the story right there"
5 Old-fashioned "cool"
6 One might speak under it
7 Co-star of Kline in "A Fish Called Wanda"
8 Start of a compilation heading
9 Times for some vigils
10 Letters on many towers
11 Busy mo. for C.P.A.s
12 Go bad
13 Three-sport event, for short
14 A chest often has a large one
15 States
16 Recharge
17 Photocopy, e.g.
18 It's the law!
19 Item said to have been burned in protest, once
24 Musical prefix with beat
29 Memphis-to-Nashville dir.
31 Emphatic assent
32 Lively dance genre
34 Hone
35 Contract details
36 Beehive State city
38 Aerodynamic
40 Bishop's jurisdiction
41 Antagonist
42 Hotel room staples
43 Top-notch
44 Booties
45 Playwright Chekhov
46 Garbage
50 Drink similar to a slushie
51 About 460 inches of rain per year, on Kauai's Mt. Waialeale
52 HBO satire starring Julia Louis-Dreyfus
53 _ bar
54 Org. that takes the lead on lead?
58 Baby fox
60 How a flirt may act
61 Football stat: Abbr.
62 NaOH
63 Radio broadcaster: Abbr.
66 Legislation that was part of F.D.R.'s New Deal
67 Ethnic group of Rwanda and Burundi
68 Two, for four
69 Coin with 12 stars
70 "Zoom-Zoom" sloganeer
71 Hollywood composer Bernstein with 14 Oscar nominations
72 Guarded
73 Like pets and parking meters
75 _ Slam (tennis feat)
76 Julius Caesar's first name
77 Words of hopelessness
78 Mature naturally, in a way
79 _ Writers' Workshop
80 Electronic Hasbro toy
81 One side of the coin
83 Arias, typically
86 Scottish folk dance
87 Alternative explanation for a lucky guess, in brief
88 Ear: Prefix
89 Letters on some badges
94 "Stillmatic" rapper
95 Seen

by Celeste Watts and Jeff Chen

96 Kind of skate
97 Brown shade
98 Kids' observation game
99 Hit musical with an "Emerald City Sequence"
104 Yoke
105 HP product
106 Narrowly beats (out)
108 Singer James
109 Drink for un bébé
110 A full moon will do this
112 Life force, in China
114 ___ Majesty
115 Hosp. areas
116 The Jazz, on scoreboards
117 Brown shade
118 Things for happy campers?
119 Picky person's pick?

THEY ALL LAUGHED

ACROSS

1 Some rappers
4 Music genre for Carmen Miranda
9 Pioneer in 35mm cameras
14 Bit of bait
18 His face overlooks Havana's Plaza de la Revolución
19 Fire ___
20 See 67-Across
21 Refurbish
22 Architectural innovation jokingly predicted by 101-Across in 1982
26 Actress Perez
27 Performer's showcase
28 Gave out
29 God of love
30 Goofy images, perhaps?
32 Kitchen brand whose name becomes an animal after adding a "t"
33 Old N.Y.C. subway inits.
36 Wish list items
38 Grooming tool jokingly predicted by 101-Across in 1979
41 "Gotcha"
43 ___ Sea, whose eastern basin has become a desert
44 Either spy to the other in "Spy vs. Spy"
45 Prop in a Shakespeare tragedy
47 Abbr. at the end of a planner
48 Classic board game derived from pachisi
50 Place to order a cassoulet
52 Writing aid jokingly predicted by 101-Across in 1967
55 Therefore
56 ___ block
57 Midnight trip to the fridge, say
58 "Yellow Flicker Beat" singer, 2014
59 Type of headsail
62 Super-duper
63 Shake off
65 Hammer out, say
66 "___ Lisa"
67 With 20-Across, yearly
68 Some sports car options
69 Painter Paul
70 "Them's the breaks!"
72 Butler played by Gable
73 Winter sport jokingly predicted by 101-Across in 1965
75 Treadmill settings
77 They're not known for neatness
78 Word connecting two place names
79 Word connecting two last names
80 Taters
81 Ragamuffin
82 Nominee's place
84 Telephone feature jokingly predicted by 101-Across in 1961
89 Porters, e.g.
92 Stampede member in "The Lion King"
93 Manual readers
94 "___ fun!"
95 Early smartphone model
96 Italian lager
98 Square thing
100 Like some rights and engineers
101 Satirical cartoonist, born 3/13/1921, known for dreaming up ridiculous inventions . . . or are they?
107 Ransacks
108 Peter the Great and others
109 Eponym of an M.L.B. hitting award
110 Jellied British delicacy
111 Goes down
112 Fender product, for short
113 Windows forerunner
114 Droll

DOWN

1 Phil of "Dr. Phil"
2 Intensity of color
3 When the president may make a pitch
4 Ump's call
5 Comedian Wong
6 Gym array
7 Sweet bread
8 Not as scarce
9 Language not traditionally written with spaces between words
10 Ambient musician Brian
11 Like Bach's first two "Brandenburg" Concertos
12 Like dice, shapewise
13 Finding it funny
14 Off the mark
15 Substance that helps a spaceship's fuel burn
16 Direct
17 It's greener the higher it is, for short
21 Glow, in a way
23 Narrow inlet
24 Part
25 ___ of Man
31 Exposed to high heat, in a way
32 Cosmetics brand with "Face anything" ads
34 Ex-QB football analyst Tony
35 Word repeated before "again"
37 Move stealthily
38 Big part of the S&P 500
39 "It's co-o-old!"
40 Toss in a chip, maybe
42 Hid
45 Org. concerned with performance rights
46 Mace, for one
48 Oodles
49 "___ From Muskogee" (Merle Haggard hit)
50 Cartoonist Dave famous for "The Lighter Side of . . ."
51 How anatomy charts are drawn
53 Mormon church, for short
54 Blow
55 "Mountain of God," in Exodus
58 Longtime name in cinemas
59 Hire calling?
60 Like slapstick comedies
61 Feature of a Care Bear's belly
64 Oodles
65 Hazard on an Arctic voyage
66 1960s style
68 Blues ensemble?
69 Slices easily (through)
71 Brush brand
72 Command+Y, on a Mac
73 Swizzle

by Jacob Stulberg

74 Cartoon speech bubble, often
75 Whirled around
76 Sting, e.g.
77 Egg holders
80 Droop
81 Most sinewy
82 Its coat of arms features a marlin and flamingo, with "the"
83 Baseball's "Big Papi"
85 Since
86 Principles
87 Russian assembly
88 Gutter nuisance in cold climates
90 Apt surname for a hot dog vendor?
91 Alone
97 Gobbles up
99 Suet alternative
100 Survivalist's stockpile
101 It might come in a yard glass
102 High toss
103 Crew's control?
104 ___ diavolo (in a peppery tomato sauce)
105 Year-round Phoenix hrs.
106 Sticky stuff

3   MORES

ACROSS

1 SAT section eliminated by the College Board in 2021
6 Firth person?
10 Best-selling book of all time
15 Get the attention of
19 Sister-in-law of Prince William
20 Lead-in to pilot
21 Stick on
22 "Goodness gracious!"
23 Nod off at a self-serve restaurant?
26 Jupiter, exempli gratia
27 [Turn the page]
28 Sooner, informally
29 Diamond stat
30 Get down and dirty, in dialect
32 Bovine disease
34 Fancy flooring for an R.V.?
38 Home of Etihad Airways: Abbr.
39 Eyeball creepily
40 Requirement
41 Hoops grp.
44 Like universal blood recipients
48 One layer of a seven-layer dip
50 What the prestigious ice sculptor had?
55 Unable to think clearly
59 Goes nowhere, say
60 Word with holy or heating
61 Grammy-winning singer Cash
63 Certain elite school
64 Appear
65 Back in the U.S.S.?

66 Org. to which Taft was elected president after serving as U.S. president
67 "Yes, that's clear"
69 "Let everyone else get some steak before taking seconds!"
74 Mooches
76 Mate
77 Grand Central info
78 Surreptitious bit of communication
81 "What have we here!"
82 Like many characters in Alison Bechdel cartoons
84 Nintendo release of 2006
85 Show runner
86 2013 Tony winner for Best Revival of a Musical
88 "We should stall!"
91 Long-stemmed mushroom
93 Egyptian god of the afterlife
94 Llama's head?
95 Button clicked to see the rest of an article
97 Not out, say
101 Target of the heckle "What game are you watching?!"
103 Why no one hangs out in actors' dressing rooms these days?
107 Played obnoxiously loudly
111 At 10 or 11 p.m., say
112 Part of lifeguard training
113 Navigation app
115 Lucky charm

116 American ___ (century plant)
117 Bathroom fixture that one never asked for?
122 Their heads get dirty
123 Dirt
124 Typos for exclamation marks if you fail to hit Shift
125 Opposite of neat
126 ___ strategy
127 Fills to the max
128 Set (on)
129 Bathroom door sign

DOWN

1 ___ salt (magnesium sulfate)
2 Mixed martial arts great Anderson
3 What a hiree should be brought up to
4 Brief summary
5 Gab
6 Knocked in a pocket, in pool
7 Handle a job satisfactorily
8 Additional
9 ___ the line
10 Trinket
11 Less certain
12 Many a maid of honor, informally
13 Create an account?
14 Not included
15 Marvel group led by Hercules
16 ___ monkey
17 Lucky charm
18 Plague
24 "My treat next time!"
25 Cheese sometimes paired with fig jam
31 Subject of the Iran-contra affair
33 Requirements for witnesses
35 Jessica of "L.A.'s Finest"

36 Believer in Jah
37 Book fair organizer, maybe, in brief
41 Longtime procedural set in Washington, D.C.
42 Foreshadow
43 Pass up?
45 Declare
46 "All in the Family" mother
47 Tissue that's prone to tearing, for short
49 Italian car since 1907
51 Enemy in the game Doom
52 Sticks in a box?
53 Style of women's leather handbags
54 Isaac and Rebekah's firstborn
56 Piece with a title like "10 Best Places to . . ."
57 First mate?
58 Recolor
62 Comparatively neat
65 Johnson & Johnson skin care brand
68 Moniker after a lifestyle change
70 Initial problem for a storied duckling
71 Man's nickname that sounds like consecutive letters of the alphabet
72 "Phooey!"
73 Japanese "energy healing"
74 Bread for dipping
75 Golden ratio symbol
79 Actress Patricia of "Breakfast at Tiffany's"
80 Phone, wallet, ___ (traveler's mental checklist)
83 Gaudy jewelry
84 Word in obituaries

by Julian Kwan

85 Eponymous member of the Ford family
87 Most cheerful
89 Fictional establishment selling Duff Beer
90 Option for an overnight guest
92 Campsite org.
95 Antacid brand
96 Forms of some mythological sea creatures
98 Turn into
99 Bob hopes?
100 Garment worn with a choli
102 Something Pharaoh's dream foretold in Genesis
103 Make a goat
104 Heavies
105 "Pearls Before ___" (comic strip)
106 Put away
108 Sculptor with a dedicated museum in Philadelphia
109 Throw out
110 Showers attention (on)
114 Lemon bar ingredient
118 Food service industry lobby, for short
119 Command to a dog
120 Male swan
121 Slow (down)

4 OVER THE MOON

ACROSS

1 Pest control product
5 Luggage label
10 Color effect in graphic design
18 Video game princess of the Kingdom of Hyrule
19 Writer Zora ___ Hurston
20 Take part in a D&D campaign, e.g.
21 Brand of fruity hard candy
23 Personae non gratae
24 URANUS
25 "Arrivederci!"
26 Jerks
27 "___ to differ!"
28 One taking the long view?
31 Tarot deck character
35 Some surgical tools
38 "Unit" of fun
39 All-star duo?
40 Comfort in not knowing, say
47 Request
50 JUPITER
51 Ships passing in the night?
52 Sch. on the Rio Grande
54 Hollers
55 Like some parties and flowers
56 "Back to the Future" antagonist
60 Hit movie released as "Vaselina" in Mexico
62 Husk-wrapped dish
65 Colorful tropical fish
66 Song standard on "Barbra Streisand's Greatest Hits"
71 SATURN
72 With 11-Down, hit 2001 film with an "!" in its title
73 Stirred up
74 Cold shower?
75 Muralist ___ Clemente Orozco
76 2021 Super Bowl champs
80 Boy, in Barcelona
81 Animated character who wears a red shirt and no pants
82 Time before computers, facetiously
85 Fleet runner: Abbr.
86 One feature of a perfect nanny, in a "Mary Poppins" song
91 MARS
92 Hesitate in speaking
93 More inquisitive
98 Jaded sort
99 Solo flier?
105 Prefix meaning "both"
106 Welled (up)
108 Like people who are much looked up to
109 Insurance fraud ploy
110 Determiner of cannabis legality, e.g.
113 Classic carnival ride
116 Cherished family member
117 NEPTUNE
118 Golding of "Crazy Rich Asians"
119 Sporty car
120 Deliver a speech
121 World of Warcraft spellcaster

DOWN

1 Leans (on)
2 Claim
3 Pastoral poem
4 ___ es Salaam
5 Navel type
6 Sticker on the back of a laptop, say
7 Home to the Sugar Bowl and Heavenly ski resorts
8 Draft pick?
9 Neighbor of Belg.
10 Word after focus or Facebook
11 See 72-Across
12 Mountain map figs.
13 Ones getting the message
14 Rio beach of song
15 Hollow center?
16 Turner who led an 1831 slave rebellion
17 Grateful sentiments, in online shorthand
18 "The Greek" of film
21 Corner space in Monopoly
22 Juggling or magic, in a talent show
26 Nobel laureate Morrison
29 Poker variety
30 "This Will Be" singer Natalie
32 Sommelier's métier
33 "Monsters, ___"
34 Be on the level?
36 "Notorious" Supreme Court initials
37 Knocked 'em dead
39 Not spoiled
41 Suffix with serpent
42 One of five in "pronunciation": Abbr.
43 Choice of sizes, briefly
44 Celebratory, quaintly
45 Deception
46 Cowboy or Patriot, for short
47 Zeros
48 Distinct melodic segment
49 Not waver from
53 Fruit also called a custard apple or prairie banana
55 Baby's cry
56 Cue at an audition
57 Land jutting into il Mediterraneo
58 Quaker
59 Community of followers
61 Thesaurus listing: Abbr.
63 Melber of MSNBC
64 Candy featured in a classic "MythBusters" episode
65 Confucian's spiritual path
67 In ___ (peeved)
68 Nintendo dinosaur who eats fruit and throws eggs
69 Bring to court
70 2003 best seller whose title is one letter different from a fantasy creature
75 Pleasures
77 Grammy winner DiFranco
78 Rendezvoused
79 ___ gow (Chinese domino game)
81 Money earned from an event, say
82 Gush
83 Archaeologist's find
84 Brian once of glam rock
86 U.S. health org.
87 "Hands off, that's mine!"
88 Austrian article
89 Sent off
90 Lose a layer
94 Bit of luau wear

by Olivia Mitra Framke

95 "No question!"
96 Magazine whose 60th anniversary issue had the cover line "Denzel, Halle & Jamie"
97 What's hard about a melon?
99 Origami shape called "orizuru"
100 Tree surgeon, at times
101 Interior chambers
102 Gem weight
103 Bonnie's partner in crime
104 Quadratic formula subj.
107 Oodles
109 Measurement in plane geometry
110 Camera type, briefly
111 As well
112 DuVernay who directed "Selma"
113 Queue before P
114 Canal locale
115 Piece de resistance?

GAME CHANGERS

ACROSS

1 Chow down on
6 "Exactly like this"
12 Word with mild or well
20 Character often found in children's books
21 Emotionally process, in modern lingo
22 Repeated cry in 1931's "Frankenstein"
23 *Perfect curveball?
25 Ivy League city
26 Jam
27 Crucial
28 White coat?
30 Course standards
31 Emergency room concern
33 *Batting coach's instruction to a lackadaisical hitter?
37 Habitual drinkers
39 Opposed (to)
40 *Apprentice groundskeepers?
46 Singer/songwriter Parks with the 2021 album "Collapsed in Sunbeams"
47 It might get pulled in both directions
50 New York's Mount ___ Hospital
51 Dark wine grape
52 Part of a heartbeat
54 Diplomatic official: Abbr.
55 Corn core
57 Cancels
60 Alacrity
61 Afternoon socials
63 Where dreams are made
65 *Overenthusiastic description of a routine base hit?
68 Stand-in for Middle America

71 Pair of socks?
72 *Umpire's aid in judging foul balls?
78 GPS approximation
79 Sgt. and cpl., e.g.
83 Airer of "Nancy Drew"
84 Old salt
86 Fury
88 State where M.L.K. marched: Abbr.
89 Some fins
92 King James on a court
94 Do as Henry VI did
96 Letters on some foundations
97 Jumpy sorts, in brief
99 *Long hours of fielding practice?
101 ___ only
103 Tilting
104 *Imperceptible fastball movement?
109 All over the place
113 Jimmy ___ (luxury shoe brand)
114 Scientist buried in Westminster Abbey
115 Pop artist who sings "Satisfied" on "The Hamilton Mixtape"
116 New ___ (cap brand)
117 Trouble, metaphorically
120 Ballgame extenders . . . and what can literally be found in the answers to the asterisked clues
124 Beekeeper
125 ___ to go
126 Run-D.M.C. and the Jonas Brothers, for example
127 Bands' performance sheets
128 Unruffled
129 ___ Domingo

DOWN

1 Bird that can spend up to 10 months in the air without landing
2 Absolute bottom
3 Digital assistant
4 Food packaging abbr., once
5 What's heard at many a coffeehouse
6 Group sometimes said to be "out"
7 French article
8 Pampering place
9 In use
10 Candle choice
11 Gumbo pods
12 Goddess with a sacred owl
13 Designers' studios
14 Its capital is Sydney: Abbr.
15 "Uh-uh"
16 Go by
17 Compete with
18 Part of EGBDF
19 Places to play cards, often
24 The Daily ___ (online news site)
29 ___ culpa
32 It plays a role in arm-twisting
33 "Venerable" saint
34 Manual readers
35 Air France hub
36 It brought Hope to the world
38 When doubled, a Nabokov protagonist
40 Pre-bar challenge, briefly
41 "Je t'___"
42 Org. with Fire and Sparks
43 It was first won by the N.Y. Mets in 1969
44 Snow blower brand
45 Word on some Oreo packages

47 Nothing special
48 Tina Turner, voicewise
49 Goldenrod, e.g.
53 Append
56 Instrument with a flared end
58 Chinese steamed bun
59 Ratio of an angle's opposite side to the hypotenuse
62 Blueprint details
64 Runs out of juice
66 Eye cream ingredient
67 Symbol on Captain America's shield
69 Villainous English king in "Braveheart"
70 Outstanding pitcher
72 Former Ford models
73 Seller of Belgian waffles and French toast (fittingly, considering the "I" in its name)
74 Super Soaker Soakzooka brand
75 Like some orders
76 Ancient halls
77 Eldest Stark son on "Game of Thrones"
80 G.I.'s garb, at times
81 Speed skater Johann ___ Koss, winner of four Olympic golds
82 One-named Nigerian Grammy winner
85 Pained sound
87 In the Renaissance, they were known as "mala insana" ("mad apples")
90 Baseball's Gehrig and Piniella
91 Most reliable
93 Russian city on the Ural River
95 Butterlike spread

by Angela Olson Halsted and Doug Peterson

98 French West Indies resort island, familiarly
100 Keep from flying, maybe
101 Profession
102 Camera inits.
104 "With any luck . . ."
105 Tag line?
106 Fancy pourers
107 Paper route hour, maybe
108 Headliner's cue
110 Land between Togo and Nigeria
111 Insider's vocabulary
112 Catch with a throw
113 Alternative to Chuck
115 Wistful sound
118 Man's name that's 123-Down reversed
119 Stanza contraction
121 Home of the world's largest carnival
122 Word with red or army
123 Man's name that's 118-Down reversed

MERGER MANIA

ACROSS

1 Men are pigs (after she's through with them, anyway!)
6 The "A" of James A. Garfield
11 Naysayers
20 Lower-cost option on a popular rideshare app
21 Egg: Sp.
22 Frontiersman's headgear
23 Result of a merger between Quaker Oats and Greyhound?
25 Maintaining equilibrium
26 Discourage
27 Soft drink concentrate, e.g.
29 "Night on Bald Mountain" or "Finlandia"
30 With 18-Down, what has four legs and sprints?
32 Musician who was booed in 1965 for playing electric guitar
34 Letters before Gerald R. Ford and Ronald Reagan
35 Luau instrument, for short
37 Zoom
39 Corner
41 Second-longest human bone, after the femur
46 Result of a merger between Kraft and Hershey's?
51 Result of a merger between Google and Planters?
53 Like the wights on "Game of Thrones"
54 Best of the best
56 Spelling ___
57 What Santa checks twice
58 R-rated
59 Rulers' staffs
61 Fire man?
63 On the ___
64 Poet Lazarus
66 Prefix with thermal
67 Bad sound for an engine
68 Result of a merger between Hasbro and Nikon?
72 Bird like the Canada goose or arctic tern
75 Lummox
76 Cheese offered tableside at Italian restaurants, informally
77 Recipe amt.
80 Eagle constellation
81 Passive acquiescence
84 Voice a view
86 Firm decision maker?
87 Revolutionary Guevara
89 Klum of "Project Runway"
90 "My love," in Madrid
91 Result of a merger between Procter & Gamble and Jacuzzi?
94 Result of a merger between Hormel and Instagram?
96 Warehouse
97 10 to 10, say
99 ___ reform, cause for the Marshall Project
100 Middling grade
101 Pub choice
103 Shot across the bow?
106 ___ Waldorf, the so-called "Queen B" on "Gossip Girl"
109 Leaves nothing to the imagination
114 Measured
116 "Been there, done that" feeling
118 Disney's world
120 Result of a merger between Ralph Lauren and Starbucks?
123 "Stop your foolishness outside!"
124 Not on
125 Chops up finely
126 Was uncomfortably hot
127 Basil-based sauce
128 ___ Allen, one of the founders of Vermont

DOWN

1 ___-de-sac
2 Ditto, in scholarly journals
3 Brexit vote, e.g.
4 Home to the Minoan civilization
5 Shine
6 "Now I get it!"
7 2021 Super Bowl champs
8 Drink up during a timeout, say
9 Tex who directed the first Bugs Bunny cartoon
10 Iraqi city on the Tigris
11 Kimono accessory
12 Natural talent
13 ___ Young-White, comedian/correspondent for "The Daily Show"
14 Lead-in to an Indiana "-ville"
15 ___ Ng, author of the 2017 best seller "Little Fires Everywhere"
16 Piehole
17 "Oops!"
18 See 30-Across
19 Part of a musical note
24 Held forth
28 "Two thumbs down" review
31 Answer to "Are you asleep?" that can't be true
33 Drift off to sleep
35 Ordinary
36 "Eh, not really"
38 1981 hit Genesis album whose name resembles a rhyme scheme
40 Balls in the sky
42 Little sounds
43 Muscular
44 "Who's there?" response
45 Nancy who served as the first female member of the British Parliament
47 Come together
48 Like some thinking
49 A.O.C., e.g.
50 Meets
52 Evening prayer
55 Come together
59 Raw material?
60 Quintana ___ (Mexican state that's home to Cancún)
62 Mayhem
65 Land governed by the House of Grimaldi
67 Obedience school command
68 More hackneyed
69 A head
70 A head
71 Best-case scenarios
72 Clipper parts
73 "You can't fire me!"
74 Italian poet Cavalcanti who influenced Dante
77 Procrastinator's problem
78 [Bo-o-o-oring!]
79 In essence
81 Where heroes are made

by Dick Shlakman and Will Nediger

82 Sass
83 Co-founder of the N.A.A.C.P.
85 Word that, when spelled backward, becomes its own synonym
88 Member of the inn crowd?
90 One of the Canterbury pilgrims
92 One doing the lord's work
93 In which you might do a deep dive
95 Mistruth
98 JAMA contributors
102 Tool in a wood shop
104 Shred
105 ___ hole
107 Battery part
108 Language group related to Yupik
109 Birkin stock?
110 From scratch
111 Quinceañera, e.g.
112 Man's name that spells a fruit backward
113 Passed-down stories
115 "Stop stalling!"
117 "The slightest" or "the foggiest" thing
119 Oscar-winning lyricist Washington
121 Classic Pontiac
122 Phishing target, for short

A RARE FIND

ACROSS

1 Not express, in a way
6 Second person in the Bible
10 One of the Blues Brothers
14 "History of the World, __" (Mel Brooks film that doesn't actually have a sequel)
15 Grp. with Bills and Chargers
18 Bridal adornment at Indian weddings
20 Buckets
21 Goggle
22 Bird that went the way of the dodo (before the dodo)
23 Mr. __, scheming socialite in "Emma"
24 See 105-Across
25 Popular action film franchise . . . or what trying to find the item in this puzzle can be described as
29 "There's no use" . . . like trying to find the item in this puzzle?
31 "The __ Holmes Mysteries," young adult series made into a 2020 film
32 Hosp. procedure
33 Keys
34 Architect Maya
35 Foreign correspondent, maybe
38 1976 greatest hits album with a palindromic title
41 Site of Hercules' first labor
45 What's-__-name
46 Experimental offshoot of punk
49 Echidna's prey
50 Service with nearly two billion users
53 __ reaction
54 Deep cut
55 Liquor store requests
56 Frees (of)
57 Quiet summons
59 Greases
61 What's at the center of some court battles?
62 City of Angels
64 Danger for an exterminator
65 Scratch the surface of
66 Certain customizable computer game character
67 Kick starter?
70 America of "Ugly Betty"
72 [Batman punches a bad guy]
73 Onetime name for China
74 They have big mouths
76 Over
77 More than umbrage
78 Two-wheeled carriage
79 "Anchorman" anchorman
80 Simple earrings
81 Duck Hunt console, for short
82 Walking with flair
84 Odd article of clothing to wear with a tank top
85 Reached
87 Man's name that anagrams to HYENAS
88 Did a Don Corleone impression, maybe
92 Consonantless "yes"
94 Actress Atwell of the "Avengers" movies
96 Product whose sizes have letters
97 Clickable images
99 "As you can imagine . . ."
103 Item hidden somewhere in this puzzle (where is it?)
105 With 24-Across, Emmy winner for "Once and Again"
106 Writer Horatio
107 Word before an explanation
108 Boxer Ali
111 Bookmarked things
112 Vowelless "yes"
113 Personal datum: Abbr.
114 Long-gone
115 Site that competes with Amazon Handmade
116 Affliction also known as a hordeolum
117 Mean

DOWN

1 Collectible records
2 __ milk
3 Packs tightly
4 Areas in many malls
5 Eldest of the von Trapp children
6 Mnemosyne's daughters
7 Benefits
8 En pointe, in ballet
9 Pizza chain since 1943, familiarly
10 Weapon for Samson against the Philistines
11 Whatsoever
12 "North" or "South" land
13 Undoing
15 Faulty
16 Subway fare
17 Impact equally in the opposite direction
19 Actor Elgort of "The Fault in Our Stars"
26 Taints
27 Sheepish response to "Where did the last cookie go?"
28 How checks are written
29 Hellion
30 "Boyz N the Hood" protagonist
36 Run an online scam
37 Feel rotten
39 Bona fide
40 Big brush maker
42 Starting point on a computer
43 Won over
44 See 50-Down
47 Become rigid and inflexible
48 Slides
50 With 44-Down, making futile attempts . . . and an extra hint to this puzzle's theme
51 Small black-and-white treat
52 Batman portrayer on '60s TV
57 Google Photos precursor
58 Workers in forges
59 Murder weapon in "The Talented Mr. Ripley"
60 What "/" may mean
63 Key used to get out, but not in
64 Man's name that means "king"
68 Palindromic leaders
69 Doctor's order
71 They may be fixed
74 Highland beauty
75 The titular bad guy in "The Good, the Bad and the Ugly"
79 Capital of Saudi Arabia

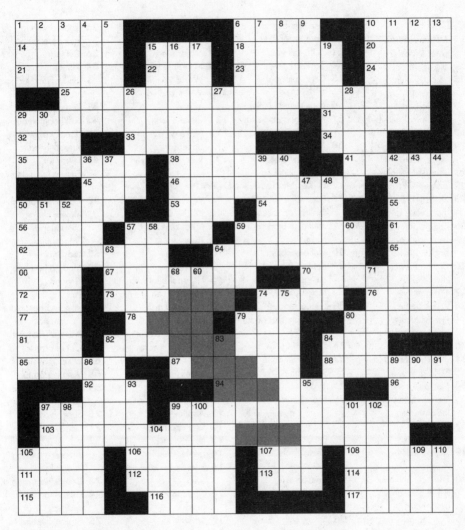

by Johan Vass

80 Singer with the 2016 platinum album "This Is Acting"
82 In good shape
83 "Know what I'm talkin' about?"
84 Secret rendezvous
86 Like child's play
89 Block where Sesame Street can be found?

90 Notable period
91 It's constantly breaking around the world
93 "The straight path"
95 German steel city
97 Like neon
98 Bar rooms?

99 It never occurs above the Arctic Circle during the summer solstice
100 One may be sworn
101 Claw
102 Seat of Florida's Marion County

104 Eugene O'Neill's "Desire Under the ___"
105 Go after
109 Word before ride or slide
110 Which card to pick from a magician?

ACROSS

1 Muhammad Ali's "Me! Whee!," e.g.
5 "S.N.L." alum Hartman
9 Start off on the wrong foot, maybe?
13 Contaminate
19 What may be in a star's orbit
21 Throw with power
22 Alleviate
23 Sheep's milk product that's often grated
25 Classic name for the land north of England
26 Course taken in shorts, often
27 "Ya don't say!"
28 765-foot-long "water coaster" on Disney cruises
30 Countertenor
31 SWAT team or Navy SEAL group, e.g.
34 Name that sounds like two letters of the alphabet
37 Epitome of smoothness
39 "Roots" author Haley
40 Shocker, at times
41 & 44 It goes around every hour
46 Gaming novice, slangily
48 Secured skates, with "up"
50 Float component
51 Act as a blueprint for, as DNA for proteins
53 Brawled, in the backwoods
55 "Howdy, everybody!"
57 Withstand
58 Fly off the shelves
59 Like bread made from almond flour
61 "Oh, hell yes!"
64 Turn red, say
65 Certain formal duds
66 Nice round number?
67 Bollywood megastar Aishwarya ___
68 "My dear man"
71 Grammy category won multiple times by Kendrick Lamar
77 Racy selfie posted for likes on social media, in modern lingo
80 Not a problem
81 Kennel club category
82 Makeup table
83 "Dead serious!"
85 "And, uh, that about covers it"
86 Supporting role
87 New students at Princeton or Yale in 1969
88 There's a famous "half" one in Yosemite National Park
90 Vessel protected by Hera
91 Uninteresting
92 Encouraging cry
94 Bottom
96 Saves, with "away"
98 "Ain't dead ___!"
99 They often come to professors with excuses
102 Hoodwink
104 Get snake eyes, say
107 Lacking experience
108 Aligns, in a wood shop
112 Set straight
113 Oscar winner for his role as a Mexican narc in "Traffic"
117 Price to pay, informally
118 Major piece
119 Miniature for a World War II buff
120 Were running mates?
121 Quite a jerk
122 Make an appearance
123 Recess for prayer

DOWN

1 Verve
2 It's 50/50
3 "That kinda stuff": Abbr.
4 Buckaroos
5 Mint
6 Fictional pilot with the line "You like me because I'm a scoundrel"
7 "Here ___ again"
8 Milk for un café
9 Onetime MTV reality series filmed near Hollywood
10 Recall regretfully
11 Auditing org.
12 Courtroom statements
13 Bone to pick
14 Lighter than lite
15 Word after soul or solid
16 "You, too?!," playfully
17 Smart
18 Wood that's resistant to warping
20 Mountain chain that stretches from Kazakhstan to the Arctic
24 Do a waving motion by the ocean, say
29 "That proves it"
32 Shade similar to verdigris
33 Distinguish oneself
34 Positioned to win
35 Shared with for quick feedback
36 Cut into
38 Region with a Unification Flag for sporting events
41 Pen pa?
42 Just hanging out
43 It really blows
45 Knucklehead
47 Flinch (at)
49 Ending for a dean's address
50 Cable network with movies like "Sharktopus" and "Mansquito"
52 Least klutzy
54 Made a boo-boo
55 "I won't ___ it!"
56 Pending
58 Risqué communiqué
60 Ancient home to Priam's Treasure
62 Out of practice
63 Quick refresher
68 Visibly scornful
69 Cold that just won't go away?
70 Super-popular
71 Gooey spread
72 Where gymnast Simone Biles won four golds
73 One-celled organism
74 Enter unannounced, in a way
75 Photog's setting
76 Name of the girl on "Game of Thrones" who said "A girl has no name"
77 Spot between programs, e.g.
78 Beehive material
79 Annual May race, informally
84 One of three characters in "M*A*S*H"

by Jeremy Newton

85 Ones behind the scenes
87 Consider, with "on"
89 High-priority item
92 Vocalist's asset
93 Directly criticized on Twitter with an "@"
95 Gillette razor name

97 Literature Nobelist Bellow
99 Bit of faulty logic
100 Sandwich supposedly named after low-income New Orleans workers
101 Begins a triathlon

103 Like the clue for 103-Down?
104 Teased incessantly
105 Kind of cavity
106 Hard vehicle to park
109 Telenovela, e.g.
110 Some drink dispensers
111 Extend (out)

114 Org. with lots of money to waste?
115 Order member
116 "Ver-r-ry interesting!"

INITIAL IMPRESSIONS

ACROSS

1 Advantage
6 Tony, e.g.
11 Plunder
18 Weighed in
20 Cow : herd :: ___ : troop
22 One with a discerning palate
23 C-Span?
25 Start brawling
26 Drink name suffix
27 Earth goddess
28 Going from point A to point B
30 Miss piggy?
31 Class acts?
33 Actress Gershon
34 Put back on the market, as real estate
37 Feel bad
38 Champagne name
40 P-trap?
44 G-force?
47 Union concern
48 Setting for C. S. Lewis's "The Lion, the Witch and the Wardrobe"
49 NPR host Shapiro
50 Words said in passing?
51 Deliberate betrayal
53 Butt
54 Father figures?
57 Guam or the U.S. Virgin Islands: Abbr.
59 Surgeons' professional org.
60 2012 Best Picture winner
61 Anastasia ___, protagonist of "Fifty Shades of Grey"
62 Make mention of
63 Top supporter?
64 Susan who portrayed the youngest child on "The Brady Bunch"
65 G-flat?
69 Deodorant type
72 Be short
73 Make music
74 Like Crater Lake, compared to any other U.S. lake
78 LeBron James in his N.B.A. debut, e.g.
79 Anheuser-Busch InBev's stock ticker symbol
80 Avocado pit, for one
81 Cause for revolution, perhaps
82 Escort's offering
83 "Yep, that happened!"
85 [And like magic . . . it's gone!]
87 First of ten?
88 Compete in pursuit of
90 Abbr. on a flight board
91 D-Con?
94 E-bond?
96 Conversely, in brief
97 Worry for a Great Depression bank
98 Ladybug, e.g.
99 Cereal box abbr.
101 Strike-out specialists?
105 See 106-Across
106 Out of 105-Across
108 Son of Zeus
109 Bird of legend
110 Fast-food chain with Famous Star burgers
113 C-sharp?
116 Black-and-white dessert
117 Take care of some personal baggage
118 Word after green or smoke
119 Things consumed for psychedelic trips
120 Men in black, say
121 Deck originally known as "carte da trionfi" ("cards of triumph")

DOWN

1 Kind of news often aired at 6 and 11 p.m.
2 Classical poem form
3 Drives home, say
4 French article
5 Floral archway
6 Pop group with a dedicated museum in Stockholm
7 "___ is mainly a catalog of blunders": Churchill
8 Means
9 "The Burghers of Calais" sculptor
10 Cruella de Vil, for one
11 Beat oneself up over, say
12 Mimic
13 Little beef
14 ___ kicks (ab exercise)
15 Pitch-correcting devices
16 Tribe of southern Montana
17 Range of knowledge
19 School administrator
21 French for "born"
24 Appalls
29 Aesthetically pretentious, informally
32 ___ card
33 Ruby, e.g.
35 Carter who portrayed Wonder Woman
36 Noncommittal response to "You coming?"
39 Load off one's mine?
41 Homonym of 39-Down
42 Trace of color
43 Wore
44 Gallivants (about)
45 Part of Q.E.D.
46 Ralph who founded the American Museum of Tort Law
51 Got ready (for)
52 Mosque leader
55 Launched
56 Product once advertised with the line "The splendor of your skin"
58 Datum for a chauffeur, for short
60 Take in, maybe
62 Supporter of Roosevelt's agenda
63 Actor whose breakout role came as a shirtless cowboy in "Thelma & Louise"
64 Singles
66 Hardly cheery
67 Hoppy request at happy hour
68 Enlighten
69 Wine barrel strip
70 Climate change, e.g.
71 Looked back on
75 Alphabetized, say
76 Wind farm output: Abbr.
77 Stink
79 Split open
80 Lorelei's lure
81 May honorees
83 Mad (at)
84 ___ Hill ('90s R&B group)
86 Decoration at el Palacio Real de Madrid

by Dan Schoenholz

89 Where livestock eat
91 Mastered
92 Divide into three parts
93 Pattern that's hard to break
95 Nasty looks
100 Lento or allegro
102 Retreats
103 Loggers' competition
104 Track
105 Rap lyrics, in slang
107 Post-O.R. destination, often
108 Doesn't just assume
110 The Rockies, on scoreboards
111 Day ___
112 Sail fixed to a bowsprit
114 "Darn!," in Dortmund
115 Baseball's dead-ball ___ (around 1900–20)

ACROSS

1 Computer file, informally
4 Wound up on top?
8 Feels it the next day, say
13 Things served in prison
18 Shout at a Greek wedding
19 Country singer McKenna
20 "Whoa, settle down"
21 More than half of humanity
23 ___ state
24 Mom's comment to her child during prenatal bonding? [Frank Sinatra, 1954]
27 Hot state
28 Bishop's hat
29 They're used mostly on corners
30 What Mom is obligated to do as her due date approaches? [The Beatles, 1969]
36 "___ the deal . . ."
37 Yes, in Yokohama
38 Bran material
39 Part of a drivetrain
40 The Renaissance, for one
42 Team ___ (late-night host's following)
43 Cancer fighter, for short
44 Henley Royal ___ (annual July event)
49 Mom's reaction to her first mild contractions? [John Cougar, 1982]
54 Midwife's advice to Mom in the delivery room? [Salt-N-Pepa, 1987]
55 Cause of wear and tear

56 Wanna-bees, e.g.?
57 ___ of Maine (toothpaste)
61 Sport whose participants call "Pull!"
62 Pet sound
63 Tennis star with the highest career winning percentage in singles matches (89.97%)
64 Stress test?
65 "Whoa boy, settle down"
66 Mom's remark as contractions grow stronger? [The Ramones, 1978]
70 Org. that delivers
73 Unenthusiastic
74 Went sniggling
75 Vaporize, say
78 Empire
80 Roughly
81 Be crazy about
82 Sappho's "___ to Aphrodite"
83 Mom's reaction as delivery draws closer? [Usher, 2012]
85 Child's response to Mom's actions? [Diana Ross, 1980]
88 Briskly
90 Actress in eight Bond films
92 Like sea horses that give birth
93 Beast with a humped shoulder
94 Utah ski resort
95 Cable news anchor Cabrera
98 Prey for a formicivorous creature
99 Simple life?

103 Nurse's remark after Mom delivers the first twin? [Britney Spears, 1998]
108 Spanish archipelago, with "the"
110 Touches
111 Witty saying
112 Doctor's comment after Mom delivers the second twin? [The Who, 1965]
117 Director DuVernay
118 Quiet
119 Settle down, say
120 Pacific crop
121 Something you might gloss over
122 Mother's Day delivery
123 Apologetic remark during a breakup
124 Hang it up
125 Consult

DOWN

1 Kind of column
2 Venue for trill seekers?
3 TV reporter's entourage
4 Like snails' trails
5 Beginning that leads to a sum?
6 Singer with the 1968 hit "Think," familiarly
7 Nibble
8 "Oh no!"
9 X
10 Drink with the flavors Poppin' Lemonade and Grabbin' Grape
11 Wyoming's National ___ Refuge
12 Spill clumsily
13 "Bye!"
14 Food delivery route?
15 Piece of equipment for a biathlete
16 Oscar ___

17 Bad thing to do in class
22 Figure (out)
25 Aesthete's interest
26 Complete
31 Hilarious sort
32 U.S. city whose name is composed of two state abbreviations
33 Struck out
34 Poorly
35 Toothpaste option
41 Solicit sales (for)
42 Fishing bait
43 Keeps the beat with one's foot
45 "Who ___ you?"
46 Woman's name meaning "goddess"
47 Relations
48 J.D. holder: Abbr.
50 What a shaken soda bottle will do when uncapped
51 Capital of Fiji
52 Not dismissive of
53 Earn
57 Quaint contraction
58 Rule for trick-or-treaters
59 Improvised
60 Wind down?
64 Janet Yellen's former post, with "the"
66 Site of offshore banks?
67 Life, briefly
68 Garr of "Tootsie"
69 Setting for a scene in the Sistine Chapel
70 Major part of the night sky?
71 It's broken off
72 Olympic athlete category
75 Lions and tigers and bears
76 Raw footage?

by Brad Wiegmann

77 Davidson of "S.N.L."
79 Stick in the refrigerator?
84 Sun follower?
85 Loving
86 Last name in shoes
87 Exam for some aspiring C.E.O.s
89 Go down the ___
90 Little bit

91 Ron who played Tarzan
95 Boundaries
96 Part of a Milky Way bar
97 Joint: Prefix
99 Book that's the source of the line "It is more blessed to give than to receive"

100 Host of HBO's "Real Time"
101 Año starter
102 Competes on a British cooking show
104 "Same here"
105 Lead-in to trumpet or drum
106 Legally foreclose
107 Tour de France stage

109 The 13th or 15th
113 Mobster's undoing
114 Places to take breaks, for short?
115 Inoculation location
116 Cleaning solution

ACROSS

1 Dude, slangily
5 Toaster Swirlz brand
9 Country singer Haggard
14 Lhasa ___ (dog breed)
18 Metallic fabric
19 "___: Legacy" (sci-fi sequel)
20 Hymn of joy
21 Loud thudding sound
23 Shot in the dark
26 Get to the point?
27 Steps up?
28 Court plea, in brief
29 Winner's sign
30 Alternative to a blitz
31 False start?
33 Improved version of an existing product
37 –
38 Skipping syllables?
40 Reward for a big hit, say
41 Two-legged stand
43 Fix for a bald spot
46 –
48 Shock
51 Oscar-winning Hanks role of 1994
54 Tiny bits
56 By-way connection
58 Voice mail prompt
59 Hasbro game requiring increasingly quick reflexes
60 Tiny bit
61 Mensch
63 Meals with Haggadah readings
64 Award to wear
65 Real deal
66 –
68 Like cabernet sauvignon
69 Go over
71 Start of many Portuguese place names
73 Be angry
75 Suffix with age
78 Highly resistant elastomer
81 –
84 Skyscraper support
88 Like some ballots
90 Breakfast drink sans creamer
92 Ill-advised move
93 Intangible qualities
94 Do
95 Anonymous surname
96 Causes of pocket buzzes
97 Loud, sharp sound
98 Like Golden Raspberry-"winning" films
100 Detectives
103 –
104 Whispered sweet nothings
106 It's a sign
108 Unsmiling
110 Like some roller chains and ball bearings
112 –
116 Leaves zip for a tip
119 One given orders around the house
121 Tract of land
122 Nickname for the Wildcats of the Pac-12
124 Smut
126 Collection on Facebook
127 Shot in the dark
131 Three-time American League M.V.P. of the 1950s
132 Varsity
133 Hurt badly
134 Disneyland transport
135 Bill blockers
136 Ta-tas
137 Polishes off
138 Fore-and-aft-rigged sailboat with two masts

DOWN

1 Photo mishap
2 Amassed
3 Congregational chorus
4 Tools for landscapers
5 "You get the idea": Abbr.
6 Food found in some bars
7 Most-often-used
8 Net wt. of many pasta packages
9 Sticker stat
10 It's water under le pont
11 Teller of the third tale in "The Canterbury Tales"
12 Surgical tool
13 Like some casts
14 Makes a scene
15 "Hallelujah!"
16 Marvelous
17 ___-3
22 Slice and dice, say
24 Takes over (from)
25 More than just a talker
32 Indian lentil dish
34 "No info yet," on a schedule
35 Carefully avoid
36 Heating option
39 Composer Bruckner
42 –
43 Unlikely Oscar winners
44 Fighting
45 Tiny bit
47 G
49 Opening for a computer technician?
50 Pro fighter?
52 Swampy stretch
53 V.A. concern, for short
55 –
57 Phenomenon by which electrons radiate from a heated filament, so named for a famous observer
59 "You can't be a real country unless you have a ___ and an airline": Frank Zappa
61 Mil. leader
62 Catch
63 Arc on a music score
65 Investment goal
67 Trucker on a radio
70 Pitchfork-shaped letters
72 –
74 When the first "Peanuts" comic appeared
75 Apple on the teacher's desk?
76 Literature Nobelist Bellow
77 Innovation in push-ups
79 It can represent a folder
80 First offer?
82 "I touched your nose!" sound
83 Coffin frames
85 Squarish
86 A jokester might say "And the pot thickens" after one
87 One of the friends on "Friends"
89 Very easy living
91 –
94 French explorer who founded Detroit
96 Duty
98 According to
99 Bad P.R. for a celeb, maybe
101 Baseball announcer's cry

by Joe DiPietro

102 One doing a Spot check?

105 Whom the Secret Service dubbed Renegade and Renaissance

107 Mike who served as a Wyoming senator from 1997 to 2021

109 –

110 Longtime Swedish automaker

111 ___ Johnson Sirleaf, Africa's first elected female head of state

113 Mammal found in the Andean cloud forest

114 Utterly lost

115 "I'm baffled"

117 Botanist's study

118 A sucker for milkshakes, say

120 –

123 ESPNU covers its games

125 Web file format, for short

128 The natural order of the universe

129 Chats over Twitter, briefly

130 Grp. mobilized by a 911 call

You Do the Math

ACROSS

1 Supply for an ultimate Frisbee team
6 2019 box-office flop described by one critic as "Les Meowsérables"
10 Picks the brain of
14 Extemporizes
19 "Why should ___?"
20 Feeling tender
21 Apartment, in real estate lingo
22 How spring rolls are cooked
23 Oscar-winning actress born Mary Louise
24 One side of a 2015 nuclear agreement
25 It's irreversible
26 University of Florida athlete
27 "That was great!"—"No, it stunk!"
31 Setting for Jo Nesbo's best-selling crime novels
32 They have stems and white heads
33 Mild, light-colored cigars
36 Have because of
38 Drive (from)
39 Recurring pain?
42 Route 70 in {Route 10, Route 95, Route 101, Route 70, Route 25}
45 Snitch
47 Hit film set aboard the spaceship Nostromo
48 Cereal grain
49 Fastener that leaves a flush surface
51 Modern party planning tool
52 Lofty
53 Collector's item
55 Word after combat or cowboy
58 What two Vikings have explored
59 Royal staff
61 Brainy sort
64 Fruits often used in sushi
66 Cattle in [cattle / pigs]
69 Burrito condiment
73 Vodka mixer
74 Hopeless predicament
79 Birthstone for Hillary Clinton, Kamala Harris and Alexandria Ocasio-Cortez
80 Toffee bar brand
82 What the nose knows
84 Major move, for short
85 ". . . unless you disagree"
87 Naturally occurring hexagonal crystals
90 "Dames at ___" (Broadway musical)
91 Was fed up
92 Comics character with the dog Daisy
95 Bear x tiger
98 "Billions" airer, for short
99 Et ___
101 Hamilton, to Burr
102 Green cards, informally
103 Offering to a houseguest
105 Hardly any
106 Car in {plane, car, train, horse, car, car, train}
113 Pong company
114 Shakespeare character who inquires "Are your doors lock'd?"
115 Greet grandly
116 Provide funding for
118 Was accepted
119 ___ mess, English dessert of berries, meringue and whipped cream
120 Its merchandise often comes with pictorial instructions
121 "Set Fire to the Rain" singer
122 Part of a golf club
123 Mathematician Descartes
124 Credit application figs.
125 PC platform popular in the '80s

DOWN

1 Grow faint
2 Coffee order specification
3 Garment whose name sounds like an apology
4 Sign of distress
5 Like many wildflower seeds
6 Boutros Boutros-Ghali's home city
7 Nearly 5,000 square yards
8 Comparative word
9 Matched up
10 What has interest in a car?
11 Sound of disdain
12 Long, loose robe
13 Leave momentarily
14 Brief evocative account
15 Diarist Nin
16 "Hello ___" (old cellphone ad line)
17 Subatomic particle
18 Some nice cameras, for short
28 Wife of Albert Einstein
29 Wipe out, slangily
30 "___ deal"
33 Has a tête-à-tête
34 Pale pinkish purple
35 Light-footed
36 Muhammad's father-in-law
37 Cause of a smudge
39 First work read in Columbia's Literature Humanities course
40 Like some news coverage
41 Squeeze
43 "Nice going!"
44 Crux of the matter
46 Rating for risqué shows
50 ___-in-the-hole (British dish)
53 Whale constellation
54 Massive ref. books
56 Have things in common
57 Like music that uses conventional keys and harmony
60 Org. whose website has a "What Can I Bring?" section
62 Summer Olympics host before Tokyo
63 They may come in a boxed set
65 Summer hrs. in Iowa
67 Co. captains?
68 First line of a Seuss classic
69 Parts of cars and stoves
70 High-profile interviewer of Harry and Meghan
71 Style of "Roxanne" in "Moulin Rouge!"
72 Drawn-out
75 Easterlies
76 Done again
77 Chef Waters who pioneered the organic food movement

by Jennifer Nebergall

78 Mrs. ___, "Beauty and the Beast" character
81 Kind of vaccine used against Covid
83 Slippery
86 Partially
88 Two-person meeting
89 Certain sots
91 Words often replaced when singing "Take Me Out to the Ball Game"
93 Disney character who says "Some people are worth melting for"
94 Less sportsmanlike
96 Where the King lived
97 Tennis's Nadal, familiarly
100 Make sparkling
103 Font flourish
104 Tease
105 Cartographic collection
106 In Touch and Out, for two
107 Texter's "Then again . . ."
108 Cloud contents
109 Trees under which truffles might grow
110 "De ___" (response to "Merci")
111 Took too much, for short
112 ___ contendere
117 ___ Moore, antipoverty entrepreneur of the Robin Hood Foundation

ACROSS

1 Gilda of the original "S.N.L." cast
7 They may need to be cut off
11 Ways of making ends meet?
16 Degree in design, for short
19 Cow's-milk cheese that's often grated
20 Sweet 16 org.
21 Honor named for a Greek goddess
23 Site of a lighthouse that was one of the Seven Wonders of the Ancient World
24 "___ pass"
25 Where snow leopards and blue sheep roam
26 King of a nursery rhyme
27 Went to bat (for)
30 Test versions
31 Good fashion sense, in modern slang
32 Appear
33 Features of some indoor arenas
35 Theater curtain material
37 Fired off, say
38 Grind
40 Money of the Philippines
42 Follow
43 One giving a khutbah sermon
46 Smaller alternative to a Quarter Pounder
48 Chicago team, in old "S.N.L." sketches
50 Ski lodge mugful
54 Fraternity letter
55 King of ancient Israel
56 Comic actress Gasteyer
57 Left, cutesily
60 Great Lakes nation
64 Pickup line?
65 Like the columns of the Lincoln Memorial
66 Cures
68 "___ we good?"
69 King of ancient Egypt
71 Tattoo artist, so to speak
73 Org. with a complex code
74 "Happy Days" network
75 Beach Boys song set to the tune of Chuck Berry's "Sweet Little Sixteen"
78 King of myth
80 4G letters
81 ___ pace
82 Not doing so hot
86 F−, e.g.
87 Discourage
89 Waze way: Abbr.
90 Piece of plastic with a gladiator pictured on it
92 Physics demonstration often done from the roof of a school
95 ___-Briggs Type Indicator (popular personality test)
97 "I will prevent disease whenever I can, for prevention is preferable to cure," e.g.
98 King of Shakespeare
99 "Keep Austin ___" (city slogan)
101 Annual presidential address, for short
103 Partner
107 "No worries"
109 "Bon appétit!"
111 Christ, to Bach
113 Place
114 Chimney channels
116 Warning on presents stashed in the closet
118 King of Skull Island
119 "Huddle up!"
121 Actress Elisabeth
122 When: Sp.
124 Early adolescent years, so to speak
125 Engage
126 Opposite of wind up
127 Infinitesimal
128 Toys with much assembly required
129 Travel brochure listings
130 Named

DOWN

1 Some hip-hop collectibles
2 On dry land
3 Join a conference call, say
4 Quick to fall asleep, in a way
5 Sense of self
6 Día de San Valentín gifts
7 Tearfully complain
8 Tabloid nickname for mother Nadya Suleman
9 Powder in the powder room
10 Course with greens
11 Machiavellian sort
12 Omits
13 Objective
14 Gateway city to Utah's Arches National Park
15 Some after-Christmas announcements
16 Home to about one in five Californians
17 Long-running sitcom set in Seattle
18 Them's the breaks!
22 Spent some time on YouTube, say
28 Nobel Peace Prize recipient who wrote "No Future Without Forgiveness"
29 Sought-after position
34 Pop
36 G.P.s, e.g.
39 City about 25 miles SE of Chicago, IL
41 ___-faire (social adeptness)
44 Level the playing field?
45 Put one past
47 One ending for a classic board game - another of which (when a player resigns) is represented visually six times in this puzzle
49 Tough spots
50 Bother incessantly
51 Scoring win after win
52 Mowry who starred alongside her twin Tia in the '90s sitcom "Sister, Sister"
53 ___ Z
55 Cubs' place to play home games
58 Wilson who wrote the lyrics to 75-Across
59 Play areas
61 The "Bel Paese," to locals
62 Borrower
63 Scale
67 Quintessentially cowardly
69 Mosaic maker
70 Remove from under the seat in front of you, say
72 Ducks known for their soft down feathers
76 Tinker (with)
77 Yes or no follower
79 "I've got it!"
83 Rob ___, British comedian and TV personality
84 Samosa tidbit
85 Part of an office phone no.

by Adam Wagner

88 Tool for a duel
91 Sidewalk drawings
92 One of the Manning brothers
93 Disentangle oneself
94 Main source of energy?
95 Breakout 1993 single for Counting Crows
96 Stay awhile
100 Only color of the rainbow not seen on the L.G.B.T. pride flag
102 Portable dwellings
104 Richie with the #1 hit "All Night Long"
105 Borrower
106 Potato cultivar that was developed in Ontario, despite its name
108 Pelvic exercise
110 Nintendo dino
112 Like diamonds from a mine
115 Father
117 Weak, as a case
119 "Oh, and another thing . . . ," for short
120 Graffiti signature
123 College, to a Brit

ACROSS

1 Earners of credits
7 One selling airtime, informally
12 Emulates a chipmunk, say
20 Like a beaming smile
22 Go out to get some juice?
23 Pork-cutting option
24 Ingredient in an Alabama slammer
25 Revise
26 Word with "two" or "three" to describe a sloth
27 Small kitchen knife
29 Abstract artist Mondrian
30 Thomas Hardy title character
31 Bottom part
32 Traveled like Charon
34 Schedule keeper: Abbr.
35 One for whom underwear is pants
36 "Wait . . . what did you just say?!"
37 Fuse
39 Three-dimensional
43 "Have You Never Been ___," #1 album for Olivia Newton-John
44 Origami designs thought to bring good fortune
45 One receiving a congratulatory email from eBay
47 Helps secure a loan
48 Recovery center
49 Refused to share
50 Scratch
51 Tablet taken before going to bed, maybe
52 Portrayer of Marvel's Hawkeye
53 Left the harbor
57 Rapper who co-founded Mass Appeal Records
58 Green liqueur
59 Dinosaur of kids' TV
60 It's nothing
61 Host
63 Signaled slyly
64 ___ Top (low-cal ice cream brand)
65 Camaro, for one
66 As one
67 Birth day presence?
68 "All in the Family" subject
71 "Don't dwell on the past"
73 Families-and-friends support group
74 Negotiate
75 Some diners . . . and donors
76 Provide a password
77 Was rife (with)
78 Matthew of "The Americans"
79 Save for later, in a way
80 Skewered
82 Like Queen Anne's lace?
83 Traditional accounts
87 Onetime hair removal brand
89 Let out or take in
90 Stage name for hip-hop's Sandra Denton
91 It's all the rage
92 "What-EVER" reactions
94 Post-distraction segue
97 Light-filled room
98 Way, way off
99 Hitchcock's forte
100 Clearing
101 Like bison vis-à-vis beef

DOWN

1 Key for Chopin's "Heroic" Polonaise
2 It might be organized
3 Foundation options
4 Eclipses and comets, perhaps
5 Joy of MSNBC
6 Parked it, so to speak
7 Maximally
8 Pacific birds?
9 Bit of thatching
10 Take sides?
11 Catapulted, say
12 Bird much seen in cities
13 Reply to a ring
14 Not in the dark
15 Adriatique, e.g.
16 Task for a sous-chef
17 Like sirens
18 Be considered perfect
19 More than just clean
21 Shopping in order to improve one's mood
28 Fire
31 They might be wireless
32 Desktop icon
33 Surname of Harry Potter's adoptive family
35 Pop star nickname, with "the"
36 Bet strategically
38 Mythical nymph
39 Reliquary
40 Inspiration for the Frisbee
41 Floored
42 Longtime Ohio State basketball coach Matta
43 Filet ___
44 Stopped smoking?
46 Half of a notorious outlaw duo
47 Added to the language
50 First little piggy's destination
52 Key hit with a pinkie
53 It helps take the edge off
54 Just going through the motions
55 Complete, as a crossword
56 Creations for Mardi Gras
58 Particles composed of two up quarks and one down quark
59 Did a TV marathon, say
62 Start of some no-frills brand names
63 In a lather, with "up"
64 Happy ___
66 Come back around
67 Bits of hijinks?
68 What Mr. Clean, Captain Picard and Michael Jordan have in common
69 Thought expressed in American Sign Language by extending the pinkie, thumb and index finger
70 Compilations of funny film faux pas
71 Soeur's sibling
72 Warehouse loading areas

by Robyn Weintraub

74 *shrug*
77 "We want all the juicy details!"
78 Maintain, in a way, as a highway
81 Michael whose initials match those of his famous comedy troupe
82 Cut through
83 "___ and Majnun" (Arabic story that inspired a Clapton hit)
84 One of the "holy trinity" ingredients in Cajun cuisine
85 Advice to one in a lather?
86 Very inclined (to)
88 Sting, perhaps
90 Taverna staple
91 Spice related to nutmeg
93 Argentite, e.g.
95 Fifth of eight
96 Show filmed at Rockefeller Ctr.

MAPLE LEAF

ACROSS

1 Writer who created Oz
5 "Obviously," in slang
10 First word of "A Visit From St. Nicholas"
14 ". . . with possibly direr consequences"
17 ___ Berliner, pioneer in phonograph records
18 Lex Luthor, to Superman
22 Raised
23 Bit of asparagus
24 Alternately
25 Lines up
26 Agitated
29 Pricey
30 M.L.B. team with a big "W" in its logo
31 Rx order
32 "Revolution," to "Hey Jude"
34 Space-scanning org.
35 It may be bitter
36 Like bees
37 Not ___ (mediocre)
39 Clear weeds, in a way
40 Part "missing" from p.s.i.
41 Mystery writer Deighton
42 Words cried after "Go"
46 Abbr. after a price in a Craigslist ad
47 Lt.'s inferior
48 Decidedly
51 Québec's ___ St.-Jean
52 Soft drink since 1905
54 Young hombre
56 Biblical verb ending
57 Instruments for Israel Kamakawiwo'ole
60 German auto since 1899
61 "That'll teach you!"
62 Pigeon English?
63 Basketball champions' "trophy"
64 Gillette brand
65 Leader of the house?
67 "Love is love," e.g.
70 Pallid
71 Outlets, e.g.
73 Something that might lengthen a sentence?
74 Moneybags
75 High school hurdle whose first two letters, phonetically, sound like one of its former components
76 Like all the answers with pairs of circled letters, punnily
81 Programming pioneer Lovelace
82 Seasons in Québec
84 15th birthday celebration
85 Tomtit is another name for it
86 Talks up
88 Classical Icelandic literary work
89 Title letters chanted in a 2011 Katy Perry hit
90 Oldsmobile Cutlass model
91 Financial org. once deemed "too big to fail"
93 Newfoundland, e.g.: Abbr.
94 Serpentine swimmer
95 Root beer brand
96 Veterans
100 Range within which you can answer the question "Can you hear me now?"
104 Six-time winner of the N.H.L.'s Art Ross Trophy, born in Saskatchewan
108 "24" and "Suits" actress, born in Halifax
111 Princess who says "Why, you stuck-up, half-witted, scruffy-looking nerf herder!"
112 Dish served on a skewer
113 Congresswoman Omar
114 Actress Lena
115 Suppliers of the milk for Roquefort cheese
116 Singer Mary J. ___
117 Moves quickly and lightly
118 Not only that
119 Rehearsal, e.g., in slang
120 Approvals
121 You can believe it
122 "Likewise"

DOWN

1 Pears with a sweet-spiced flavor
2 Part of B.A.
3 Deploy
4 Alberta city named for an eagle-feather headdress
5 Like some birds or dolls
6 Excite
7 Rank
8 Stops talking, with "up"
9 Mettle that may merit a medal
10 Two-player game invented in Toronto
11 Sardonic
12 ___ of Parliament
13 Stops talking, with "up"
14 "Nice burn!"
15 Battle ___
16 Seasonal destination near Quebec City
19 Program introduced by the Trudeau government in 1984, colloquially
20 Approximate weight of the Liberty Bell
21 Spots
27 Advocacy grp. that filed for bankruptcy in 2021
28 Words at an unveiling?
31 Cry after an award is announced
33 Woman's short hairstyle
36 Portrayer of Senator Vinick on "The West Wing"
38 Level or bevel
43 Like some outlets
44 Desert planet of "Star Wars"
45 Be batty, in a way?
49 Canuck, e.g., for short
50 Capital of Qatar
52 Like bells in carillons
53 Part of L.C.D.
54 Some salon supplies
55 Like Rochester and Syracuse, but not New York City
58 Novel convenience?
59 Band whose 1999 hit "Smooth" spent 12 weeks at #1
66 Sleep stage
68 Overturns
69 "Very high," on a fire danger scale
70 Iowa Cubs baseball classification
72 Et ___ (footnote abbr.)
74 Federal regulatory org.
77 Rose or lilac
78 "Where ___ go wrong?"
79 Novelist Gaiman

by Stephen McCarthy

80 Pound sound
83 Thrown together
85 They might help with changing your locks
87 One with a phony personality?
90 Snake oil, purportedly
92 Passes
95 Central route thru town
96 Leers at
97 Frederick who composed "Camelot"
98 Helps a dish washer, say
99 One source of oil
100 Cheer
101 Shout, informally
102 ___ Wars, conflicts of 1839–42 and 1856–60
103 It may be perfect or simple, but not both
105 Big elevator maker
106 $15/hour, e.g.
107 What most spiders have eight of
108 Hitchhiker's need
109 International fashion magazine
110 Climb, as a rope

16 FAMILIAR SURROUNDINGS

ACROSS

1 Home for The Devil
6 Fairy tale villain
10 Ballet-inspired fitness method
15 Web designer's code
19 Dream interrupter, maybe
20 Pitcher Hershiser
21 They might dog a dog
22 "___ there!"
23 Prisoner accidentally causes a power outage?
26 Police unit, informally
27 "Hoo boy!"
28 "Your guess is as good as mine"
29 Small songbirds
30 In a manner of speaking
31 Kind
33 Year, in Brazil
34 Cherokee and Navajo
37 Southern university beefs up campus security?
42 Unlike bread on Passover
45 Pierce-Arrow competitor
46 Popular Hyundai
47 "O mio babbino caro," e.g.
48 Key part: Abbr.
50 Keenness of judgment
53 Chinese zodiac animal
54 Fellow imposes a strict palm fruit regimen?
59 Something that can be tried or cracked
60 Dead giveaway?
61 Put away some groceries?
62 ___ school

63 Convenient transport through urban traffic
64 Go bad
65 One seeing things with a critical eye?
67 ___ cannon (sci-fi weapon)
68 Good spice to add to guacamole (try it!)
71 Wizard of ___ (nickname for a good massage therapist)
72 U.F.C. fighting style
73 Heretics flout them
77 Early Ron Howard role
78 Actress de Armas writes "Mr. Gas" and "Ms. Rag"?
82 World's best-selling musical artists of 2020
83 Target of a pop-up blocker
84 Financial planning option, for short
85 Like the verse "Roses are red, violets are blue . . . ," in brief
86 Body of water that's home to the world's largest marine reserve
88 The Cougars of the N.C.A.A.
91 New York has 28 of them
94 Smartphone advises on poker bets?
98 High-hat attitude
99 "Told you so"
100 Off-road ride, for short
101 Org. whose plans are up in the air?
104 Georgia-based insurance giant
106 Unnamed somebody
109 Ones making you duck down?

111 Kinks song that Weird Al Yankovic parodied as "Yoda"
112 Doctor acquires antibiotics?
115 A short one by Ogden Nash reads "Parsley / is gharsley"
116 Macabre illustrator Edward
117 One kind of plastic
118 Indian wedding adornment
119 Even ___
120 Connecticut-based insurance giant
121 Break
122 Work from Roxane Gay or Jia Tolentino

DOWN

1 Snacks from some trucks
2 Honolulu's ___ Stadium
3 Sought feedback from
4 Willy, in "Free Willy"
5 Telecom with a pink logo
6 Reaction to a stomach punch
7 Chow
8 Add new caulking to
9 Roosevelt credited with saying "No one can make you feel inferior without your consent"
10 Closest of pals, for short
11 Hillary Clinton vis-à-vis Wellesley College
12 Move to a new table, maybe
13 Hip-hop duo ___ Sremmurd
14 What ". . ." may represent
15 José Martí, by birth

16 Social media pic designed to attract sexual attention
17 False
18 Some strong solutions
24 DuPont patent of 1938
25 Skip it
29 Boston airport
32 Work in the kitchen?
35 Abounded (with)
36 St. Kitts, St. Lucia and St. Vincent
37 Saint on the big screen
38 Pulitzer winner ___ St. Vincent Millay
39 Spur
40 Shake an Etch A Sketch, e.g.
41 Full
42 How kids might describe dad jokes
43 Important stretches
44 "___ Too Proud" (hit musical about the Temptations)
49 Visits overnight
51 Ingredient in a Negroni
52 Sporty trucks, in brief
55 Lots
56 Lets hit it!
57 What ". . ." may represent
58 ___ March
59 Word that appears with confetti when texted on an iPhone
63 Big name in synthesizers
65 Cardamom-spiced brew
66 !!!
67 They may be checked at the door
68 Yoga pose with an arched back
69 "High-five!"
70 Like fuchsia and turquiose

by Michael Lieberman

71 Actor Aziz
74 Spanish hand
75 Spanish love
76 Application figs.
78 Practiced
79 Birds' bills
80 What an integral can be used to calculate
81 One of the Obamas

83 Jellied garnish
87 Low bows
89 Kind of question
90 Old wheels
92 ___ Park, Colo.
93 Raw deal from a restaurant?
95 Categorize
96 "There's no one on me!"

97 Document with two accents
101 Water clover and adder's-tongue
102 Fight setting
103 Purity test
104 Popular dog 105-Down
105 See 104-Down

107 Daughter of Ned Stark on "Game of Thrones"
108 Smelt things?
110 Payment often made around January 1
112 Tour grp.
113 Little eggs
114 Business card abbr.

GRAVITY'S RAINBOW

ACROSS

1 Rackets
6 Spruce or fir
15 Japanese city that shares its name with a dog breed
20 Home to the Ho Chi Minh Mausoleum
21 Homemade headgear for pretend pirates
22 Conducted, as a campaign
23 Undo, legally
24 Highly specialized knowledge
25 Color whose name is derived from "lapis lazuli"
26 Frequent comics collaborator with Jack Kirby
28 Belief
29 Hubbubs
31 "See? I knew what I was talking about!"
32 Gives an edge
33 Indignant denial
34 Bozo
35 "I 30-Down the fool!" speaker
37 GPS suggestion: Abbr.
38 What might follow you
39 1966 Donovan hit
43 Sinatra, to fans
47 Band whose "Gold: Greatest Hits" has sold over 30 million copies
50 Raised a false alarm
52 Tennis's Nadal, informally
56 Fruit with crimson-colored flesh
59 Guest feature?
60 Popular folk rock duo
62 Place for a canal or a kernel

63 1968 self-titled folk album
65 A.L. West team, on scoreboards
66 Rubik with a cube
68 Ice cream holder
69 Cal's game-winning kickoff return against Stanford in 1982, familiarly
71 World's deepest river
73 Little tasks that crop up
75 Wood shop item
77 Investigate, à la Sherlock Holmes
79 Wunderkinder
82 Implement for an Amish driver
86 Features of classic cars
87 It's covered in paint in the Sherwin-Williams logo
89 Oscar-winning song from "Slumdog Millionaire"
90 "Likewise"
91 Media watchdog agcy.
92 "Strange Magic" band, for short
93 Medium for Kehinde Wiley's "President Barack Obama"
94 Took a load off
95 Mars
100 Harmful bits of sunlight
105 Remove calcium deposits from
106 Sharp shooter, for short?
108 Harder to grasp
109 Changes by degrees
111 Whole bunch
112 You might cry if you slice it
115 Word rhymed with "ami" by Lafayette in "Hamilton"

116 Like Merriam-Webster's inclusion of the word "irregardless," originally
119 College admissions fig.
120 Delta hub, on luggage tags
121 Birth control option, briefly
122 In the blink of ___
123 Deli or bar order
124 Stags or bucks
125 Biblical possessive
126 Alcoholic's affliction, briefly
127 Complicated, as a relationship
128 Retired flier, for short
129 Explosive stuff

DOWN

1 California-based soft drink company
2 Divisions of long poems
3 Historical records
4 Place for a pitcher
5 "I'm such a dummy!"
6 Olympic poker?
7 Military hospitals, briefly
8 Period of history
9 Back in
10 Fresh, in a sense
11 A one and a two
12 Bursts in on
13 And the rest, for short
14 Twin in Genesis
15 Prizewinner
16 Instrument often played for comedic effect
17 Tennessee Williams's "The Night of the ___"
18 Babysitter's handful
19 "___ Fideles"

27 ___ Simmons, real name of the late rapper DMX
30 See 35-Across
36 Affectionate attention, briefly
37 One enforcing traveling rules
39 Kind of jacket
40 "Ish"
41 Xbox 360 competitor
42 Chicken
43 Total domination, in gamer-speak
44 Whole bunch
45 Racy
46 Polite form of address similar to "Mr." or "Ms."
47 Criminally aid
48 Yawn-inducing
49 Make yawn
51 Campus leader
53 With the bow, musically
54 Bungle
55 Vipers with upturned snouts
57 Part of a religious title that means "ocean"
58 Southern California county
60 "Mood ___" (Duke Ellington classic)
61 Quit drinking
64 Golf's ___ Ko, youngest golfer to be ranked #1
67 In draft form
70 High degrees, for short
71 Setting for many a Super Mario Bros. level
72 Temporarily out
74 Pesach observers
76 Most peaceful
78 Groups of bees?
79 "You can't expect me to believe that!"

by Ross Trudeau and Lindsey Hobbs

80 Laughable
81 Typical way to take a multivitamin
83 Is legally entitled
84 "It's a possibility for me"
85 Family members that get talked down to?
88 Kind of massage

89 Travels
96 ___ River, part of the Texas/Oklahoma border
97 Even-tempered
98 Skedaddled
99 They might be made after a fight
101 Runs again

102 Without fail
103 State flower of Illinois or New Jersey
104 ___ Faire (event with jousting, for short)
107 Is mad about
109 Source of the milk for chèvre cheese

110 The "R" of R.B.G.
113 Ready for business
114 Condé ___
117 What might make a ewe turn
118 Spanish monarch

ACROSS

1 Like "American Pie," "American Psycho" and "American Beauty"
7 Proposed portrait for the $20 bill
13 Like sports fans who paint their faces, say
18 Drink with tapioca pearls
19 Peach relative
21 Run off (with)
22 Upbeat sentry's emotion?
24 Many, informally
25 Regarding
26 More, on a music score
27 Auspice
28 King's collaborator on the Grammy-winning blues album "Riding With the King"
30 Take the next step in an online relationship
31 Actress Blanchett
33 Scotland's ___ Lomond
35 Winter Olympics maneuver
36 Some H.S. yearbook staff
37 Bacteriologist's emotion upon a new discovery?
40 Jess's best friend on TV's "New Girl"
43 Glib
44 Maker of Regenerist skin cream
45 Any member of BTS, e.g.
47 Pellet shooter
50 What Kit Kat bars come in
51 "I'm glad to hear it"
53 It's full of hot air
54 Mongolian shelters
55 Novice window-washer's emotion?
58 Scathing review
59 Complete set of showbiz awards, for short
60 Clownish
61 Really play that saxophone
62 Egypt's Sadat
64 Powerhouse in international men's ice hockey
66 Haul away
67 Art gallery tour leader
68 #46
69 Modern reading option . . . or where to read it?
71 ___ Building, Boston's first skyscraper
73 Apt anagram of GIFT
75 Brownish-gray
76 Jester's emotion after the king's laughter?
79 Like Ignatius J. Reilly in "A Confederacy of Dunces"
80 English-speaking
82 A fan of
83 Dionysian ritual
84 Ashleigh ___, 2019 French Open champion
85 Apathetic
87 Duchess of ___ (Goya model)
88 One-named winner of the 2021 Grammy for Song of the Year
89 Notation on a party invite
90 Wild horse's emotion?
94 Huge tub
97 One who's able to rattle off digits of pi, perhaps
99 Wine: Prefix
100 Like Eeyore
101 Hard-to-please type
102 Result of a snow day
105 Eddie Murphy's org. in "48 Hrs."
107 Lifelike video game, for short
108 A mighty long time
109 ÷ symbols, in typography
110 Cat's emotion while sitting in its human's lap?
114 Stuck
115 Brazilian beach made famous in song
116 Coming or going
117 Hits the paper airplane icon, perhaps
118 PC support group
119 Blocks

DOWN

1 Fired up
2 Quiets down
3 Wheel of Fortune's place
4 Airport info, for short
5 Lesser-known song
6 Kind of tire
7 Pay with a chip-based credit card, perhaps
8 As much as
9 Actor Wilford of "The Natural"
10 Old-style copies
11 Easy as pie
12 Column of boxes on a questionnaire
13 "Chill out!"
14 Hair loss
15 Evil genie's emotion?
16 ___ facto
17 "MacGyver" actor Richard ___ Anderson
18 Subpar athletic effort
20 Cable option for film buffs
23 Relentlessly competitive
29 Death Valley was once one
32 The Gettysburg Address, e.g.
34 Massage therapist's substance
37 Some recyclables
38 Jumping the gun
39 Turn over
41 One might take you in
42 Gusto
43 Finished a hole
46 Justin Timberlake's former group
47 When said three times, hit song for 46-Down
48 Famous toon with a Brooklyn accent
49 Farmer's emotion during a dry season?
50 As compared to
51 Eat (at)
52 Commercial lead-in to Clean
56 Responded to the alarm
57 New Mexico art hub
60 One of his paradoxes claims that two objects can never really touch
63 Home mixologist's spot
65 Interior design
66 Big name in lawn care
67 Oppose
69 Silk Road city near the East China Sea
70 What "10" might mean: Abbr.
71 Sleeping spot for a guest, maybe
72 It's way above the recommended amount
74 Youngest recipient of the Mark Twain Prize for American Humor (2010)
75 Apply sloppily
77 St. Cloud State University's state: Abbr.
78 Laze
79 Follow

by Howard Barkin

81 Identified, in Ipswich
86 Birth control options
87 Rescue dog, e.g.
88 Estrogen or testosterone
91 Move from aisle to window, maybe
92 Recent delivery
93 Took steroids, informally

94 Brio, to Brits
95 Staves off
96 Auditory : sound :: gustatory : ___
98 Bursts in on
101 Willem of the "Spider-Man" series
102 Delicious food, in modern slang

103 Theatrical award
104 Nobel pursuit?: Abbr.
106 Putin's parliament
111 N.Y. tech school
112 Castle door destroyer
113 Actor who was once crowned "America's Toughest Bouncer"

NO RUSE

ACROSS

1 Art of riding and training a horse
9 "Mea culpa"
14 Campania's capital
20 Put in other words
21 Bob Marley's "___ You Be Loved"
22 Mark in the World Golf Hall of Fame
23 Lacking self-assurance
24 Onus for a magician's disappearing act?
26 Study of how gels gel?
28 All together
29 Little, to a Scot
30 H
31 Fizzle (out)
33 Miscellaneous task
37 Irish writer Behan
39 Increased, with "up"
44 Actress Polo
45 Pablo Neruda's "___ to Wine"
47 They'll put you head and shoulders above everyone else
49 Constellation almost above the North Pole
50 Autobiography subtitled "The Girl Who Stood Up for Education and Was Shot by the Taliban"
53 Red card
54 ___ Khan, prime minister of Pakistan beginning in 2018
55 Sports broadcast feature
56 Angry Wisconsin sports fans?
59 Fire sign?
61 Like n, where n = 2k (and "k" is a whole number)
62 Unagi, at a sushi bar
63 President Bartlet of "The West Wing"
64 Singer Astley
66 Total-itarian?
69 Law enforcement, slangily
71 Tajikistan, e.g., once: Abbr.
73 "How was ___ know?"
75 Loll
77 Many a marble bust
80 Getting "Amscray!" under control?
85 Like yoga instructors
87 Greet the day
88 One of the Earps
89 –
91 Bathroom cabinet item
92 Certain bridge positions
94 McEachern a.k.a. the "Voice of Poker"
95 Cake topper
96 Wealthiest professional sports org.
98 Abrogates
100 Party animal?
102 Reveals
104 Reply to an oversharer
105 One in a hundred: Abbr.
106 Parrot
110 Power of a cowboy's shoe?
116 Odysseus' wife whispers sweet nothings?
119 Bliss
120 With wisdom
121 In a sense, colloquially
122 Activity for some pen pals
123 Port on the Black Sea
124 Colorful food fish
125 Giveaways during some pledge drives

DOWN

1 What the doctor ordered
2 Where Johnny Cash shot a man, in song
3 Bruins legend Phil, to fans
4 "Cut it out!"
5 Pronounced with authority
6 Twitter handle starter
7 Davis of "Thelma & Louise"
8 Icelandic saga
9 Chicken ___ (discontinued fast-food snack)
10 Dramatic accusation at a dentist's office?
11 Stickers
12 City council representative: Abbr.
13 Onetime White House inits.
14 Lunchtime liaison
15 Bands you might listen to in the car?
16 Salt's musical partner
17 Where "khop jai" means "thank you"
18 God who "loosens the limbs and weakens the mind," per Hesiod
19 Call at home
25 Not gross
27 Île be there?
31 ___ paneer (dish with puréed spinach)
32 Way in
33 "The Adventures of Milo and ___" (1989 film)
34 Cyber Monday offerings
35 She might take care of a kid on a sick day
36 Rock star who wrote the poetry collection "The American Night"
37 Contradict
38 "Mon ___!"
40 36-Down's anagrammatic nickname
41 "Gay" city in a Cole Porter song
42 Hallmark.com purchase
43 Opposite of "takes off"
46 Something to leave to beavers?
48 Precipitous
51 Grammy-nominated D.J. Steve
52 Thomas ___ Edison
57 Join with rings
58 Smudge
60 Vaper's purchase
65 Neighborhood where you might get kimchi, for short
67 Goddess of the dawn
68 Obama chief of staff Emanuel
70 Campaign pros
71 ___ Gilbert, co-developer of a Covid-19 vaccine
72 Smile with one's eyes, per a modern coinage
74 Long past
76 Some fencing swords
78 Something to play fetch with
79 "Well, golly!"
80 Biting
81 Spongy toys
82 Resets to zero, as a scale

by Ashish Vengsarkar

83 ___://
84 John Winston ___ Lennon
86 Professor 'iggins
90 Eaglelike?
93 Appetizers filled with potatoes and peas
97 One of the Jacksons
99 Word following English or green
101 Kind of wonder?
103 Cred
105 Campaign (for)
106 Itself: Lat.
107 World's oldest alcoholic beverage
108 Pulitzer-winning playwright from Independence, Kan.
109 Seriously annoys, with "off"
110 Tora ___, Afghanistan
111 Not overlooked
112 Defendant's plea, for short
113 Determination
114 Fork point
115 Storied cauldron stirrers
117 Spanish "that"
118 Admit (to)

DIG IN

ACROSS

1 Certain music royalties collector, for short
6 Viva ___ (aloud)
10 Dirty look
15 Even once
19 Part of R.I.
20 Big exporter of saffron
21 Sci-fi intro to "forming"
22 Foul
23 "Enjoy the food!"
25 Sportscaster who memorably asked "Do you believe in miracles?"
27 Crush
28 Emmy-winning FX series created by Donald Glover
29 "Curses!"
30 Challenger astronaut Judith
31 *"With enough butter, ___"
34 Commanded
36 Fuel economy authority, for short
37 Main artery
38 *"A party without cake is ___"
48 Retin-A target
49 Healthful property of a beach town
50 Chicken or veal dish, in brief
51 Merit
55 Boardroom plot?
57 Hangout rooms
58 Pair of quads
59 The Powerpuff Girls, e.g.
60 Filmmaker with a distinctive style
62 Affixes, as a cloth patch
64 Something that's gone bad if it floats when placed in a bowl of water

65 *"If you're alone in the kitchen and you drop the lamb, you can always just pick it up. ___?"
71 Word mistakenly heard at a Springsteen concert
74 Under way
75 Beethoven's Third
79 Reverse
81 Tons
82 Seriously hurt
86 Move quickly, informally
87 ___ o'clock (when happy hour begins)
88 Host's offer at a housewarming
89 Spongelike
91 Focal points
92 *"I enjoy cooking with wine. Sometimes I ___"
96 "Same here"
99 Word with noodle or nap
100 ___ lepton (elementary particle)
101 *"The only time to eat diet food is while you're waiting for ___"
108 Stamps (out)
113 One of Abraham Lincoln's is in the Smithsonian
114 "Welcome to the Jungle" rocker
115 Born with a silver spoon in one's mouth
117 Cause of a smartphone ding, perhaps
119 Chef quoted in this puzzle's starred clues
120 Guitar part
121 Member of la famiglia
122 Letters on an F-22 Raptor
123 One given onboarding

124 1975 Wimbledon champ
125 Like voile and chiffon
126 What may make the grade
127 Direct

DOWN

1 Shady spot
2 Less-than-subtle basketball foul
3 Temporary road markers
4 "I don't give ___!"
5 Pharmaceutical picker-upper
6 Penthouse perk
7 "Coffee ___?"
8 Stone memorial
9 Suffix with exist
10 Actor Jason who was once on Britain's national diving team
11 Four-stringed instruments
12 Financial adviser Suze
13 Dry with a twist
14 Milk: Prefix
15 NASA spacewalk
16 Try to win
17 Page who became the first openly trans man to appear on the cover of Time magazine (2021)
18 L.A. neighborhood referenced in Tom Petty's "Free Fallin'"
24 Coolers
26 Comedian Minhaj
28 How some bonds are sold
32 Himalayan legends
33 Fetch
35 Provided tunes for a party, in brief
38 Backbone of Indian classical music
39 Earth tone
40 Body sci.

41 Toon first introduced in the 1945 short "Odor-able Kitty"
42 Neighbor of Oman: Abbr.
43 Japanese honorific
44 Florida attraction with 11 themed pavilions
45 "His wife could ___ lean"
46 Family name in Steinbeck's "East of Eden"
47 "That's it for me"
52 Exist
53 Outfit
54 Drink garnished with nutmeg
56 Quizzical responses
58 Part of NGO: Abbr.
61 Change from portrait to landscape, say
62 Neither red nor blue: Abbr.
63 Benchmark
66 Locks-up shop?
67 Any set of elements in a column on the periodic table
68 Japanese port near Sapporo
69 War zone danger, for short
70 "A Room of One's Own" novelist
71 Mac
72 Gastric acid, on the pH scale
73 Tribute in verse
76 Classic Langston Hughes poem
77 First name in fashion
78 Saharan
80 Snacks that sometimes come in sleeves
82 Words to live by
83 The Cardinals, on scoreboards
84 Large Hadron Collider bit
85 Many a rescue dog

by Jesse Goldberg

89 It's not the whole thing
90 Mount ___, California volcano
93 Critical
94 Rank for a rear admiral
95 What the Unsullied warriors are on "Game of Thrones"
96 She turned Arachne into a spider after losing a weaving contest
97 Wags a finger at
98 Separate
102 Tough period of the school year
103 Bayt ___ (destination for a Muslim pilgrim)
104 Krispy ___
105 Crooner Mel
106 Handy
107 Caffeine-rich nuts
109 Still alive, in dodgeball
110 Laissez-___
111 N.J. city on the Hudson
112 Meal at which parsley is dipped in salt water
116 Serious divide
118 Candy aisle name
119 Protrude

STAR SEARCH

ACROSS

1 Symbol of royalty in ancient Egypt
4 Wouldn't stand for it?
7 They have springs in the middle
12 ___ Perez, former Democratic National Committee chair
15 Nutritional fig.
18 Apple tablet option
20 Popular analgesic
21 Belgian city that hosted the 1920 Summer Olympics
23 One of the rooms in Clue
24 N.B.A. superstar Durant
25 Voting "aye"
26 Gilbert and ___ Islands (former colonial names of Kiribati and Tuvalu)
27 Give way
28 Levy of "Schitt's Creek"
29 When the Lascaux caves were painted
32 Furthermore
33 Much of Goya's output
35 Japanese beer brand
36 San Francisco's ___ Valley
37 In which "Stella" means "star"
38 Seaweed used to wrap sushi
41 Descriptor of almost a million and a half Californians
44 Porridge, essentially
48 Real surname for the authors Currer, Ellis and Acton Bell
51 With a yawn, say
52 Less certain
54 Onetime material for tennis racket strings
55 "That much is clear"
56 Symbol of Mexico
57 Country with roughly 6,000 islands
59 Where a pop-up leads
61 Alpha and Beta Ursae ___ (pointers to 68-Across)
64 Noodle soup
68 Guiding light
72 Gentille figure of a French folk song
74 Lord's title
75 Originally from
76 Place to take a suit
77 Executive producer of HBO's "A Black Lady Sketch Show"
80 Risk
81 "___ Lang Syne"
82 Pesky insect
84 Something to notice in passing?
87 It's between micro- and pico-
88 Horace's "Hymn to Mercury," for one
89 New York political family
91 Fifth-century conqueror defeated in the Battle of the Catalaunian Plains
93 Rap's Lil ___ X
94 Reliable supporters
95 Glazer of "Broad City"
97 Online source for film facts, in brief
99 Repugnance
102 Disguised
105 Author ___ Carol Oates
109 Wine that may be made spumante or frizzante
111 Little
112 Bested
114 Gritty, in a sense
115 Ones committing a party foul . . . or the images depicted in this puzzle's grid?
118 Camping gear brand
119 Letters before an alias
120 Surprising wins
121 Jeu d'___ (witticism)
122 Little one
123 Female mallard
124 Grommet
125 Black-eyed ___ (flowers)
126 Kind of protein in tempeh

DOWN

1 They get the wheels turning
2 Like proverbial milk
3 Poet Neruda
4 Company that makes recoverable and reusable rocket boosters
5 Overdue amount
6 Content of a Kinder Egg
7 Like many chardonnays
8 Last czarina of Russia
9 Celestial figure depicted in this puzzle's grid, in Roman folklore
10 Unforgivable acts, say
11 iPhone button with an up arrow on it
12 Duty
13 About to enter the stage, say
14 Subject of Hokusai's "Thirty-Six Views"
15 Delight (in)
16 Go on and on
17 Avant's opposite
19 Celestial figure depicted in this puzzle's grid, in African American folklore
22 Celestial figure depicted in this puzzle's grid, in Babylonian folklore
30 Joe and co., e.g.
31 Sharing maternal lines
33 Excoriated
34 Akira Kurosawa film
38 Peacock streaming inits.
39 Italian time unit
40 Utter nonsense
42 Like five-star hotels vis-à-vis three-star ones
43 Gather
45 Rose of rock
46 Nickname on a ranch
47 Spanish title: Abbr.
49 Tower topper
50 Digital writing
52 Buffoon
53 Brawler's memento
58 Is at the Forum?
60 Steamy place
61 ___ Special Administrative Region of the People's Republic of China
62 For all to hear
63 Unit in thermodynamics
65 Chump
66 Unaccounted for, briefly
67 Fumble
69 Went into syndication, e.g.
70 Singer Aguilera's alter ego
71 Star performances, maybe
73 This is a test
75 "Gee, that's swell!"
78 Like Vulcans, typically
79 Central Asia's ___ Mountains
82 "Gloomy" guy
83 "That's just unacceptable"

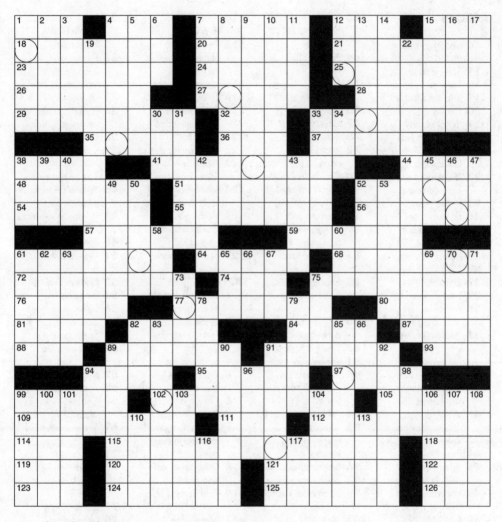

by Chandi Deitmer

85 1969–74, politically
86 Tree that lends its name to a programming language
89 Matured, in a way
90 Like the three-toed sloth, among all animals

91 New wings
92 Tweaks
94 Clear, as crystal
96 Like Parmesan, but not mozzarella
98 Bouncy jazz genre
99 Noted book club leader
100 Male mallard

101 Certain caucus voter
103 1938 prize for Pearl S. Buck
104 Big name in trading cards
106 W.W. I Belgian battle locale
107 Green with the 2010 hit "Forget You"

108 Enlighten
110 Roger's cousin?
113 Ireland, poetically
116 Smartphone network std.
117 Home to the Nittany Lions, for short

THE INSIDE DOPE

ACROSS

1 Kind of court
6 Decorative inlay material
11 Screening
15 Took off
19 Shooter's target
20 Facility
21 What pi may be used to find
22 Much family history, e.g.
23 *Feature of some kids' cereals
25 Shelter supplies
26 Feeling
27 Rita Hayworth title role of 1946
28 Monarch's bane
29 *Regular provider
31 Bollix up
32 Interior look
34 Aniselike herbs
35 "___ dreaming?"
37 *Holder of the world record for the longest ovation on the operatic stage (80 minutes)
41 W.W. II noncombatants
43 Spirit
44 Eremites
45 "The Guns of August" figure
49 Weekend warrior's woe
50 Grauman of Grauman's Chinese Theater
51 Swift gift
52 Reagan attorney general
53 Where you can feel the heat
55 Part of a tennis racket
57 Accusatory words
59 H look-alike
60 *Let the mind believe what it likes
64 Parter of the waters
65 Soyuz destination
66 Governessy
67 Covers up
70 Behind
72 Room sharer, often
74 Group west of the Atlantic: Abbr.
76 *Bastion of brotherhood
80 Uniters with 51-Down
81 Hug and kiss, to a Brit
83 Cracker topper
84 Bird baked in a pie
85 1920s anarchist in a celebrated trial
87 Some cottons
91 Tennis's Shriver
93 Kierkegaard's "The Sickness ___ Death"
94 "My Way" lyricist
95 Mexican revolutionary ___ Hidalgo
96 Brush makeup
97 Earth Day subj.
98 *Elementary school test package
102 Slice of history
103 Approaches aggressively
106 Portrait photographer Arbus
107 Ralph ___, 1974 N.L. batting champ
109 *Dress for the return of cool weather
111 Indeed
113 Overdo it, in a way
115 Requirement for some degree candidates
116 ___ avis
117 *Not even close
120 Dungeons & Dragons figure
121 List ender
122 Ones being shot at
123 Heinrich who wrote "Atta Troll"
124 Moneybags in "The Wind in the Willows"
125 Comfy retreats
126 Unpadded
127 Synthetic fabric

DOWN

1 Grp. influential in campaigns
2 Wide-eyed
3 *Alaskan cruise sighting
4 Midway, e.g.
5 Preliminary events
6 Cowboys' org.
7 Bean who was the fourth man to walk on the moon
8 Gave up at last
9 Ran amok
10 Add instead of subtract, e.g.
11 Some tubes
12 Lover boy?
13 Lights
14 Speeds up
15 It's sour
16 Disney duck
17 Documentary filmmaker Morris
18 Gets off the bottle
24 Title on a child's bookshelf
29 Object of a vain wait
30 Lee who directed "Brokeback Mountain"
33 Pay increase to keep up with inflation, in brief
35 Up to one's ears
36 Former Portuguese colony in China
38 Put right
39 Core groups
40 Piddling
42 Title with a tilde
46 *Wasn't clear, as one's future
47 Where Monferrato wine comes from
48 Behind
51 Uniters with 80-Across
52 Finds at Pompeii
54 Songlike
56 Suffix with sheep or goat
58 Soapstone, e.g.
61 Mideast's Gulf of ___
62 Mauna ___
63 Firecracker parts
68 Cabinet inits. since 1947
69 Show annoyance with
71 Chef's hat
72 Sportsman of the Year co-winner of 1998
73 ___ the Great
75 Like some electronics
77 Politician's projection
78 Seminole's archrival
79 Virulent virus
82 1945 Colette novel
86 Spread some holiday joy
88 Quaint garden fixtures

by Lynn Lempel

89 O.K.
90 Where Napoleon planned his Hundred Days campaign
92 Welds
95 Reached the due date
96 Helmsman
99 That: Sp.
100 "Do I have a volunteer?"
101 Company whose production goes in cycles?
103 Going on
104 Load of ships?
105 Santa ___, Calif.
108 Rodeo competitor
110 "The Nanny" actress Drescher
112 Poor returns?
114 Island-dotted lake of Northern Ireland
117 Not fair
118 Food additive
119 ___ Aviv

ACROSS

1 "Come on . . . be good, kids"
7 Kind of jacket
11 Actor Gulager
14 Occurs to, with "on"
19 Emulate Earhart
20 Bean town?
21 Alley ___
22 Traditional whale hunter
23 Like some titmice
24 Went too far
26 Pretty cool
27 Mark who won the Masters and British Open in 1998
28 The old frontier you and I don't remember?
30 Is covered in dew, perhaps
32 Mahmoud Ahmadinejad, e.g.
33 Longtime Bob Hope broadcaster
35 ___ d'amore
37 Like some traffic
38 Donkey Kong, for one
39 Place to gamble in N.Y.C.
41 Job ad abbr.
43 Center of success?
44 Rap's Dr. ___
45 Climate that's copy-protected by law?
49 Ralph Nader and Ross Perot
52 Brought on
53 Sound from a fan
54 ___ Tunes
55 U.K. record label
57 Richness
60 Like some grasses
61 Porridge ingredients
63 Scratches (out)
64 Took too many pills, briefly
65 Merlin on an Imax screen?
67 Fall mos.
71 Currency whose symbol is "$"
72 Like Java man
73 Lose one's marbles
78 What to follow in the forest
80 Stat for Warren Spahn: Abbr.
81 Pull out formally
82 F.B.I. director appointed by Clinton
83 Jimmy of DC Comics
87 Bond poster
89 Eyelid moistener at a museum?
93 Some colas, familiarly
94 Small wts.
95 "Well, ___-di-dah!"
96 Asian school of thought
97 U.S.O. show attendees
98 Cuddly sci-fi critter
100 Algonquian tongue
101 Court call
103 Twangy
105 Mover left or right
107 Rouse a beloved English queen?
110 Nocturnal insect
113 Buggy drivers
115 In the world
116 National airline of Afghanistan
117 Coca-Cola trademark
118 Singer Des' ___
119 10-year host of "Entertainment Tonight"
120 Boasts of
121 Seventh-grader, often
122 Many, many mos.
123 Pamplona shouts
124 Tangle up (in)

DOWN

1 Group with a secy. gen.
2 Certain gamete
3 Better half takes the stage?
4 Christmas on Capri
5 "S.N.L." alum Cheri
6 Married in error?
7 Scent maker
8 Add pep to
9 "What ___!" ("This place needs cleaning!")
10 Go-___
11 Able to be followed
12 Bath scrubber
13 So far
14 "Goll-lee!"
15 Many a "Star Trek" character
16 Tush made of shuttle thread?
17 Bit of trail mix
18 Pork place?
25 Grabbed surreptitiously
29 Graduation or confirmation
31 Following
34 Not just ask
35 Florida county seat
36 Not on deck
38 Had something
40 Go "waaaah!"
42 Got things wrong
44 Harriet Beecher Stowe novel
46 Elite
47 Didn't walk or go by subway, say
48 ___ Epstein, Red Sox G.M. starting in 2002
50 Mr. Right, with "the"
51 Enjoy the theater
56 Word before and after "a"
58 Prell competitor
59 Currency exchange abbr.
61 Painter Mondrian
62 Milk source
63 Former Israeli president Weizman
65 3.5, e.g.: Abbr.
66 Actress Papas
67 Viscera
68 Rodeo locale
69 Stick one's foot in Chardonnay?
70 Good winter entree
73 Some toothpastes
74 Where to get a mil. commission
75 Development of amnesia?
76 In ___ (stunned)
77 None too bright

by Stella Daily and Bruce Venzke

79 Illustrator for Charles Dickens
81 Fabric that needs serious mending?
84 Bequests
85 Circus props
86 Supposed makers of crop circles
88 Suffix with buck
90 Bird whose name sounds like its soft call
91 Tricks
92 Get more soap suds out of
99 Angers
100 Metal that may ignite if scratched
102 Try
104 Dr. J was one
105 Spinning dizzily
106 Part of DKNY
108 Tribal chief
109 "The Simpsons" bus driver
111 They're not good for QB's
112 Nasty wound
113 Back
114 Big mouth

24 TRIANGULATION

ACROSS
1 Magazine that features "Alfred's Poor Almanac"
4 I.R.S. form 1099-___
8 Early pulpit
12 "The Simpsons" character who often refers to himself in the third person
18 Speedy steed
20 "___ tale's best for winter": Shak.
21 Reddish-brown
22 How Mulan dresses in much of "Mulan"
23 Fielder's cry
24 Something to play
26 Numbers game
27 They're left behind
29 Turns in
31 Old infantry spears
32 Saw things
33 "___ Blas" (Lesage novel)
34 "Where ___ go wrong?"
36 Procter & Gamble brand
37 One succumbing to 6-Down
39 Bird: Prefix
40 It might be silver
42 Be in another form
44 "Don't worry about me"
46 Archbishop Tutu
48 Censures
50 Some players in a kids' game
52 Single, for one: Abbr.
53 As quickly as possible
54 Sinai borderer: Abbr.
55 King in a Steve Martin song
56 Star in old westerns
58 Home of Canadian P.M. Stephen Harper
59 Freight weight
60 "Great" boy detective
62 When the sun is directly overhead
64 Combined
67 Facilities
69 Creepy sort
73 Thin-framed, big-footed woman of cartoons
75 Indian bread
77 Lilliputian
78 Chest protector
81 Subject of this puzzle [and proceeding counterclockwise]
83 Summons: Abbr.
85 Words of honor?
86 Thought
87 "Notes ___ Scandal," 2006 film
88 Skateboarder's accessory
90 Rim in which a gem is set
91 Guessing game
95 Flat ___ (some proponents of I.R.S. reform)
96 Big picture?: Abbr.
97 Jazz singer Nina
99 Songwriters' org.
100 Gag reflex?
101 Córdoba kinswoman
103 Bring (out)
104 Bagel topper
105 Strip joints?
108 Buttonholes
110 New York governor after Pataki
113 Place
115 Drink whose name is Tahitian for "good"
117 Like any points on a circle, from the center
119 X-ray ___, joke shop offering
120 Sandinista leader
121 Pipsqueak
122 Judge, with "up"
123 Went like the dickens
124 Mixed economy advocate
125 Salty septet
126 Disney World transport
127 Galas

DOWN
1 "Speed-the-Plow" playwright
2 Greet the day
3 Whence the line "Into the eternal darkness; into fire and into ice"
4 Medieval weapon
5 "That ___ it should be"
6 See 37-Across
7 PC data reader
8 Three-time A.L. M.V.P., familiarly
9 Pouty look
10 Working out of
11 What those in agreement are said to be of
12 Court figs.
13 Bats
14 ___ Hawkins Day
15 "Seinfeld" character
16 "Catch your breath"
17 "___ pro omnibus, omnes pro uno"
19 1950s stereotype
25 Joan Rivers's daughter and TV co-host
28 Place for surfing
30 Star Wars, initially
33 Flit (about)
35 Highlighted, as text
38 Second showing
40 Wish one could
41 Comprehensive
43 Spanish pronoun
44 Query to the Lord in Matthew
45 Quark-plus-antiquark particle
47 "Love of loves"
49 In the blink of ___
51 Not just hungry
53 Oaf
56 Inebriate
57 See 81-Across
61 Place for a swing
63 Maria Muldaur's "___ Woman"
65 Like some diet colas, in brief
66 Makes up?
68 Power in Hollywood
70 Like things
71 Chest material
72 Listens to
74 "That makes sense!"
76 Bottom of the ___
78 The Owls of the N.C.A.A.
79 "Do what you want"

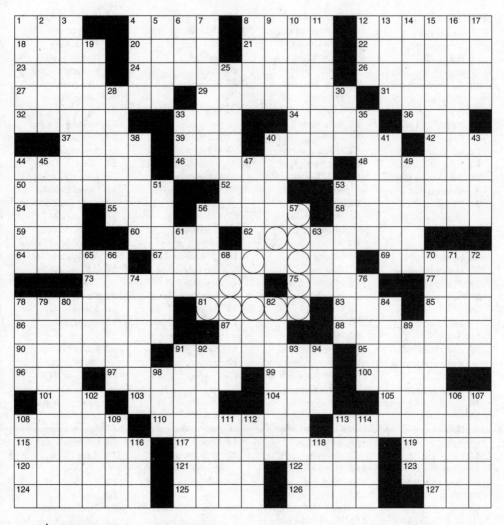

by Natan Last

I NEED MY SPACE

ACROSS

1 Literary elephant
6 Succeeded in
11 Hot
17 Drag show accessory
20 ___ Stadium, home of the University of Hawaii Warriors
21 Baseball Hall-of-Famer Edd
22 Admonish
23 Suffix with absorb
24 Like a useless photo lab employee?
27 Stephen of "Breakfast on Pluto"
28 Dejected
29 Trespasses
30 Lineage
31 Imported by plane
33 TV oil baron
35 "Let's go, Miguel!"
36 Wally's TV brother, with "the"
38 Take on
39 Offers breakfast to students before first period?
43 Marriage ___
44 Part of A.A.R.P.: Abbr.
45 First word of "Jabberwocky"
46 Put a rider on, e.g.
47 It may be false
48 Game stopper
50 Place for a panel
52 Director Anderson
53 Beer sources for genteel guests?
57 Extremely inept person, slangily
59 Sharp turn
62 ___ Arbor
63 Through
64 Cartoonist Bil
65 Sauce thickener
66 Name in a hymn
67 Worthless talk, in slang
69 It may charge you a fee
70 Casino surface
71 Mattress brand
72 Reminder to a forgetful judge on bowling night?
78 Early invader of Britain
79 Esq.
80 Sette minus quattro
81 Utter
82 Give ___ of hope
83 Functions
84 1977 George Burns film
86 Fix
87 Letter addenda, for short
90 Band with the 1989 hit "Stand"
91 Own (up)
92 What talk show guests have before the broadcast?
95 Yowl
96 Playboy's look
97 Sloops' headsails
98 Sported
99 Poker game with four hole cards
102 See 26-Down
104 Ring stats
106 Guest beds, often
107 Sign outside a church lavatory?
113 Stately trees
114 Work units
115 Satirical paper, with "The"
116 They may be scattered
117 Short-hop plane
119 Potential hangar buildup
120 On the safe side
121 Music with jazzlike riffs
124 Ruby ___
125 Where a Monkee changes after a game?
130 "___ Poetica"
131 Handily defeated
132 Church support
133 1964 Quinn role
134 Still
135 Tasty bit
136 PC key
137 Beginning

DOWN

1 Barnyard calls
2 ___-Romeo
3 Laredo or Nuevo Laredo
4 "Now it's clear!"
5 Cereal topping
6 Torts
7 Responses to punches
8 Crackpot
9 Religious retreats
10 1976 horror film whose score won an Oscar
11 Talks from a Rev.
12 Toll hwy.
13 Sports legend whose #4 was retired
14 Day spa accessories
15 Unfold
16 "Finding ___," 2003 film
17 Eccentric friend on "Designing Women"
18 Seldom-used golf club
19 Over
22 1969 Oscar-nominated film role
25 Little job for a body shop
26 With 102-Across, dashboard warning light
32 Loud hits
34 Exert, as influence
35 ___ 1, Yuri Gagarin's spacecraft
36 Jaguar alternatives
37 Seventh-brightest star in a constellation
39 Offer to buy at auction
40 Meteorological effect
41 Steam shovel inventor William
42 Guthrie's follower at Woodstock
43 TV host Kelly
48 Diva's effect
49 Host of public radio's "This American Life"
50 Cubs' protector
51 Survey info
52 Increase, in a way
54 Poland Spring competitor
55 Owen ___, John Irving character
56 "A maid with hair of gold," in an old song
57 Goes it alone
58 Attempt to trick
59 "Beetle Bailey" soldier
60 Analogy part
61 U.S. possession since 1898
65 Kind of hall
66 Schmo
67 Rap enthusiast, in slang
68 Rob of "Melrose Place"
70 Damager of the ozone layer
71 Pouting person's action
72 Bygone leader
73 Fabled race loser
74 Reason for an office visit
75 "___ my fault!"
76 Impulse
77 Paper purchases
83 Turnaround, slangily
84 Bauxite, e.g.
85 "Right Place Wrong Time" singer, 1973
87 Seminar leaders
88 Expensive strings
89 Dict. listings
91 Brothers
92 Beginning, as of an idea
93 Seine tributary
94 Stirred up, as memories

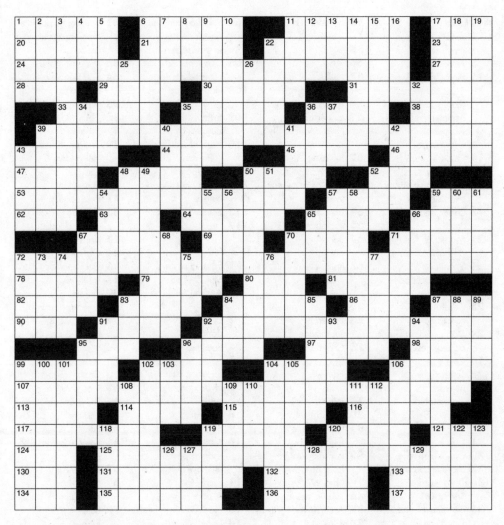

by Mike Nothnagel

95 Blanket holder
96 Golden Triangle
   country
99 Prescription
   phrase
100 "Le Misanthrope"
    playwright
101 Place for an elbow
102 One pulling in

103 Road bend
104 Italian province
    or its capital
105 Singer with the
    #1 country album
    "80's Ladies"
106 Playful movement
108 Company with
    a star logo

109 Source
110 "This one's ___!"
111 Physical therapy
    equipment
112 "Now it's clear!"
118 The first prophet
    of God, in Islam
119 Awful
120 Feel compassion

122 Kind of beef
123 Part of a Latin 101
    conjugation
126 Gridiron units: Abbr.
127 Java
128 Giant born in
    Louisiana
129 1989 Gold Glove
    winner Darling

26   JUST FOLLOW DIRECTIONS

ACROSS

1 Artist's digs, maybe
5 Totally accurate
11 Pineapple desserts
18 "__, gorgeous!" (Fanny Brice's comment to herself when looking in the mirror)
19 One of wine's Gallo brothers
20 Autobiographical short story by Edgar Allan Poe
21 Marisa of "What Women Want"
22 1974 Mocedades hit
23 Careful consideration
24 Men's fashion accessories
26 Cork shooter
28 "Biography" network
29 Accelerated
30 Threw off the scent
31 Check list?
32 Canonized mlle.
33 More encouraging
34 Third word of "America"
35 Blue Devils' and Tigers' org.
38 Contact lens solutions
40 They're better than one
45 Elton's johns
47 Blind element
48 Stereotypical reaction to Elvis
50 Magneto's adversaries, in comic books
51 Lugs
53 Spread in a spread
55 –
56 Passé
57 –
59 Classic Toyota sports cars
61 __ Bradshaw, "Sex and the City" role
62 Wynken, Blynken and Nod, e.g.
63 Turf, as opposed to surf
64 Dancer Alvin
65 Malodorous
67 Become part of
68 Imp
71 Place to get dates?
72 Fronded plant
73 Fictional submariner
75 Civil rights march site, 1965
76 Family
77 –
78 Wise
80 –
81 Repeated John Gielgud role
83 Popular song from Broadway's "The Wiz"
86 Titanic message
87 Arctic diver
88 Runs
90 Eponymous German electrophysicist
92 Begets
96 Things on strings
97 Deterge
101 Prefix with -zoic
102 Sitcom title role for Brandy Norwood
103 1997 Jim Carrey film
104 What a man and a woman become in marriage
106 Two-wheeled covered carriage
108 Hops-drying kilns
109 Establishing a business
110 Hero of Bellini's "I Puritani"
111 Anticipate
112 Mary Tyler Moore co-star
113 Seinfeld, for one
114 Feast

DOWN

1 Sainted pope of A.D. 683
2 Ancient Mexican people
3 Evidence of dandruff
4 Facilities
5 –
6 Slips
7 Hydrocarbon suffix
8 Execrate
9 Bone formation
10 Mathematical sequence of unknown length
11 __ Bator
12 A pop
13 Na_2CO_3
14 Dental filling
15 Literature's Lorna
16 Lose little by little
17 –
18 U.R.L. lead-in
20 Israeli P.M. Olmert
25 They may be funny or bright
27 Neighbor of Switz.
30 Educator Maria
31 Subatomic particle that is a nuclear binder
33 Mideast money
34 Bad dancer's handicap
35 "Enough!"
36 Collected
37 Mistress
39 Bridges in Hollywood
40 The "ten" in "hang ten"
41 Reactionary
42 Flower also called a naked lady
43 Hero maker
44 Old dirk
46 Unblemished
48 Lineage
49 Failings
52 Breezes (through)
54 Quite wrong
56 Business position
58 Word before and after "after"
60 Cross product
61 Geom. figure
64 Disco term meaning "galore"
65 Punch
66 French Sudan, today
67 Raspberry
69 "__ Angel," 1933 film
70 Scratch sheet listings
72 Slams
74 Fannie __ (securities)
77 Jupiter or Mars
79 __ Gay, W.W. II bomber
82 Ointment ingredient
83 Subject of the book "Last Flight"
84 Setting for "Driving Miss Daisy"

by Matt Ginsberg

85 –
88 Call, or call on
89 Turkish pooh-bahs
91 Lake ___, third-largest lake in Africa
92 Imagine, informally
93 Sectioned, as a window
94 Prince Valiant's wife
95 Tapestry threads
96 –
97 –
98 Month before Iyar
99 "Socrate" composer
100 First, in Frankfurt
102 Relig. title
103 Lady's man
105 Anchorage-to-Fairbanks dir.
107 Great ball of fire

ACROSS

1 Inferior
10 Puzzle page favorite
15 S. Amer. land
19 Like some addresses
20 Communist's belief
22 Part of a blouse that touches the waist?
23 The real scoop about lipids?
24 They're better than F.G.'s
25 Portion of a drag queen's wardrobe
26 Bumptious
27 Toy company that launched Rubik's Cube
28 Bad ___
29 Snowmobile parts
31 Professional with an x-ray machine: Abbr.
33 Underage child of a military officer?
38 Nonsense of a market pessimist?
44 Affirm
45 Oven maker
46 Caught in ___
47 Biblical birthright seller
48 Oscar winner Hunt
50 Glad Wrap competitor
51 Pianist Dame Myra
52 Missy Elliott's "___ What I'm Talkin' About"
53 Toil of a Broadway show?
55 Match for a bad guy?
58 Owns
59 Fine-tune
60 Italian port on the Adriatic
61 Make ___ of
62 Sam's Club competitor
64 Yes
68 Watchdog org.?
72 Fixes
74 Hair behind the ears, maybe
75 Email directive: Abbr.
78 What can produce a "boing!"?
82 Ardor of a new employee?
84 Bookstore sect.
85 "Our Gang" affirmative
86 Stop early
88 Botulin, e.g.
89 "___ la Douce," 1963 film
90 Charlie's Angels, e.g.
91 Tally mark
92 Torn
93 Comeback of a Japanese game?
95 Singer Johnny's gallop?
98 It can be measured in gigs
99 So
100 "Yo!"
101 Over
105 Molière's Harpagon, e.g.
108 Prosperity
110 Go the other way
113 Privilege of liberals?
115 Road in Yellowstone?
118 Become level
119 Darlin'
120 Give it ___
121 Say yes
122 Reason to take Valium

DOWN

1 Trampled
2 Accidents
3 "___ Alive!" (1974 thriller)
4 One looking for a lift?
5 Wilts
6 Comic Rudner
7 New Testament book
8 "The way of nature"
9 Popular street name
10 Patriot Putnam of the American Revolution
11 When planes are due, for short
12 Equivocator's choice
13 Child-raiser's cry?
14 Start of a cheer
15 City WNW of Stillwater
16 François Truffaut's field
17 West Point rival, for short
18 ___ nitrate
19 Polo Grounds legend
21 Words sung before and after "is just"
26 Literally, "fish tooth"
28 Rambunctious
29 Lewis Carroll creature
30 Hawaii's ___ Coast
32 Habiliments
33 "Happy Days" character
34 Province of central Spain
35 Villain in "Martin Chuzzlewit"
36 "National Treasure" group
37 Turkish hospice
38 Believers in the spiritual unity of all people
39 Roadside sign abbr.
40 Obscure
41 Gas bill info
42 Roofing items
43 Yearns (for)
49 Refuse holder
54 It's pitched
56 Times gone by
57 Current
60 Be angry
63 It's kept within the lines, usually
65 Sully
66 "At the ___ Core," 1976 sci-fi film
67 Laredo-to-Fort Worth dir.
68 Comparable in size
69 Veep after Hubert
70 Destinations of some limos
71 Perfecto, e.g.
73 One taking a quick look
75 Handyman
76 Squeeze-dry
77 Al ___
79 Must, informally
80 Ukulele activity
81 Playable
82 ___-totsy
83 Venture
87 Erymanthian ___, fourth labor of Hercules
94 Artist Max
96 Pure

by Bill Zais

97 Restrained
99 Sports car since '53
101 Italian wheels
102 Moola
103 Miles away
104 ___-bitty

106 "The Lay of the Host of ___" (old Russian epic poem)
107 Elisabeth of "Leaving Las Vegas"
108 Small warbler
109 Makes (out)

110 Speeds
111 Alamo battler?
112 1,000 smackers
114 Actor Stephen
115 West Coast hrs.
116 Wow
117 "Riddle-me-___"

POLITICAL LEADERS

ACROSS

1 Words "beautifully marked in currants" in "Alice in Wonderland"
6 Common ___
9 Make an example of
13 Destination in Genesis 8
19 With 105-Across, what the answer to each starred clue starts with
21 *Again
23 *Baseball's Willie Mays, with "the"
24 *Fiancé
25 Glycerides, e.g.
26 Football Hall-of-Famer Ernie
28 Home of Faa'a International Airport
29 Lie
30 Jury pool
31 Watch-crystal holder
32 Villain
33 Ring results, briefly
34 Bigwig
38 "Awesome!"
41 Next-to-last round
42 Little of France?
43 St. Louis, e.g.
44 Brawl motivator
45 Crunch's title
46 Rod holders
50 Photocopier choice
51 Hollow-point ammo
53 *Metal used for swords
55 Stage awards
56 Butlers and maids
57 Be about to fall
58 *Symbol of rejoicing for someone's long-awaited return
61 *Brownish-orange
65 Lady-in-waiting in "Othello"
66 Lovers of expensive furs may put them on
67 West Coast wine city
68 *Kind of ratio
72 Divine
74 New York's ___-Fontanne Theater
75 Supermarket lines?
76 "We Need a Little Christmas" singer
77 Hoop grp.
78 Alma mater for Neil Armstrong and Pat Nixon: Abbr.
79 Close of day, to poets
80 Gutter locale
81 Thomas Mann's "Der ___ in Venedig"
82 Attempts
85 With 20-Down, airshow activities
86 Jim who wrote "Ball Four"
88 Indy champ Bobby
90 Dentist's concern
91 ___ of vantage (good position for viewing)
96 Split
98 Split
99 Like wiping one's dirty mouth on one's sleeve
100 *Decelerating
102 *Composer's due
104 *Whatever happens
105 See 19-Across
106 Cantankerous
107 Not including
108 Inexact fig.
109 Magazine holders

DOWN

1 Mississippi quartet
2 ___ of thousands
3 "___ Remember"
4 "Real Time" moderator
5 Tip reducer?
6 Variety of leather
7 Exercised power over
8 All the parts of a column except the bottom
9 Stick
10 Accustom
11 Actress Harper
12 Diplomats' place: Abbr.
13 Ball handler?
14 "Not I!" hearer
15 Titular Verdi role
16 Laugh-a-minute
17 Both: Prefix
18 Curling goal
20 See 85-Across
22 Author of the Oprah's Book Club selection "We Were the Mulvaneys"
27 I's opposite on a clock
30 Improvises
31 Bar personnel
32 Light from a headlight
33 Rears
35 Cracker topper
36 What 35-Down may do
37 Jessica of "7th Heaven"
38 Done with
39 Tourist mecca near Venezuela
40 Relinquish
41 Passing remark?
42 Sch. fair organizer
46 Schumacher of auto racing
47 The "E" in H.R.E.: Abbr.
48 Violinist Mischa
49 This, in Havana
50 Cox's call
52 Spot
53 Manhattan street leading to the Williamsburg Bridge
54 Guarantees
56 Sensory receptor in the ear
59 "Mon ___!"
60 Loud, abrupt sound
61 Dog of old comics
62 Denier's reply
63 Aerobics technique
64 Winning
66 +
68 +
69 Impair through inactivity
70 Atahualpa, e.g.
71 It may be + or −
72 Act of kindness
73 Soothsayer's subject
76 "Death in the Afternoon" figures
80 Muse of music
83 Creator of "Hägar the Horrible"
84 Hero

by Henry Hook

85 Part of many a Halloween outfit
86 Noble partner
87 Fictional TV planet
89 ___ Fleming, central character in "The Red Badge of Courage"
90 Dots on a map
91 Home of 67-Across: Abbr.
92 Top
93 Not so friendly
94 Capital of East Flanders
95 Fits (inside)
96 Reed instrument: Abbr.
97 Pork cut
98 Liver in Lyon
99 Braggadocio
100 "No seats left"
101 FedEx competitor
103 Still

ACROSS

1 Theme of this puzzle
9 Accord competitor
15 Is afflicted with sigmatism
20 Emphatic refusal
21 Tulsa native
22 French pen filler
23 Film (1954), actress (2003)
25 Nothing, to Nero
26 Brief
27 Comments around cute babies
28 East ender?
29 "We can't delay!"
30 Visually assess
31 Morsel
33 Fish in fish and chips
35 Isabel Allende's "___ of My Soul"
36 Florence-to-Rome dir.
37 Director (2003), actor (1962)
39 Interject
40 Rests
41 12 meses
42 Low tie
44 Like the Wild West
47 Pen with a cap
48 Abbr. at the bottom of a letter
49 Places for runners
52 Work ___
53 Granny, in Gelsenkirchen
55 China's largest ethnic group
57 Nineveh's kingdom
59 Smeared
61 Film (1992), actor (1958)
64 Follower of weekend news, briefly
65 ___ bran
66 Friend in a western
68 "The Age of Anxiety" author
69 Rent
70 Philosopher Kung Fu-___
71 Actor (1934), actor (1995)
73 Destination of the Bounty in "Mutiny on the Bounty"
76 Comedy club annoyance
78 Olive ___
79 Troll dolls, once
81 Beau ___
82 Milo of "Ulysses"
83 Kind
85 "___ Diaboliques"
87 Big pan
89 Lead role in "La Cage aux Folles"
91 Venezuelan export
92 Object of veneration in ancient Egypt
93 Cool
94 Actress (1986), director (1962)
98 Mail order option, for short
101 Sport jersey material
102 Author Huxley
103 Wallop
104 Kwik-E-Mart owner on "The Simpsons"
105 Pantomime, say
107 Tahoe, e.g., for short
108 Future school?
109 See 113-Down
111 Soil improver
112 Actress (1983), supporting actor (1999)
116 Humble
117 Rebel
118 Checks
119 Surgical aid
120 Jerks
121 Forensic experts

DOWN

1 Investment options, for short
2 Dolls
3 Password, e.g.
4 Reactions to fireworks
5 Former N.F.L. guard Chris
6 Overawe
7 Santa ___
8 Spin
9 Rus. and Ukr., once
10 Response to "pow!" in cartoons
11 Big name in grooming aids
12 Winter wear
13 Detective superintendent Jane of TV's "Prime Suspect"
14 Knack
15 Jay that chatters
16 At first
17 Film (1993), actress (1987)
18 Ready
19 Three-time French Open champ, 1990–92
24 Household item with a neck
29 One flying over Hawaii
31 Stakes
32 Linda Ronstadt's "___ Easy"
33 Villa in Mexico
34 Like the inside of a sphere
37 Gat
38 ___ alai
40 Slender
43 Org.
44 Basutoland, today
45 World books
46 Song (1942), supporting actress (1994)
47 Capital known as the Venice of the East
48 Swamps
50 Informal eating place
51 More racy
54 Sierra Club founder
56 Prized horse
58 Elated
60 Area between hills
62 Geezer
63 Inspiration
67 Kind of vow
71 Reunion gatherers
72 "Us" or "them" in "It's us against them"
74 "Didn't we just have that?"
75 Global energy company
77 Make the beds, dust, etc.
80 March around camp, e.g.
84 Term of respect abroad
86 ". . . as old as yonder ___": James Joyce
88 Late news?
90 Part of a Latin 101 conjugation
91 Works

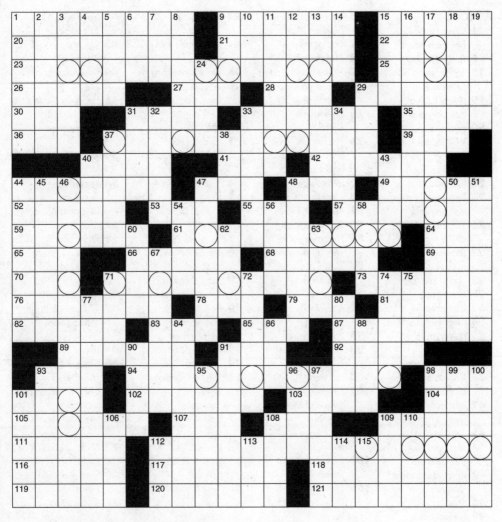

by Nancy Nicholson Joline

ACROSS

1 Offer for an R. J. Reynolds brand?
8 Rules, for short
12 1970 Simon & Garfunkel hit
19 Away from a teaching post
20 Forster's "___ With a View"
22 Joining
23 Cube holder
24 IUD part
25 Realm of Otto von Bismarck
26 1802 acquisition of 25-Across
27 Settles on, in a way
28 Top of a platter
29 Papa pad?
32 Composes
34 Org. that oversees quadrennial games
37 Sporty Mazda
38 Canola and sunflower oil?
41 Best fraternity pledge tormentor?
45 Jack who said "Just the facts, ma'am"
47 Rugged coastline feature
48 "My!"
49 Casual attire
52 Not the most exciting school athletes?
56 Social gathering with the Rockettes?
59 "Like a Rock" singer Bob
61 Cosmetician Lauder and others
62 Get decked out
63 Waste maker

65 Puts up again, as bowling pins
67 Squiggly letter
68 Got sober?
70 Flutter
73 Shows past the doorstep
75 Student of Bartók
76 The lion in "The Lion, the Witch and the Wardrobe"
78 Clap hands on
81 Pan-fry
83 C.I.A. noggins?
85 Hit boxer John with a haymaker?
87 "___ Calloways" (Disney film)
89 "Damien" subtitle
90 Mount Rigi, e.g.
91 Head set
93 Fog in Zürich?
96 How-to films for a dairy farm?
100 ___ nerve
102 First song on "More of the Monkees"
103 ___, meenie, miney, mo
104 Side view of salmon?
109 "Soon It's ___ Rain" ("The Fantasticks" song)
111 Reliquary
112 Temple of Isis locale
116 Facial growths
118 Phrase of agreement
119 Words heard after opening a gift, maybe
121 Hazel, e.g.
122 Ice Cube né ___ Jackson

123 It started around 1100 B.C.
124 Do a mailroom task
125 Professional org.
126 Transcribe some Dickens?

DOWN

1 Colorful carp
2 Enough, for some
3 Plaudits, of a sort
4 "Sure, I'm game"
5 Exposed
6 One of Donald's exes
7 Susan of "Looker"
8 Train storage area
9 ___ Tubb, the Texas Troubadour
10 Nabber's cry
11 Rather, informally
12 Silver prizes
13 Physicist Fermi
14 ___ Real, Spain
15 The "se" in per se
16 The King's "princess"
17 Common pasta suffix
18 Eastern title
21 Like some Sp. nouns
27 "The Sopranos" Emmy winner Falco
30 No man's land, in brief
31 Vladimir Putin's onetime org.
33 Michael of R.E.M.
34 Wagner heroine
35 Extras
36 Mooches
39 It commonly follows a verb: Abbr.
40 Disrespect

42 Salespeople, informally
43 Lukas of "Witness"
44 Sheet music abbr.
45 Locks on a dome
46 Chef Lagasse
50 Cornerstone abbr.
51 Must
53 Winners' signs
54 August hrs.
55 Some football blockers: Abbr.
57 "See ___?"
58 Plane part
60 Signs a lease
64 "Julius Caesar" setting
66 Deejay's bane
68 Classic soft drink with orange, grape and peach flavors
69 Shad delicacies
70 "So-Called Chaos" singer Morissette
71 Like Niels Bohr
72 Kind of inspection
73 Orch. section
74 Old French coin
76 Means of defense: Abbr.
77 Come across as
78 Canned meat brand
79 "And that's ___" ("Believe you me")
80 Christina in the 2005 revival of "Sweet Charity"
82 Speech stumbles
84 Informal greetings
86 Zoo feature, in England
88 Finnic language

by Patrick Blindauer and Tony Orbach

92 Fashion inits.
94 Ring bearer
95 Here, on the Riviera
97 Fife player
98 Bread for tacos?
99 Plywood layer
100 ___ Book Club
101 7, 11 and 13
105 Bologna bone
106 Mandela's native tongue
107 Hijacked cruise ship Achille ___
108 Bar at the bar
110 "I'd hate to break up ___"
113 Having a taste of the grape
114 Run up ___
115 NASA cancellation
116 Econ. measure
117 Your and my
119 Snap
120 Cyrano's nose

SPLITS AND MERGERS

ACROSS

1 Upper end of a soprano's range
6 Life work?
9 In support of
12 Bishopric
19 Basketballer nicknamed the Diesel
20 Attribute (to)
22 Joins up
23 Concave button
24 "Over my dead body!" / Alert [split]
26 Exchange words? / New beginning [merger]
28 ___ Maria (coffee liqueur)
29 Gift-wrapper's need
30 Strummed instrument
32 "___ my doubts"
33 Animated film character voiced by Matthew Broderick
35 Fine fellow
36 Undecided, you might say
38 Deal (out)
39 Annoying obligations / "No need to check" [split]
42 1980s "NBC News Overnight" anchor / Feared insect [merger]
44 At full speed
45 "Mazel ___!"
46 "The History ___" (Tony-winning play)
47 Harsh
48 Return flight destinations?
52 Off-limits
55 Get down
56 Plant manager?
58 Figure just above the total
59 Black hole's boundary / Despite the fact that [split]
62 Group migration
64 Like Eton attendees
65 Author of the "Earth's Children" series
66 Social reformer Lucretia
67 "Great Scott!"
68 A little cross?
70 Double sugar / Travel freely? [merger]
74 Get dressed (up)
75 "Feh!"
76 Insects found in trunks
77 Takes off
78 Bag
80 In the cooler
81 Unread messages, usually
83 Mountain SE of ancient Troy
85 It has many sides
86 Commuter's source of entertainment / Actor John or David [split]
90 Martini ingredient / Delta site [merger]
94 Burt's "Stroker Ace" co-star
95 "The Seagull" ingenue
96 Water, to Watteau
97 Fictional blue humanoid
98 Aggressive patriot
99 Fishtank accessory
100 Prefix with potent
102 MapQuest suggestion: Abbr.
103 Franz Liszt, e.g. / Didn't go straight, maybe [split]
106 "Come back now, y'hear?" / Park employee [merger]
110 TV journalist Van Susteren
113 Commentator
114 Using company resources
115 Great white ___
116 Took too long, as a meeting
117 Superhero name ender
118 Broke bread
119 Finger-lickin' good

DOWN

1 ___ polloi
2 Overnight site
3 Patrician
4 Della sells hers in "The Gift of the Magi"
5 See 26-Across
6 Keen producers
7 Quarantine
8 Scale's range
9 Taylor's deputy on TV
10 Kimono securer
11 ___ room
12 Gap filler?
13 Occupy
14 Blast furnace input
15 Peacemaker maker
16 #1 hit for Marty Robbins
17 Add surreptitiously
18 Some phosphates, e.g.
21 Observance
25 See 24-Across
27 Modern political acronym
30 Navajo enemy
31 See 42-Across
33 Abrupt increase on a graph
34 Assuages one's guilt
37 Prepares, in a way, as chicken
39 Adult insect
40 California county with Point Reyes National Seashore
41 See 39-Across
43 Origin
44 Complete
47 It's not needed in hydroponics
49 It's clipped at both ends
50 Philippic
51 Game similar to bridge
52 Really appeals to
53 Earthly paradise of Celtic legend
54 Caviar source
55 W.W. II light machine gun
56 See 70-Across
57 Bleeped word
60 Reagan's first secretary of state
61 See 59-Across
62 Pros who practice
63 Violinist Itzhak
66 Four-legged female
69 Napped fabrics
70 "Goodbye, Mr. Chips" star
71 ___ Sea, connected to St. George's Channel
72 It's split
73 At a distance
76 ___ bourguignon
79 See 90-Across

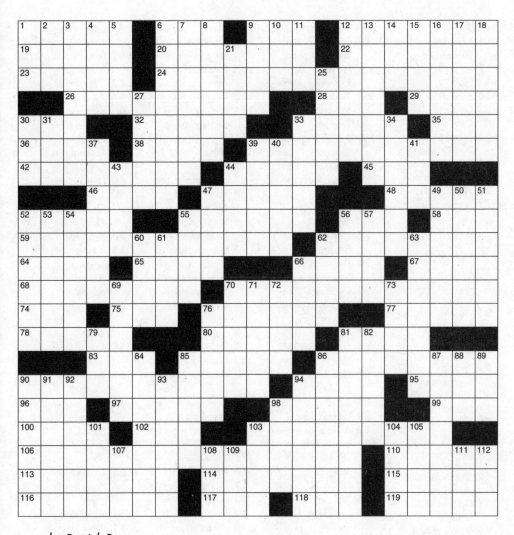

by Patrick Berry

81 1953 3-D film starring Fernando Lamas
82 Earlier
84 Seat separator
85 See 106-Across
86 Stop up
87 Some campaign fund-raisers
88 See 86-Across
89 Cereal grass
90 Himalayan cedar
91 ___ Quimby, girl of children's lit
92 Chinese province bordering Vietnam, Laos and Myanmar
93 Change genetically
94 ___ franca
98 2007 title role for Ellen Page
101 "___ be O.K."
103 Chemistry Nobelist Otto
104 See 103-Across
105 Precinct
107 ___ landslide
108 Country singer McGraw
109 What retroviruses contain
111 Preschooler
112 To some extent

ACROSS

1 Place for bluegrass
7 #1 on the charts
12 Blast
20 Kia sedan
21 Café con ___
22 Certify
23 Broad comedies involving hogs?
25 Like traditional Catholic Masses
26 N.H.L.'s Tikkanen
27 Entertainment center at many a sports bar
28 Where bluejackets go
30 Movement that inspired '60s fashion
31 Good viewing spot for a canyon
32 Bickering
33 Bookcase lineup
34 Beautifully illustrated report of a computer failure?
39 Clark's partner
40 It's put on some houses
41 "It'll ___ you"
42 Stockholm-bound carrier
45 First-year J.D. student
46 Makes eyes at
49 All-time top-selling Atari video game
51 Cake maker's boast?
53 Short-legged, thickset horse
55 Not badgering, say
56 Flood survivor
57 Nursery rhyme call sung to an old French melody
60 Short breaks
61 French director's comment about his submission to a film festival?
67 Wide-headed fastener
68 Smears
69 Ang Thong resident
70 How some kids spend the summer
73 "Peer Gynt" mother
74 Bird call on a farm?
79 They're developed by a muscleman
82 Lip cover
83 Nebraska county with an Indian name
84 Super Bowl XLII M.V.P. Manning
85 Gen. Lee, in brief
86 Loyal
88 Lobster claw
89 A Simpson without access to his volume of the "Odyssey"?
94 Rocker Morissette
96 Till compartment
97 Succulents that soothe
98 Easy wins
99 Starter starter?
100 Sign that's often lit
101 Film editor's job
104 Most heterogeneous
106 Former Tennessee senator's Halloween costumes?
109 Prestigious
110 Curt
111 Name on some euros
112 Sources of a cosmetics oil
113 King in 1 B.C.
114 Body-sculpting undergarment

DOWN

1 Be down
2 Narrative writing
3 Razor brand
4 Cartoonist Browne
5 Breakfast menu heading
6 Brave words?
7 Mason of a sort
8 Griffin who loved game shows
9 Virginia is in it: Abbr.
10 Cover
11 Redcoat's ally
12 Do for a V.I.P.?
13 South American tuber
14 Creatures with three hearts
15 Opening remarks at a coffee makers' convention?
16 Paying guest
17 "Do ___?"
18 Baseball catchers
19 Time on la Côte d'Azur
24 Banking initialism
29 ". . . to name just a few": Abbr.
31 Not straight
32 Seller's terms
33 Symbol of blackness
34 Coup start
35 Clinton's attorney general
36 Pitcher
37 Give ___ up
38 Also addresses, as with an email
42 Long-necked instrument
43 Opposite of reject
44 Payroll dept. ID's
46 Light wind?
47 Sacred cup
48 Christine of "Running on Empty"
49 French cleric
50 ___ consequence
52 Check holder: Abbr.
53 Monthly charge
54 Couple in a rowboat
57 Tournament passes
58 ___ Boy, classic figure in Japanese anime
59 One of Dumas's Musketeers
61 "___ inside" (slogan)
62 Louis Vuitton competitor
63 Rat-___
64 Some Wharton alums
65 Tooth holders
66 Hawaiian Punch rival
67 Sticky stuff
71 Where a dope unloads a ship?
72 Words on a deathbed, maybe
74 Bass ___
75 Popular snack cakes
76 Talked-about twosome
77 Part
78 Tree in bloom in a Van Gogh painting

by Elizabeth C. Gorski

80 Five-dollar bills, slangily
81 Photocopier option: Abbr.
82 Fraternity members
86 Highest grade
87 Was not cooped up
88 Love
89 Whence the line "To sleep: perchance to dream"
90 Stopped fasting
91 Vented
92 Minnesota's St. ___ College
93 Fabrics that shimmer
94 Stood
95 Led Zeppelin's "Whole ___ Love"
99 Norms: Abbr.
100 ___ buco
101 Bloke
102 ___ Reader
103 Bygone autocrat
104 Touched
105 "Didn't I tell you?"
107 Clearance rack abbr.
108 Valedictorian's pride, for short

COMMON INTERESTS

ACROSS

1 Track figure
8 Din-din
12 Nautical line
19 Ally makers
20 Search high and low
22 Like some grievances
23 Home of the newspaper Haaretz
24 Electrical engineers and news anchors?
26 World travelers and wine connoisseurs?
28 Wrestling locale
29 Cheer greatly
30 Some Millers
31 It may be pinched
32 Zealous
34 Business card abbr.
35 Oriole or Blue Jay, for short
36 Completely bungle
38 Hercules or Ulysses
39 Eyed
42 Classic Hans Christian Andersen story, with "The"
44 Geologists and music video producers?
46 Meal crumb
47 Congestion site
48 Some volcanic deposits
52 College students and mattress testers?
57 Greeted
58 Outdoor cover
59 Robert who introduced the term "cell" to biology
60 Where the antihelix is
61 Under
64 Itinerary word
65 Choir stands
67 Despicable sort
69 Executed
70 Stop
72 The Gamecocks of the Southeastern Conf.
73 Machinates
76 Prominent D.C. lobby
78 Wallop
79 Twelve ___
81 Supercool
82 Old West outlaws and aspiring thespians?
85 Bit of gridiron equipment
87 Obviously sad
88 Boffo
89 Beat-era musicians and orthopedists?
91 Show on the small screen
96 Home of the Rachel Carson National Wildlife Refuge
98 PC screens, for short
99 Certain investigators, for short
100 Champ just before 36-Down
101 Tough spot
102 Lavishes gifts (on), say
104 U.N. chief ___ Ki-moon
105 Desex
106 Huge, in poetry
109 Shak. is its most-quoted writer
110 Fort Knox officials and pop singers?
113 Comedians and parade directors?
116 Defeat in a derby
117 Office newbie
118 "___ joking!"
119 Lettered top
120 Set out
121 Cold war inits.
122 Activity in which spelling counts?

DOWN

1 Like a guardian
2 Kept from home
3 Flew
4 Bay ___ (residents of Massachusetts)
5 Walter ___, author of "The Hustler"
6 Prince in "The Little Mermaid"
7 Answer
8 Mortgagee's concern
9 Sharp
10 Craggy peaks
11 Boulogne-___-Mer, France
12 For all to play, in music
13 With 105-Down, a short play
14 Salon option
15 Cambodian money
16 Florid
17 Stroked
18 Car with an innovative "rolling dome" speedometer
21 Ad-libs and such
25 Honcho
27 Western tribe
32 Stepped aside, in court
33 Gave
36 1976–80 Wimbledon champ
37 Not touch
38 Sounds of anger or jubilation
40 Factory shipments: Abbr.
41 Hurdle for some college srs.
43 Sharpeners
44 Estuary
45 Assist in shady doings
47 Blood ___
49 Extravagant
50 Mournful
51 Sudden floods
52 Much smaller now
53 Exterminator's option
54 Gangster's gun
55 Nickname once at 1600 Pennsylvania Ave.
56 Hurried
57 Member of the familia
62 Needing bleach, say
63 Campaign feature
66 Eked (out)
68 Feels indignant about
71 Egg holder
74 Religious pilgrimage
75 Rebounds and steals
77 Hurt so bad
80 Fruit-flavored soda
83 ___ Magica
84 "Essential" things
86 A.T.M. need
87 Without oomph
90 Certain chamber group

by Robert W. Harris

91 Oversee
92 Heat-related
93 On
94 Dog after the winter, e.g.
95 How Calvin Coolidge spoke
96 You can say that again

97 Lacking scruples
99 Less accurate
101 Kids
103 Expressed delight
104 Some South Africans
105 See 13-Down
107 Symbol of thinness

108 Attire not for the modest
110 Striped animals
111 Wands
112 Prefix with zone
114 "Imagine that!"
115 Note to be used later

ACROSS

1 Lively, in mus.
5 101, in a course name
10 "Little ___ in Slumberland" (pioneering comic strip)
14 One on two feet
19 Literature Nobelist Morrison
20 Word on a wanted poster
21 He's seen on the ceiling of the Sistine Chapel
22 Serengeti grazer
23 Pedicurist's need
26 Antics
27 Zingers
28 Toot one's horn
29 Scrooge's nephew in "A Christmas Carol"
30 Wearer of uniform #37, retired by both the Yankees and the Mets
34 Entered pompously
38 Clears
39 Relating to flight technology
41 Carnival site
42 "Inka Dinka ___"
43 Close overlapping of fugue voices
45 Prince ___, Eddie Murphy film role
47 Caboose, e.g.
48 Frolicking
52 Whispering party game
54 Vardalos of the screen
55 Diva's delivery
56 Holiday celebrating deliverance from Haman
59 Narrow inlet
60 Textile factory fixture
62 ___ fide
63 Lingo suffix
64 Unfortunate development
65 Bone-dry
66 Divider of wedding guests
68 Champion figure skater Irina
72 Leaves for lunch?
75 Author Janowitz
77 Professor 'iggins
78 Picassos and Pissarros
80 55-Across, e.g.
81 Bewitched
83 Penlight battery size
84 ___ radiation
86 DeMille output
87 Early millennium year
88 Manual transmission position
91 French dome toppers
93 Big shot after making a big shot, maybe: Abbr.
94 Kind of question
95 Peter Shaffer play based on the lives of Mozart and Salieri
98 "___-haw!"
99 Make haste
100 Like sugar vis-à-vis Equal
102 H.S. subject
106 Heartbreaking situations
109 Kitchen implement used with a little muscle
112 In the mail
113 K.G.B. predecessor
115 Popular Toyota
116 Users of 118-Across
118 Bats, balls, gloves, etc.
122 False appearance
123 Capital of Italy
124 Annie of "Ghostbusters"
125 Blade of Grasse
126 Lugged
127 Zenith
128 Company-owned building, e.g.
129 Sch. research papers

DOWN

1 Place for a fan
2 Writer Peggy known for the phrase "a kinder, gentler nation"
3 Actually existing
4 Stately dance with short steps
5 Tempts
6 Elite athlete
7 Error indicator
8 Suffix with adverb
9 Hit TV show with the theme song "Who Are You"
10 Port west of Monte Vesuvio
11 Fall setting
12 A, B and C
13 Mantra syllables
14 Come-hither look
15 Coming-clean words
16 Protective mailer
17 Music producer Brian
18 License to drill?: Abbr.
24 Milano of "Who's the Boss?"
25 Carbolic acid
29 Top-rated TV series of 2001–02
31 Consort of 21-Across
32 Capone henchman
33 "They're in my hot little hands!"
35 BlackBerry rival
36 Land of Ephesus
37 Acknowledge tacitly
40 Heads in the Pantheon?
44 Variety
46 Poet Omar ___
48 Rhyme scheme of "Stopping by Woods on a Snowy Evening"
49 "Star Trek: T.N.G." counselor Deanna
50 Some business attire
51 Yellow Teletubby
53 Composer Satie
57 Letters before many a state's name
58 Brush up on
61 Whiteboard cleaner
64 Subj. that deals with mixed feelings
67 Bearing nothing
69 Japanese eel and rice dish
70 "King Lear" or "Hamlet": Abbr.
71 Boxer's measurement
73 Touched down
74 Medics
76 Nonbeliever
79 Classic Dana fragrance for women
81 Representations of a winged woman holding an atom
82 Big name in skin care products

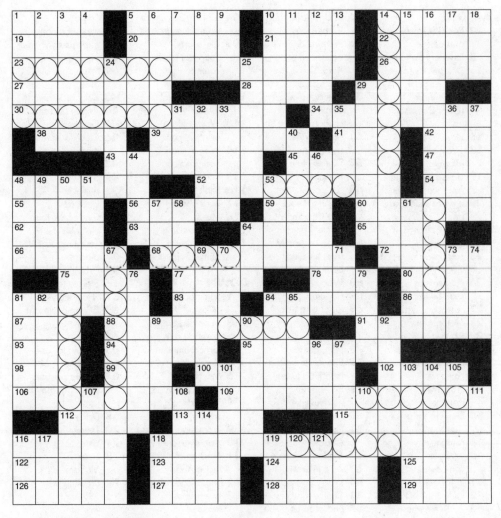

by Paula Gamache

84 Entire range
85 Amazon parrot
89 Opener for a crystal ball gazer
90 Dine at a diner
92 F equivalent
96 Not dis
97 Declaim
101 Estimated: Abbr.

103 Chemical cousin
104 Lug: Var.
105 Online protocol for remote log-in
107 Discontinue
108 Absorb
110 Like lip-glossed lips
111 Deserves

114 Cause for an R, perhaps
116 Badge holder: Abbr.
117 Status ___
118 Main
119 Day ___
120 Dawn goddess
121 Divisions of gals.

COULD YOU REWORD THAT, PLEASE?

ACROSS

1 Rocker Ocasek and others
5 Dwellers along the Dnieper River
10 "A ___, petal and a thorn" (Emily Dickinson poem)
15 Rtes.
18 1969 self-titled jazz album
19 United We Stand America founder
20 Eastern seaboard rte.
21 Greek discord goddess
23 Tax break for Gumby?
26 Publication read by drs.
27 "Steady ___ goes"
28 Motor levers
29 Abjures
31 Money replaced by the 49-Down
33 "Bien sûr!"
34 Primitive wind instruments
35 Blessing for a shipboard romance?
40 Without compassion
41 Indisposed
42 Be indisposed
43 Architect whose epitaph says "Reader, if you seek his monument, look around you"
44 It's short for a long car
47 World's longest wooden roller coaster, at Kings Island
51 Battery type
52 "Hawaii Five-O" airer

55 Bridge writer Culbertson
56 Perhaps doesn't believe witty Rogers?
58 "Let's ___!"
59 Like some single-sex schools
61 Near-grads: Abbr.
62 Dinner plate scraping
63 ___'acte
64 "On First Looking Into Chapman's Homer" poet
65 Tribe originally from the Deep South
68 Wood shop device
69 Rigor of a fever
70 "Yoo-___!"
72 "Alley ___!"
73 "Oh, please"
75 Enough to hold a lotta iPod tunes
76 End-game maneuvers?
80 Turncoat
81 Somalia neighbor: Abbr.
82 Modern address
83 Zero interest
84 W.W. II vessels
85 Choice marbles
87 End of some 82-Acrosses
88 "Hands Across the Sea" composer
90 Writer ___ Rogers St. Johns
92 Excavate in the white cliffs?
99 "A Little Bitty Tear" singer, 1962
101 United
102 Flamenco cheer
103 Current gauge

104 1910s–'20s Dutch art movement
108 Like many "Survivor" contestants
109 Short ride
110 Drab Oriental fabric?
113 Word before or after "on"
114 Was a good Samaritan to
115 Rock genre
116 Blink ___ eye
117 Born abroad
118 Musts
119 Plant swelling
120 Communism battler, with "the"

DOWN

1 Summarizes
2 "Maybe"
3 Minor league baseball category
4 Greet someone
5 Hot Springs, e.g.
6 March fast?
7 Metropolitan ___
8 What people are saying, briefly
9 Promotion
10 Apt. overseer
11 Mechanics give them: Abbr.
12 Taro dish
13 Like half of all terminals
14 Leader with a goatee
15 Say "hallelujah!"
16 Sketch sewing-kit stores?
17 British fruitcake
22 Fresh
24 "Same here"
25 Prime minister raised in Milwaukee
30 Snail shell shape
32 Personification

34 "Be a ___!"
36 Kind of alcohol
37 Expressed wonder
38 Hops drier
39 "Apologia pro ___ Sua"
43 Kelly or Whitman
44 Waste of a sort
45 Crooked
46 Clown's parade memoir?
48 Twaddle
49 31-Across replacer
50 Decamp
51 One of the four elements
53 Toweling-off place
54 Urban grid
56 Start to lead?
57 "Holy moly!"
60 Onetime telecom giant
63 Listener
65 Friday, for one
66 Dictionary, often
67 Where private messages may be sent?: Abbr.
68 Delay
70 Towel stitching
71 Olive ___
73 Dear ___ Madam . . .
74 Breath: Prefix
76 1990–91 war site
77 Shortly
78 Braided
79 Wood shop device
84 Night owl's TV fare
86 "The House of the Spirits" author, 1982
87 Grunts
89 ___ law (early legal code)
90 Cause to blush

by Daniel C. Bryant

91 Criticize harshly
92 ___ Melodies
93 "I ___ appreciate . . ."
94 In installments
95 In hijab, e.g.
96 "L'chaim!"
97 Figure skater Sokolova and others
98 Little stinger
100 Steakhouse shunner
104 Not natural
105 Terminal figs.
106 Leap on a stage
107 Good soil
111 Summer offering
112 20-Across terminus: Abbr.

36

HOW INSULTING!

ACROSS

1 Polish Peace Nobelist
7 Story development
10 Tongue of Jung: Abbr.
13 Variety show potpourri
18 Scrubs
19 Head of Great Britain
20 Where "I shot a man" in Johnny Cash's "Folsom Prison Blues"
21 Something to believe in
22 Foul weather condition?
25 1980s U.N. ambassador Kirkpatrick
26 Date
27 Sounded wowed
28 Plume source
29 Child protector?
30 Some moralizing about getting off a balance beam?
34 Quitter's assertion
36 Former Giants giant
37 Saloon door sign
38 "Do your thing, Jack the Ripper"?
43 Provides tools for, as a crime
46 Hefty competitor
47 Matériel
48 Hardships
50 Numbskull
54 Cheerful chorus
55 Wampum
57 Classic soft drink
58 Apartment 1-A resident, maybe
59 Sophistication of clubs like Sam's and BJ's?
62 Wool source
66 Title for Michael Caine
67 Declines
68 Concerns of someone who's choking?
75 Prepare
76 Used a bus, e.g.
77 March master
78 Fraction of a min.
82 Delta 88, e.g.
83 Asian shrine
85 Mid 10th-century year
86 Another, in Andalucia
87 Bruce who played Watson
88 Her Royal Daunter?
91 Eucharist plate
94 Suffix with ball
95 Take off, as a brooch
96 Coleslaw-loving children?
104 ___ nothing
105 Player of filmdom's Mr. Chips
106 With all one's strength
107 Welsh rabbit ingredient
110 Airbus, e.g.
111 Find chewing gum under a desk, perhaps?
114 Passage practices
115 Chihuahua drink
116 Prominent Chihuahua feature
117 Samantha's cousin on "Bewitched"
118 In other words
119 Bygone map letters
120 Hook shape
121 Texas team

DOWN

1 Rolls of dough
2 Broadway Rose-lover
3 Crosses the international date line from east to west
4 Work measurement unit
5 James I and Charles I
6 Northeast state of India
7 1979 film parodied in "Spaceballs"
8 Sonata movement
9 Subordinate person
10 Sci-fi, e.g.
11 Over
12 Swiss dish of grated and fried potatoes
13 Place in Monopoly
14 Continue
15 Doing the same old same old
16 Joint parts
17 Insertion in an operation
20 Just
23 Even if, briefly
24 More humid
31 Bagnold, Blyton, Markey, etc.
32 Postal creed word
33 Some NCOs
34 Rock's ___ Pop
35 Popular pop
39 '50s teen star
40 Incenses
41 Car financing co.
42 "As we have therefore opportunity, let ___ good to all men": Galatians
43 Tommie ___, 1966 A.L. Rookie of the Year
44 Nobel physicist Niels
45 Actor Bana of "Munich"
49 Prelims
50 Import tax
51 Magnum ___
52 "Coming Home" co-star
53 Stacking contest cookie
56 Puzzled (out)
58 Metal refuse
59 Sideless wagon
60 Nonexistent
61 Seals are part of it
62 Do that's picked
63 Advent song
64 More than nudge
65 9 to 5, e.g.
69 Go on too long
70 Venetian V.I.P. of yore
71 Wannabe's model
72 Rx writers
73 Judy Garland's real last name
74 "La ___ Bonita" (Madonna song)
78 Diamond center
79 Efficiency device
80 ". . . ___ saw Elba"
81 Mass. neighbor
83 Worrisome engine sound
84 Highway or Pet lead-in
87 Like a relative notified in an emergency, maybe
89 ___ while

by Cathy Millhauser

90 Preserves fruits
91 Sans a healthy glow
92 Remove by cutting
93 Porterhouse alternatives
94 Honshu metropolis
96 Banana liqueur drink shaken over ice
97 Old Norse works
98 Magician Henning and others
99 Run up
100 Oral flourishes
101 Starfleet V.I.P.'s: Abbr.
102 Japanese yes
103 "Once You ___ Stranger" (1969 thriller)
108 TV host known for his mandibular prognathism
109 History chapters
112 Word between two surnames
113 Leftover for Rover

37 SPACED OUT

When the puzzle is done, the letters in the following squares spell a bonus phrase: 7A - 3rd letter, 31A - 5th, 65A - 4th, 104A - 6th, 136A - 3rd, 151A - 1st, 149A - 4th, 133A - 4th, 100A - 1st, 62A - 1st, 29A - 6th

ACROSS

1 Thing in a case
4 1960s–'80s Red Sox legend, informally
7 In the cellar
11 Org. that promotes adoption
15 "Poor venomous fool," in "Antony and Cleopatra"
18 Pumpkin-picking time: Abbr.
19 "Sons and Lovers" Oscar nominee Mary
20 Expected
22 King of comedy
23 Going rate?: Abbr.
24 1941 Henry Luce article that coined a name for an era
28 Barcelona Olympics prize
29 Tevye creator ____ Aleichem
30 Eight-time Norris Trophy winner
31 Protein acid, informally
32 Have ____ to pick
33 Celine Dion's "I'm Your Angel" duet partner
34 Closeout come-on
39 Designated driver's drink
40 Badges, e.g., in brief
41 ____ candy (some pop tunes)
42 Work of Seigneur de Montaigne
43 "Your Moment of ____" ("The Daily Show" feature)
45 Truncated cones, in math
49 Streaming
52 Novel that ends "Don't ever tell anybody anything. If you do, you start missing everybody"
61 Not to mention
62 Atlas section
63 "Roll Over Beethoven" band, for short
64 1990s–2000s English tennis star Tim
65 Rocky Mountains resort
66 Wide-eyed
67 First principles
70 "I'm king of the world!," e.g.
71 Exceeded the speed limit?
72 "Tancredi" composer
75 Artful deception
78 State quarters?
80 Actress Ullmann
81 Suffix with billion
82 1972 Harry Nilsson hit
90 Windsor, e.g.
95 Switch finish?
96 Absorb a loss
97 1984 Heisman winner
99 Orient
100 Chickadees' kin
101 Laughing gas and water, chemically
103 Mess up
104 Lover in "The Merchant of Venice"
106 Genuine: Ger.
107 Prime eatery
111 Sloughs off
113 You can't take it with you
114 Upstate N.Y. sch.
115 Tribute in jest
118 Managed
119 Sneak a peek
121 Boot part
125 Stanley Cup finalists of 1982 and 1994
131 Couple
133 Long-legged wader
134 He played Krupa in "The Gene Krupa Story"
135 "You did it!"
136 Lorenz Hart specialty
137 Pricey sports car, informally
138 Head of a special government inquiry
143 Hard wood
144 Math. class
145 Actress Watts
146 Home on "Gilligan's Island"
147 Inflation meas.
148 On the other hand
149 Charles de Gaulle alternative
150 Varsity QB, e.g.
151 Sign at a smash
152 Possessed

DOWN

1 "Number 10" Abstract Expressionist
2 Made a comeback?
3 "A Streetcar Named Desire" role
4 "Dee-lish!"
5 "These ____ the times that . . ."
6 Closed (in on)
7 Money
8 Botanist Gray
9 Center of many revolutions
10 Certain X or O
11 Subbed (for)
12 Dive
13 Glances
14 "____ takers?"
15 Spanish sherry
16 Offshoot
17 Snap
21 Mother of Judah
25 Popular portal
26 Kupcinet and Cross
27 Application letters
29 Some namesakes: Abbr.
32 Without obligation
35 Change of a mortgage, slangily
36 Paul Bunyan story
37 Ministry of ____, in "1984"
38 Ryder Cup team
40 Time ____
43 Tase
44 When many get a St.-Tropez tan
46 Biblical queendom
47 Joint part
48 Royal Navy foe of 1588
50 Willow used in basketry
51 Hills of Yorkshire
52 Spree
53 Monster hurricane of 1989
54 Libido
55 Lowly workers
56 Do voodoo on
57 Skull and Bones members
58 Latitude
59 Bleeth of "Baywatch"
60 Unabridged
67 Executive's charter, maybe
68 Infiltrator
69 Flat-bottomed boat
73 Despot ____ Amin
74 Lead-in to "the above" or "your business"
76 Like some twins
77 ____ center
79 Mystery element
82 Leaps across the ballet stage
83 "Vega$" star Robert
84 Nick Nolte movie based on a Kurt Vonnegut novel
85 Some advanced researchers, for short
86 Traditional almanac data
87 Bikini blast
88 Sorry sort
89 Parisian "to be"
91 Jean who wrote "Please Don't Eat the Daisies"
92 "So long, dahling"
93 "The fix ____"
94 Virginie ou Pennsylvanie
98 Subject of the book "Many Unhappy Returns": Abbr.
102 ____ Zagora, Bulgaria
104 Infant's food
105 "Certainement!"

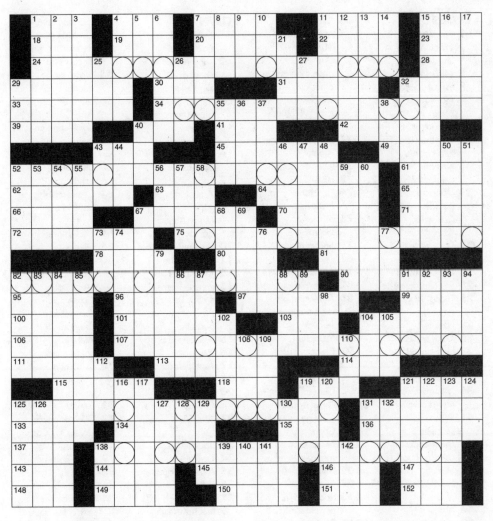

by John Farmer

Oops!

ACROSS

1 Program executors, for short
5 Miracle-___
8 Tribal council makeup, often
14 Casual attire
19 Like the carol "Away in a Manger," originally
21 Wine sometimes blended with Cabernet Sauvignon
22 Be
23 Turn away
24 Foot, slangily
25 2% alternative
26 *Long, long time
28 Loot
30 Yank or Tiger
31 Half-baked
32 *Stick with a needle, maybe
34 *Absence at a nudist colony?
41 What a Tennessee cheerleader asks for a lot?
42 Stuck
43 Neighbor of Ga.
44 *Bugs
50 Jazzy Jones
51 *Wee
54 Below par
55 X-ray ___
56 "What a moron I am!"
57 Gawk at
58 Whatchamacallit
60 Monterrey mister
62 Suffix not seen much in London
63 Least bold

65 Like the answers to the 10 asterisked clues, more often than any other English words, according to a 1999 study
69 Narrative
71 ___ choy (Chinese vegetable)
72 Contract specifics
73 Luster
74 Tip of the Arabian Peninsula
76 Massage target?
77 Spicy cuisine
81 Debt acknowledgment
82 *Conspicuous
86 Trying period for a doctoral student
87 *Supplant
91 Clean air org.
92 Baseball's ___ league
93 Gen ___
94 *Doggedness
97 *Oblige
103 Commotion
104 Series of rounds
105 Is undecided
107 *Event
113 Root used in perfumery
115 Farmer's ___
117 Attempts
118 T-shirt style
119 Follows
120 Like some pens
121 Swift's "A Modest Proposal," e.g.
122 Plain
123 Alternative to dial-up
124 French noblemen

DOWN

1 Symbol of happiness
2 Long-haired sheepdog
3 Regulated bus.
4 Writer/illustrator Silverstein
5 Mustang competitor
6 Photoshop options
7 Tops
8 Ambulance figure: Abbr.
9 Many August babies
10 Disarming words?
11 Rocker John
12 Violinist's need
13 Pen, to Pierre
14 1950s Braves All-Star pitcher Burdette
15 Relaxes, in a way
16 It's bowed
17 Archipelago part
18 Cubic meter
20 Laredo-to-Galveston dir.
27 "Bro!"
29 Cliff
33 Spanish "a"
34 Karl Marx's one
35 Alphabet quartet
36 Expose
37 Product with TV's first advertising jingle, 1948
38 Word of encouragement
39 QB Manning
40 "Illmatic" rapper
44 Most massive
45 The whole wide world
46 Show up again
47 Judged, with "up"
48 They're seen in many John Constable paintings

49 ___ machine
51 Orator's no-no
52 Restaurant chain since 1958
53 Close, as a relationship
56 Laura of "Jurassic Park"
58 Some shampoos
59 Running mate with Dick
60 Like cotton candy
61 Commercial come-on
62 Type
64 Ticklish one?
65 Freeze
66 Target of many a Bart Simpson prank call
67 Rice-A-___
68 Marmalade component
69 Without adjustments
70 Dynasty of Confucius and Lao-tzu
75 Trendy
77 Olive or apple
78 Goldie of "Cactus Flower"
79 Actor Baldwin
80 "Ah, yes"
83 O.K. mark
84 When Earth Day is celebrated: Abbr.
85 ___ profundo
86 Anthem contraction
88 Rare imports, maybe
89 Crucial sleep stage
90 Cock-a-doodle-doo
92 Examination
94 Opposite of "nod off"
95 Marked permanently

by Oliver Hill

96 Parish priests
97 Previously mentioned
98 Toes' woes
99 Parish priests
100 Matriarchs
101 __-garde
102 Brusque

106 Ooze
108 Dorm heads, for short
109 "Heavens!"
110 International chain of fusion cuisine restaurants

111 Course after trig
112 Somme times
114 Heavens
116 Literary inits.

39

POPLAR MUSIC

ACROSS

1 Craving, slangily
6 Crèche figures
10 Impromptu Halloween costume
15 Spray withdrawn in 1989
19 Try to steal the scene, maybe
20 "Darn it!"
21 Mountain chain
23 Nick name?
24 1977 Dolly Parton song for tree fanciers?
26 Bridal collection
28 Not ___ many words
29 Nominal promotion of a military officer
30 Sugar substitute?
31 Modern pentathlon event
32 Inner circles
33 1965 Yardbirds song for tree fanciers?
39 ___ volatile
40 Bellowing
41 Nirvana seeker
42 World capital, founded in 1538, formerly known as Chuquisaca
44 Suffix with myth
48 Went like a shot
50 1957 Jerry Lee Lewis song for tree fanciers?
53 Outer limits
54 Stand
56 Rush hour sounds
57 Port of Iraq
58 One trillionth: Prefix
59 Rossini subject
60 Air Force athlete

61 1964 Bobby Goldsboro song for tree fanciers?
68 It's spotted in the wild
69 Like a lot of Australia
70 Lay on the line
71 Brain parts
72 Tippy transport
74 Bank deposit?
75 Old-time oath
79 1982 Joan Jett and the Blackhearts song for tree fanciers?
82 Jazzy Nina
84 Altar procedure
85 "Sesame Street" regular
86 Beaufort scale category
88 Neighbor of Chad
89 Flight formation
90 1959 Chuck Berry song for tree fanciers?
92 Source of some coffee
96 Italian bread
98 Source of creosote
99 Sugar or flour
100 Doozy
101 Do police work
107 1978 Linda Ronstadt song for tree fanciers?
110 Palate part
111 Sing "Bye Bye Birdie," e.g.
112 Hurt badly
113 16th-century English dramatist George
114 Badlands sight
115 Exorcist's enemy
116 Red army?
117 Sp. misses

DOWN

1 Witty remark
2 "A Jug of Wine . . ." poet
3 Off-limits item
4 Words of reproach
5 Strand
6 Key fort?
7 Stretch
8 Ashram leader
9 Chemical suffix
10 Teatime treat
11 Theater audience
12 For this reason
13 Dot follower, often
14 Tito Puente played them
15 "Sink or Swim" author
16 Permission
17 Sign of spring
18 Go into hysterics
22 ___ Lad, doughnut shop on "The Simpsons"
25 Cry of dismay
27 Insignificant amount
31 "A Letter for ___" (Hume Cronyn film)
32 ___ Jr., West Coast hamburger chain
33 Discombobulate
34 Mill material
35 Cross
36 Thanksgiving serving
37 Enters cyberspace
38 Dungeons & Dragons character
39 Sing like Fitzgerald
42 Impassive
43 Nut holder
44 "___ else fails . . ."

45 ___ Systems, networking giant
46 Helpful pointer
47 Musical Rimes
49 Underlying meaning
51 Place for an easel
52 One way to be taken
55 R.N.'s station
58 Purple stuff, perhaps
59 Power of film
60 Happy gatherings
61 Play-by-play partner
62 Theodor Escherich's discovery
63 Ledger entry
64 Anacin alternative
65 ___-Poo of "The Mikado"
66 1970s–'80s baseball All-Star Manny
67 Rap star ___ Jon
72 Chick on the piano
73 Rough condition to face?
74 Criticize
75 Eastern ruler
76 Energetic
77 From the top
78 Laura of "Blue Velvet"
80 Ran through again
81 Give the once-over
83 Cliques
87 Prizes
90 Sufficient, informally
91 Dance specialty
92 Dickens title starter

by Richard Silvestri

93 Soul singer Lou
94 Via ___ (Roman road)
95 Be noisy
96 Words before bed or rest
97 Not at all familiar
99 Email annoyance

100 "The Informer" author O'Flaherty
101 Kind of meeting in "O Brother, Where Art Thou?"
102 Give off
103 Camper driver
104 Something one can never do

105 Salmon tail?
106 Actress Charlotte and explorer John
108 Grand ___, Nova Scotia
109 John's "Pulp Fiction" co-star

40 DONE WITH EASE

ACROSS

1 Rooter at the Meadowlands
8 Lean and bony
15 Superman, to his father
20 Common solvent
21 Filled
22 Acid in proteins
23 State of a bottle-fed baby?
25 Woody Allen title role
26 Afternoon hr.
27 Construction bit
28 Bleacher
30 Comme ci, comme ça
31 Was visibly irked with
35 Shower with flowers, say
36 Soft drink brand
38 A platform in front of Elsinore, in "Hamlet"?
44 Contemporary of Duchamp
47 "Doctor Faustus" novelist
49 Jazz virtuoso Garner
50 The toe of a geographical "boot"
51 Massage therapist's office?
55 Like a Rolex watch
57 Fashion designer Bartley
58 Brown alternative
59 "You can ___ horse to water . . ."
61 Sentimentality
62 "Puppy Love" singer, 1960
63 Jawaharlal Nehru's daughter
65 Rouge roulette number

67 Group of yo-yo experts?
70 One willing to take a bullet for Martin or Charlie?
76 Neighbor of Hung.
77 Fixes firmly
79 Shade on the French Riviera
80 Calypso offshoot
83 Actor Alain
86 It has banks in Bern
87 Urban area in a Cheech Marin film
89 1965 Peace Prize recipient
91 Little Bo-Peep's charges?
94 Catty comments?
95 87 or 93
97 Turn on an axis
98 Alphabet trio
99 Musicians at a marsh?
103 Numerical prefix
105 Corrosive chemical, to a chemist
106 Strong and deep
108 Oversight
112 Limo feature
117 "Road" picture partner for Bob
118 "Same here!"
119 "The joke's ___!"
120 St. Paul sixth graders?
125 Indonesian island
126 Victimizes
127 Brewing needs
128 Do
129 Calendar divisions
130 ___ Row

DOWN

1 ___ Kádár, 1950s–'80s Hungarian leader
2 Low-price prefix
3 "The Love Boat" actress Lauren
4 Squash, squish or squelch
5 Head
6 Gloucester's Cape ___
7 Chick
8 Cuban-born jazz great Sandoval
9 Fix
10 3.9, e.g.: Abbr.
11 Final: Abbr.
12 Gift with a string attached?
13 Over
14 Fix-up
15 Buzzers
16 Green card, informally
17 Leslie Caron title role
18 Home of the Chisholm Trail Expo Center
19 Front of a mezzanine
24 ___ big way
29 Casually showed up
31 Land west of Togo
32 The less you see of this person the better
33 Intro to business?
34 Alpine region
37 German biographer ___ Ludwig
39 ___ of the above
40 Romaine
41 Online periodical, for short
42 Warsaw Pact counterforce
43 Automaker Ferrari

44 Key of Elgar's Symphony No. 1
45 Get the class back together
46 ___-boo
48 "Bye Bye Bye" band, 2000
52 Cousin of a camel
53 "Aren't I amazing?!"
54 Skirt type
56 Called
60 Good blackjack holdings
63 Like G8 meetings: Abbr.
64 "There's no such thing ___ publicity"
66 Subdue
68 "My man!"
69 Resort to violence
71 "Three cheers" recipient
72 Ideal sites
73 Like some pyramids
74 Lined
75 Don, as a sari
78 "Luncheon on the Grass" and others
80 Well
81 Baby-bouncing locale
82 Sanyo competitor
84 Words to live by
85 Hornet, e.g.
87 Extracted chemical
88 "___ of Six" (Joseph Conrad story collection)
90 Hrs. on the 90th meridian
92 Addie's husband in "As I Lay Dying"
93 Stretch . . . or a hint to this puzzle's theme?
96 Shop grippers
100 "And I'm the queen of England"

by Tony Orbach and Patrick Blindauer

101 Director Mark of "Earthquake"
102 Particles in electrolysis
104 Slide presentation?
107 Amazon ___
109 They might be bounced off others
110 Troubadour's stock
111 Wimp
112 Scribbles (down)
113 Body of troops
114 "Well, I declare!"
115 Summer hangout
116 Poop
118 Seaborne lackey
121 Org. interested in schools
122 Albany is its cap.
123 That's "that" in Tijuana
124 Pro ___

ACROSS

1 Site of campus workstations
6 Ancient pueblo dwellers
13 Norm of "This Old House"
18 Muse with a wreath of myrtle and roses
19 Together
20 Tell things?
21 Bill formerly of the Rolling Stones
22 Fight imaginary foes
24 Richard ___, 2002 Pulitzer winner for Fiction
26 ___ B'rith
27 Sylph in Pope's "The Rape of the Lock"
28 Pressure, of a sort
32 "Sixteen Tons" singer, 1955
36 Do better than
37 In the capacity of
38 X-ray units
41 Nails
42 Notch shape
43 "Would you like to see ___?"
45 Italian restaurant chain
47 Game pieces
48 Some badge holders
49 "Alice in Wonderland" sister
50 It's a laugh
51 Each
53 "Lawrence of Arabia" composer Maurice
54 ___-doodle
56 Start of the names of some health care plans
58 Daily grind
60 Place for a vine
61 Bent over
63 How headings are often typed
65 Surfing spot
66 Immigrant's class: Abbr.
68 "Survivor" setting, often
69 Blood-typing letters
70 Fire
72 Some M.I.T. grads: Abbr.
73 Buster?
75 Certain T-shirt design
77 Sure application spot
79 Drug-free
80 National Chili Mo.
81 Blue shade
83 "Pearly Shells" singer
85 Refrain syllables
86 Loud laugh
88 Take to Vegas, maybe
90 Valuable find
92 Mideast call to prayer
93 Airport with a BART terminal
95 Steer
97 Kids
98 Kind of score
99 "Deadwood" figure
100 Untouched
101 Meaningless amount
103 Quick stumbles
104 Dealer's handout
107 Starts, as rehab
110 Upper ___
111 Shade provider
114 Outplays
115 Former L.A. Ram who holds the N.F.L. record for most receiving yards in a game (336)
119 Response to "Any volunteers?"
123 Pretends
124 "Back door's open!"
125 Explorer of sorts
126 To date
127 In order
128 Post with a column

DOWN

1 Missal location
2 "Geronimo!," e.g.
3 Escape
4 Defender company
5 Test extras
6 Electrolysis particle
7 Match ___ (tie game, in France)
8 Aardvark
9 ___ Phillips, who played Livia in "I, Claudius"
10 Old film pooch
11 "Fan-tastic!"
12 Suffix in some pasta names
13 Hosts
14 To the point
15 Opening track of 'The Beatles' Second Album"
16 Cobbler's tool
17 Eds. read them
19 "No problem!"
20 Oscar-winning Brody
23 Jack of "Eraserhead"
25 Good nickname for a cook?
28 Galley marking
29 Peripatetic sort
30 Einstein subject
31 Short-billed rail
33 Push for more business orders
34 House of Lancaster symbol
35 Jilts
39 Sloping surfaces next to sinks
40 Pacifier
44 Cheese ___
46 Good farming results
48 Klinger portrayer on "M*A*S*H"
52 ___ pro nobis
53 Awarding of huge settlements to plaintiffs, in modern lingo
55 Some greetings
57 Zoologist Fossey
59 Early anti-Communist
62 Mix
64 The Nutmeg State: Abbr.
66 Hug
67 Marathoner Alberto
71 Control: Abbr.
74 Actor James
76 Indian tribe encountered by Lewis and Clark
78 Sign of the cross
82 "Were that so!"
84 Plain as day
87 Excellent debt rating
89 Rappel down
91 Edsel driver's gas choice
93 "Bambi" author

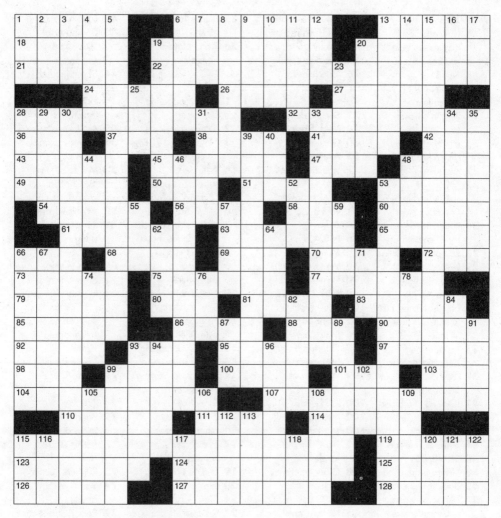

by Brendan Emmett Quigley

SPY GLASS

When this puzzle is done, the seven circles will contain the letters from A to G. Starting with A, connect them alphabetically with one continuous line, and you'll get an image of a 39-Across.

ACROSS

1 How architects' models are built
8 Lou Bega's "___ No. 5"
13 Ottoman V.I.P.'s
18 Foyer item
19 Plug in a travel kit
21 It may give you a cold shoulder
22 Alarming
23 *1969
25 Auditioned for "American Idol"
26 Italian town known for its embroidery
28 End of a plumb line
29 Law assignment
30 Garbage hauler
32 "True"
35 Neighborhood next to N.Y.C.'s East Village
37 Ecuador and Venezuela are in it
39 [See instructions in Notepad]
41 Relating to a blood line
45 Sub systems
47 Suffix with urban
48 *1973–85
50 Moles' production
52 Subj. for bilinguals
54 Like some video, to cable customers
55 Warhol's "___ of Six Self-Portraits"
56 Lambs' kin
58 Aside (from)
61 "Smooth Operator" singer
62 French seas
63 Powder site, maybe
64 First mate
65 "Put ___ writing!"
67 Layer
68 *1987–89

71 Figures at many a wedding reception, briefly
74 Kite flier's wish
75 Muscle mag displays
76 Sneaky
77 Semitic deity
78 Med. plans
80 Gut course
82 Alexander Hamilton's last act
83 "By the power vested ___ . . ."
84 Aches
86 N.B.A.'s ___ Ming
88 Ventured (forth)
90 Writer born May 28, 1908
93 Speech pauses
95 Surprisingly
96 Brings out
97 Offering from St. Joseph
99 Willy Wonka's creator
100 ___ buco
102 Mexican beer
103 A great deal
105 "Lost" filming locale
108 Global currency org.
110 2003 best-selling fantasy novel by teen author Christopher Paolini
113 Beethoven's third?
115 *1995–2002
119 New Jersey city, county or river
121 Name-drop, maybe?
122 Least restrained
123 Artist Watteau
124 Ward off

125 Singer Jones and others
126 Piano players' hangouts

DOWN

1 Old propaganda propagator
2 Ocean menaces
3 *1962–67, 1971 and 1983
4 Attire with supersized pockets
5 "Exodus" hero
6 ___ 9, first spacecraft to land softly on the moon
7 Deviled things
8 Chairman's supporter?
9 Natl. Poetry Mo.
10 Brief encounter?
11 Programme airer, with "the"
12 Knee sock material
13 Wood shaper
14 Like some wrestling
15 Tennis star Mandlikova
16 Edwards and others: Abbr.
17 Eye doctor's concern
19 Shakes up
20 Hungers
24 On
27 California's ___ Valley
31 "___ #1!"
33 Title for 48-Across and 3-Down
34 Lennon's mate
36 Nears, with "on"
38 "The Allegory of Love" writer, 1936
40 Kurchatov who oversaw the Soviet atomic bomb project

42 Lowly one
43 Composer of "Dido and Aeneas"
44 Spearheaded
45 Sign of approval
46 White-collared thrush: Var.
49 Authorizes
51 Butterfly experts, perhaps
53 March 25, in the Christian calendar
57 It can be fragile
59 Residences, in slang
60 Drs.' org.
64 Ship-to-ship communication
66 In song, "Once you pass its borders, you can ne'er return again"
68 Fights
69 Cable TV inits.
70 Baton Rouge sch.
71 *2006–
72 Bond common to the answers to the six starred clues
73 Runners' locales
74 It's full of holes
77 Rock guitarist once married to Goldie Hawn
78 Commander
79 Plan for dinner
81 1998 Sarah McLachlan hit
82 Alpha
84 Disapproving cry
85 Bluesy Smith
87 Night lights
89 Rich soil

by Elizabeth C. Gorski

91 Homeland protection org.
92 Main mailbox locale: Abbr.
94 Sweater flaw
98 Castle and Cara
101 Game played with a 40-card deck
104 "Romanzero" poet
105 Phone co. employee
106 Suffix with billion
107 Jalopy
109 Univ. house
111 Autumn birthstone
112 Second start?
114 Clinches
116 Hanna-Barbera art
117 German direction
118 ___ Na Na
120 Disco guy on "The Simpsons"

43   EXTRA SYLL-UH-BLES

ACROSS

1 Diane of "Alice Doesn't Live Here Anymore"
5 Picture holder
10 ___ alai
13 They may be big fellers
17 Prefix with business
18 West African coins
20 On one's ___
21 World capital formerly a pirate stronghold
22 Waistband sold in stores?
24 Issue to avoid
26 Bad things to share
27 Wiser from an ethical perspective?
29 Miller brand
30 Two points?
31 Wellborn folks
32 Fighting force trained by Pavlov?
38 Qualifying races
39 Auto superseded by the Rambler
40 Actress Susan of "L.A. Law"
41 Leading man?
45 Some cloisonné pieces
46 Distresses
47 Put through demeaning rituals
49 City just west of Silver Springs
50 Salon selections
51 Kilo- times 1,000
52 Mardi ___
54 Skirts worn by both men and women
56 Freelance autopsist?

59 Renaissance painter Uccello
61 Lady Bird Johnson's given birth name
62 Private
63 Catchy song parts heard on "Name That Tune"?
66 Country with a camel on its coat of arms
67 Sign
68 Captain Hook's mate in "Peter Pan"
69 X3 and X5 maker
72 Pack carriers
73 T. ___ Price (investment firm)
75 Intervals
76 Animation
77 Minus
78 Club wielders' grp.
79 Stud farm visitor
80 Crème de la crème
81 Stones and brickbats?
86 Appointed
90 Attorney general during Reagan's second term
91 "Metropolis" director
92 Store that peddles political influence?
95 Like glass doors, often
98 Its bite is worse than its bark
99 Boiled lobster's feature?
102 Be part of the opening lineup
103 High dudgeon
104 Ankle covering
105 Barrett of gossip
106 Lots of talk

107 Smidgen
108 Only beardless one of the Seven Dwarfs
109 Fall around Christmas

DOWN

1 Testing facilities
2 Flu symptom
3 Washes without water
4 Record keepers, of a sort
5 Mobile phone company
6 Bottom of the barrel
7 Weave's partner
8 Rimbaud's "___ Saison en Enfer"
9 "___ the Wanderer" (1820 gothic novel)
10 Composer Pachelbel
11 Gone from the company, maybe
12 Like many large cos.
13 Evildoer
14 To the rear of
15 It's in the spring
16 Alibi
19 Premium vodka brand, for short
21 N.F.L. star Grier
23 Bug-ridden software releases
25 Miniature
28 Down Under jumper
30 Buchanan's secretary of state
32 Sound of a failure
33 Lifesaver
34 Architect Jones
35 Ornamental piece of drapery

36 Timber-dressing tool
37 Actress Witherspoon
41 Squirrels' cache
42 Word to which a common reply is "Bitteschön"
43 "Tattered Tom" author
44 Ensign holder
46 Bacterium that needs oxygen
47 Submit
48 John of "The Addams Family"
49 Self-descriptive fruit
51 Cheek teeth
52 ___ Park, historic home near Philadelphia
53 Vin color
55 Organic compounds with nitrogen
56 French aristocrats
57 Nudge
58 Founding member of the Dadaists
59 Place to keep Mace
60 Not quite right
63 Get better
64 Slowly
65 Motivate
69 Fighting words
70 Fly-catching aid
71 Depression causes
74 Granola tidbit
75 Willing
76 Appliances with lids
78 Belarus port
79 Think that might is right?
80 It may come with attachments

by Patrick Berry

81 Not just sit there
82 Projected onto a screen
83 Last number in a column
84 Ohm of Ohm's law
85 Queen of mystery
86 2005 Best Picture winner
87 ___ Sorrel (woman in a love triangle in "Adam Bede")
88 Available by the pint, perhaps
89 Rubberneck
93 Alter pieces?
94 ___ Roberts, first inductee into the Romance Writers of America Hall of Fame
95 ___-Ball
96 Inadvisable action
97 Chew on
100 Per la grazia di ___ (by the grace of God)
101 Brand at a gas station

ACROSS

1 Bear-named villainess in Superman films
5 Cause of a full stop for sailing ships
13 Ritzy Rio neighborhood
20 Column on a questionnaire
21 Blasted, with "on"
22 Wreaked havoc on
23 They tremble in the slightest breeze
25 Apple pie order
26 Strip
27 Hoedown sites
28 Geneviève, e.g.: Abbr.
29 Beginning of a cowboy song refrain
30 Loathing
31 "Star Wars," e.g.
32 Parliamentary measure of 1774
35 It's pitched
36 Abbey area
37 Introductory course?
39 Grassy plains
40 Ten-millionth of a joule
41 Too much ink
42 Arctic bird
43 Run out
44 Period in which we live
47 Addams who created the Addams family
51 Drang's counterpart
53 Sidesplitter
54 Word before and after "yes"
55 Reason for lights going out
56 Trio of comedy
58 Takes off
60 "All ___"
62 Mrs., abroad
63 Recoiling from
65 Pursue
68 Hikes
69 Compound that's subject to tautomerism
70 Vending machine tricker
72 Packard's partner
73 Scintillas
75 Chess opening?
77 Canine cry
79 Cries shrilly
80 ___ Mawr
81 "The Spirit of Australia" sloganeer
84 Engorge
86 Wildly
87 Implements using fulcrums
88 Red, e.g., once
91 Credit card magnet
94 Birthstone for some Libras
95 Stage direction
96 Relative of Welsh
97 Daughter of James II
99 Shadow
100 Attacks
101 Tea holder
102 Grasp
103 Teem
105 Washing machine setting
106 Title girl of a Willa Cather novel
109 Graham Greene novel set in Saigon, with "The"
111 Woodworker, at times
112 Without paraphrasing
113 Pig product
114 Backwoods valleys
115 Freezing mixtures
116 Scroll holders

DOWN

1 Two wiggling fingers, maybe
2 Drunkard
3 White-hot
4 Invite to a movie, say
5 Classic 1965 novel set on the planet Arrakis
6 Arts and Sciences major: Abbr.
7 Gypsum variety
8 Amount to take
9 "It Happened One Night" director
10 Mideast city that was once a British protectorate
11 Monocle, basically
12 Members of 82-Down
13 Ready to blow
14 Like forget-me-nots
15 Gardner of "Mogambo"
16 Where G.I.'s fought Charlie
17 "Ararat" director, 2002
18 Doc
19 Mavens
24 Computing-Tabulating-Recording Co., today
28 Slangy greeting
31 Primer pooch
32 Wharves
33 South African who twice won the U.S. Open
34 Hidden drawback
36 El ___ (1942 battle site)
37 Glide
38 "___ House," 1983 Madness hit
41 Is a second-story man
42 Stuffed shirts
43 Really mean
44 What, to Camus
45 Capital on the Dvina River
46 Suffix with zillion
48 Low-cost stopover
49 Stops on le métro
50 Word next to an arrow, maybe
51 Daze
52 Cozy and warm
55 St. Lawrence and others
56 In Harry Potter books, nonmagical offspring of wizard parents
57 Treaded transport
59 Sign of a brake problem
61 Patrick of "X-Men"
64 Place between hills
66 Fruit named for its appearance
67 Fever causes
71 Spray under the sink
74 1973 #1 hit for the Rolling Stones
76 Tour de France stage
78 Close
81 More upset
82 Sawbones' org.
83 Play a sax solo, maybe
85 Hosp. staffer
88 1988 Tracy Chapman hit
89 Just for the heck of it

by Will Nediger

90 Offers
91 Sport with a service line
92 Seek aid from
93 Many a tux
94 Beginning of all New York ZIP codes
95 Wild animal ID
96 Battle of ___ Bay, 1898
98 Gets warmer
99 Karate-like exercises
100 The Beatles' "And I Love ___"
103 Plaintiff
104 Lean and sinewy
105 Solitaires, e.g.
107 It's well-supplied
108 Palm Springs-to-Las Vegas dir.
109 Home shopping channel
110 Watch unit: Abbr.

45

ACROSS

1 Fills to almost overflowing
8 Unposed photo
14 Search blindly
19 What some shoot in a golf round
20 Decked out
22 Alternatives to Yodels
23 Memo about Stephen King's "Christine"?
25 Bob Marley's "___ the Sheriff"
26 Drop from the invitation list, say
27 Dig in
28 Staple figure in origami
30 Emmy-winning Ward
31 Meeting of the minds?
32 Memo about an inveterate perjurer?
37 Like the Honda Element
38 BBC : Britain :: ___ : Italy
39 Part of ½
40 Want to undo
41 Absentee
44 Kind of line
46 "Now I see!"
48 Memo about a dating guide?
50 Way around Paris
53 Contingencies
54 Onetime MSN rival
55 Board
57 An essay may be on one
61 Loon
64 Memo about where tariffs are imposed on incoming ships?

68 In the slightest
69 Mocks
70 Apple gadget
71 Memo about stores for animal appendages?
74 Falls on the border
76 Strategic W.W. I river
77 Mower part
78 Wee bit
79 D.C. bigwig
80 City on the Ruhr
82 Memo about a religious outpost for prisoners?
88 1492 voyager
91 Editorial take
92 Have mercy (on)
93 Bearded beast
94 Source of wool
99 Timecard abbr.
100 Flirtatious sort
101 Memo about why to buy an air purifier?
105 Box office sign
108 Canned
109 Lightly moisten
110 Journey part
111 "Right on!"
112 Ready to roll? . . . or not ready to roll?
114 Memo about a lyricist?
119 Top echelon
120 Ignore the usual wake-up time
121 Clothing chain since 1994
122 It's distracting
123 John James Audubon, e.g.
124 "Ain't gonna happen!"

DOWN

1 Short and often not sweet
2 Some are Dutch
3 Give some zing
4 Hoity-toity type
5 Special ___
6 Fourth members of a musical group
7 At will
8 Inflexible, as some rules
9 Suffix with stock or block
10 Go-ahead signal
11 ___ Malfoy, Harry Potter antagonist
12 Buries
13 Special military assignment
14 4, on a phone
15 "Arrested Development" actress Portia de ___
16 Candy bar whose name is an exclamation
17 It may be used for banking
18 They're left behind
21 1958 hit whose B-side was "La Bamba"
24 Articulate
29 Biggest section in a dictionary
32 Rice-A-___
33 All of a crowd, maybe
34 When repeated, Mork's TV sign-off
35 Prefix with byte
36 Whaling adverb
37 Kid's greeting
41 Threefold
42 Proves otherwise
43 Like Albany or Chicago

44 Low-___
45 Bordering on
47 Frank
49 One of a comedic trio
50 LeBlanc of "Joey"
51 One with a pole position?
52 General on a Chinese menu
56 Long lines on a timeline
58 Turkey is part of it
59 Music players
60 Rule before a revolution, maybe
62 Popular table wine
63 Clay, by another name
64 No longer working: Abbr.
65 Specialized fishermen
66 Grand ___, setting for "Evangeline"
67 HDTV maker
69 King ___ Carlos of Spain
72 Figure-watchers' figs.
73 World Cup cheer
74 Where Forrest Gump did a tour
75 "Gotcha," to a beatnik
78 Boom maker
81 Put (away)
83 K–12 grades, collectively
84 ___ loading
85 How a ringtone may be set
86 Discman maker
87 ___ Ed
88 Like many nonanimated Disney films
89 Banished

by Jeremy Newton

90 Having digits
95 Isr. neighbor
96 They do impressions
97 First Ford
98 Invariably
100 Filet type
102 Schiller's "___ Joy"
103 Babydoll
104 Old western actor Van Cleef
105 Makeup applier's boo-boo
106 One of the Canterbury pilgrims
107 Ham ___
111 Years in old Rome
113 Old Ottoman title
115 Univ. in Troy, N.Y.
116 Family nickname
117 Shine, in product names
118 Fingers

CHAIN REACTION

ACROSS

1 Third Crusade siege site
5 Citadel trainee
10 Where houses traditionally have no walls
15 Isn't idle
19 Leeway
20 Like galleys
21 Run ___ of
22 Great Lakes salmon
23 FOOD COURT ___ CIRCUIT BOARD
25 CIRCUIT BOARD ___ ROOM SERVICE
27 Music may come in it
28 Stock market worker
30 Like some sacrifices
31 Stove option
32 Is for a group?
33 Clothing lines
34 Life's partner
37 ___-midi (French time of day)
41 Like many dorms nowadays
42 Laughable
43 ROOM SERVICE ___ LIGHT TOUCH
46 Code unit
49 Covert sound
50 "Beetle Bailey" character
51 What greedy people want
52 Cause someone's insomnia, maybe
54 "Git!"
55 LIGHT TOUCH ___ BELL PEPPER
57 Pet animal of Salvador Dali
58 Sponge

60 Sylvia Plath poem that begins "I know the bottom, she says. I know it with my great tap root"
61 Weightlifter's rep
62 Impassioned
63 Corporate division
65 Fabric border
68 Give up
69 Young newt
70 Some dates have one
71 Long-armed Sumatrans
73 BELL PEPPER ___ BRUSH FIRE
76 Was idle
77 Track take
78 "It's been real"
79 Protection
80 Iota
81 "Father ___," hit 1990s British sitcom
82 BRUSH FIRE ___ SMART CAR
84 Songwriter Carole Bayer ___
85 "Comin' ___ the Rye"
86 French word before deux or nous
87 Dialogue units
88 Bore
92 Third-century year
94 D-Day mo.
95 Tale of a trip to Ithaca
96 Shaped, as wood
100 Julia who starred in "Sabrina," 1995
104 SMART CAR ___ PIANO BAR
106 PIANO BAR ___ TRAILHEAD

108 Composer Thomas
109 Irving Berlin's "___ My Heart at the Stage Door Canteen"
110 Tennessee teammate
111 Final Four game
112 Tomorrow's opposite: Abbr.
113 Send
114 Some seconds
115 Too: Fr.

DOWN

1 Tennis lobs, e.g.
2 Prince Albert, for one
3 Gift that might cut
4 Newly developed, as technology
5 Pullover shirts
6 Dweller along the Mekong
7 Once, old-style
8 Mugful
9 Work of prose or poetry
10 More conservative, as investments
11 In front of, in dialect
12 Farm call
13 Best, in a way
14 Played the enchantress
15 Gulf of Guinea capital
16 Alternatives to RCs
17 ___ park
18 Blisters, e.g.
24 "Stop it!"
26 Place for an opinion
29 Code unit
34 Give insider info
35 Protect

36 TRAILHEAD ___ COUNTERTOP
37 Turkey's tallest peak
38 Read carefully
39 Throw a fit
40 Heaven on earth
41 Vikki who sang "It Must Be Him"
44 Soap plant
45 Some camera lenses
46 COUNTERTOP ___ POST OFFICE
47 Oaxaca gold
48 Hanoi holiday
50 Teahouse treats
52 Cut decoratively
53 Brass
55 Heavy hitter
56 Area around the mouth
57 A tremendous supply
59 2, 4, 6, 8, etc.
63 Calyx part
64 They were seen at Black Power meetings
65 Like Iran's Ahmadinejad
66 Satan is often seen with one
67 Records
70 Bull or Buck, e.g.
71 Make a choice
72 Paris's ___ La Fayette
73 Farm tower
74 Ball in a basket
75 "Syriana" actress Amanda
78 Tote
80 It's in front of a mizzen
82 Something to pop

by Pamela Amick Klawitter

83 Write on a BlackBerry, maybe
84 Eat noisily
85 Recipe abbr.
88 Fee for many a doctor's visit
89 Put on a pedestal
90 City on the Rhone
91 Key
92 Split
93 Garçon's handout
94 Bordello patrons
97 Channel for interior decorators
98 Buffalo's county
99 Go out with
101 Button next to a *
102 Fictional captain
103 IV ___
105 A way to vote
107 Drivel

ACROSS

1 City once called Eva Perón
8 Jim Belushi's costume in "Trading Places"
15 Cross stock
19 Napoleon's relatives
20 Woo
21 Reform Party founder
22 Impatient kid's plea at a zoo?
24 Minneapolis suburb
25 Four: Prefix
26 Wipe out
27 Animal with an onomatopoeic name
28 More kempt
29 Big name in computer printers
31 Worrisome type at a china shop?
33 X-rated
36 Sea route
39 "That hurt!"
40 Count with a severe overbite
43 Villa ___ (town near Atlanta)
44 Dwellers along Lake Victoria
48 Seeking the right women's tennis attire?
50 Love overseas
51 Maker of the old Royale
52 "Get it?"
53 Insinuating
54 Warning sign on a pirate ship?
57 Gold medalist skier Hermann
59 Miss Piggy's pronoun
60 "Presto!"
61 Source of some inside humor?
67 Name on a plane
69 The dark side
70 Young hog
71 Tree doctor?
75 City WSW of Dortmund
77 Geom. point
80 24-hr. convenience
81 Dope
82 Your basic "So this guy walks into a bar . . ."?
85 Disastrous drop
88 Rabbit's title
89 Certain hand-held
90 ___-majesté
91 Brand-new to the language
93 Gulf
94 Use of steel wool, e.g.?
98 Palate appendage
101 Butch Cassidy, for one
102 ___ crow
103 Peaks
105 Swingers' stats
109 "Be that as ___ . . ."
110 Cheez Whiz you could blow up?
113 What a rake does
114 Thaw
115 Traveler's temptation
116 Once, in the past
117 Hellish
118 Bears witness

DOWN

1 In case
2 Workout aftermath
3 Churchyard unit
4 Jack who wrote the lyrics to "Tenderly"
5 Intend (to)
6 Nursery items
7 Cartoon dog
8 Father of Deimos and Phobos
9 Apple or pear
10 Comedic Philips
11 Punch with a kick
12 Take apart
13 Become blocked, in a way
14 Christie contemporary
15 Took a two-wheeler
16 "A Masked Ball" aria
17 Music for a baseball team?
18 Movie lover's cable channel
21 Have a quick look from the hallway, say
23 Geiger of counter fame
28 Alternative to J.F.K. and La Guardia
30 Rain hard
31 "___ teaches you when to be silent": Disraeli
32 Prepare to chat, maybe
33 Some hand-helds
34 Golden pond fish
35 Be something special
37 Padded
38 Laugh, in Lille
41 Type of eye surgery
42 Practically pristine
44 Thurman of "Kill Bill"
45 "When You ___ Love" (1912 tune)
46 Actress Patricia
47 Concession stand purchase
49 Opera's ___ Te Kanawa
50 Settled (on)
54 Luau fare
55 Converse competitor
56 Holler's partner
57 Use shamelessly
58 Gray area?: Abbr.
59 Co. with a butterfly logo
61 Nature's aerators
62 Nikita's no
63 White wine apéritif
64 Soyuz launcher
65 Lots
66 South Pacific kingdom
67 "Voice of Israel" author
68 Org. with peace-keeping forces
72 Stock ticker's inventor
73 1958 Best Actor David
74 "___ Day" (1993 rap hit)
75 Flush (with)
76 Arid
77 Perfume brand
78 Boxing stats
79 There are 435 in Cong.
82 Seed cover
83 Ben-Gurion carrier
84 Author portrayed in the miniseries "The Lost Boys"
86 Indiana city near the Michigan border
87 Spoils
88 Illegal record
91 Sly
92 Boneheaded
94 Deceit
95 Out-and-out
96 When doubled, sings

by Tony Orbach and Patrick Blindauer

97 Something to believe

99 Roxie's dance partner in "Chicago"

100 "___ or lose . . ."

103 Lead-in to girl

104 Battle of Normandy city

106 Streisand, to friends

107 "___ first you don't succeed . . ."

108 Orch. section

110 Wallet items, informally

111 Darth Vader's boyhood nickname

112 Chess piece: Abbr.

ACROSS

1 Town at the eighth mile of the Boston Marathon
7 1971 Tom Jones hit
16 Dict. fill
19 Charlie Chan player J. ___ Naish
20 Acted briefly
21 Online activity
22 V.I.P. in a limo?
24 Penn Station inits.
25 Sycophant's reply
26 Articles by nonstaffers
27 Singer Winehouse
28 Glass-enclosed porches
30 1999 film with the tagline "Fame. Be careful. It's out there"
32 Way of the East
33 Open
35 Dirty
36 Stories about halting horses?
39 Kisses, on paper
41 Team building?
42 1954 event code-named Castle Bravo
43 Swedish Chemistry Nobelist Tiselius
45 Detailed, old-style
47 Produce for show
51 Roundabout
53 Corduroy feature
56 Certain guy, in personals shorthand
58 Causes of meteorological phenomena?
60 "Q: Are We Not Men? A: We Are ___!" (hit 1978 album)

61 Eponymous German brewer Eberhard
63 Says, in teenspeak
64 Stir
66 They're in control of their faculties
67 Etc. and ibid., e.g.
69 Unequaled
70 Missile's course
72 Trudge (through)
73 Baton wavers
76 Miffs
77 Iceland?
81 Fully or partially: Abbr.
82 French-Belgian border river
83 Start of a sign on a gate
84 Scatterbrain
86 National League East player
88 Kind of atty.
90 Explorer ___ da Gama
94 MDX and RDX maker
96 National League East player
98 Barrier Ahab stands behind?
102 Literally, "back to back"
104 Lure
106 60-Across producer
107 Long-distance swimmer Diana
108 Something little girls may play
110 Fifth pillar of Islam
111 Body layer
113 Internet address letters
114 "What are you, some kind of ___?"

115 Cry after writing a particularly fun column?
119 Office note
120 Settle
121 Arab League V.I.P.'s
122 Eur. carrier
123 Small plane, perhaps
124 Common town sign

DOWN

1 "Treasure Island" illustrator, 1911
2 Showed delight over
3 River crosser
4 Eng. neighbor
5 U.S.A.F. Academy site
6 One who lifts a lot
7 Little stubble
8 Residence on the Rhein
9 Summer setting in MA and PA
10 Extremely arid
11 In ___ (really out of it)
12 Pitch maker?
13 "___ losing it, or . . . ?"
14 Investigators: Abbr.
15 Goes up and down
16 45, e.g.?
17 Connecticut town where "The Stepford Wives" was filmed
18 Italian road
21 Sen. McCaskill of Missouri
23 "Are you ___?!"
29 Like some good soil
31 Clergy attire

33 Out into view
34 Rock's Richards and Moon
37 Orchestra sect.
38 High, in the Alps
40 Legal suspension
44 Overthrowing, e.g.
46 Lead-in to while
48 Cutting remarks?
49 Slogan holder, often
50 It has a blade
52 Is shy
54 1887 Chekhov play
55 Tomb raider's find
56 Derisive
57 Where ax murderers' weapons are on display?
59 Lines on a musical staff
60 1973 Helen Reddy #1 hit
61 Tylenol rival
62 Troupe org.
65 Calls one's own
67 Ray, e.g., in brief
68 Like the bad guy
71 Phnom Penh money
72 Shaved, in a way
73 Bygone station
74 Part of N.C.A.A.: Abbr.
75 Indication of big shoes to fill?
78 Dip
79 Wishy-___
80 Words with snag or home run
83 Carpenter's supply
85 Dow Jones fig.
87 Blue blood, informally
89 "Flags of Our Fathers" setting
91 Pourer's comment

by Brendan Emmett Quigley

92 Catfight participants
93 Boot Hill setting
94 Title family name on TV
95 Eye part
97 Tiny laughs
99 One with bad looks?
100 Letters on a cross
101 Polite turndown
103 Best
105 Training staff
109 Fen-___ (banned diet aid)
111 Exhausted
112 Michigan town or college
116 Season for les vacances
117 Little bird
118 Third-century Chinese dynasty

49 PARTING THOUGHTS

ACROSS

1 Having chutzpah
6 Home of the Braves: Abbr.
9 Hale-___ (comet seen in 1997)
13 Take a chance
19 Page facing a verso
20 Arthur Miller play about the Salem witch trials, with "The"
22 Enigmas
23 Take heat from?
24 Downhill racer
25 Poet John who wrote "Lives of X," an autobiography in verse
26 Last request, part 1
29 Rains in Spain
30 Twigs, perhaps
31 Animal more closely related to the mongoose than the dog
32 Inhuman
35 Groundbreaking inventions?
36 Cabinet inits. since 1979
38 Part of a range: Abbr.
39 Records
40 Not maj.
41 Endorsers, typically
44 Election ending?
45 Request, part 2
52 Barney's buddy, in cartoondom
54 Veiled comment?
55 "Sense and Sensibility" author
56 "Thumbs way up!" review

57 Unlike drive, reverse has just one
59 Lord's land
61 With 95-Across, chef whose recipes are used on the International Space Station
63 National Institutes of Health location
65 Request, part 3
66 How good investors invest
68 Profitless
69 Bill
71 On Soc. Sec., typically
72 "The King and I" setting
73 Park ___
76 Disfigure
77 God, in Granada
79 Request, part 4
84 ___ culpa
85 Actress Mimieux of "Where the Boys Are"
86 Supply in a loft
87 Alludes (to)
89 Lambert airport's home: Abbr.
92 "___ pig's eye!"
93 Created
95 See 61-Across
96 ___ ballerina
98 Salma Hayek, for one
101 1970s Renault
102 End of the request
108 European carrier
109 Part of many an autobiography's author credit

110 Morticia, to Fester, on "The Addams Family"
111 Gander : goose :: tercel : ___
112 More chic
113 Clothing retailer Bauer
114 Erica Jong's phobia, ostensibly
115 "Yonder window," according to Romeo
116 Uno + due
117 Actions

DOWN

1 Very dry
2 First female attorney general
3 Sch. known for its discipline
4 Having grooves
5 'Hood inhabitant
6 Existing
7 Crowd in Calais?
8 Grease up
9 Propaganda technique introduced by Hitler in "Mein Kampf"
10 M.D.'s who deliver
11 What dead men don't wear, per a 1982 film title
12 Tasty tubes
13 Suggestive
14 W.W. I's so-called "U-Boat Alley"
15 Reptilian, in a way
16 ___ Abdul-Jabbar
17 Tab, e.g.
18 "Shogun" sequel
21 Soft

27 Not exactly
28 One of two title roles (in the same film) for Spencer Tracy
32 Bellyache
33 Peppy
34 Desire, for one
35 Sign in the stands
37 Noted bunny lover
40 Jason's jiltee
41 Matador's move
42 Social worker
43 Scattered (about)
46 Pirate whose treasure is recovered in Poe's "The Gold-Bug"
47 Keeper of a flame?
48 Total
49 Dickens's shortest novel
50 Bad guys
51 Count (on)
53 Benin, until 1975
58 Matter of law
60 Lassitude
62 Deep bleu sea
63 Bigmouth, for one
64 Pollen producer
66 Hair-raising
67 Ein Berliner, often
69 "Picnic" playwright
70 Clarifying words
74 ESPN sportscaster Dick
75 Treebeard, e.g.
78 Manuscript encl.
80 Ace's specialty
81 Slaves
82 Spinachlike plant
83 Won back
88 Unseen part of the moon

by Matt Ginsberg

89 Marijuana cigarette, slangily
90 Like some Afghan leaders
91 In the cards
93 Ecological groupings
94 Not AWOL
95 Poe poem that ends "From grief and groan to a golden throne beside the King of Heaven"
97 Word of thanks
99 Quickly
100 Edison rival
101 Cubic decimeter
103 Spend time (with)
104 Cut, say
105 Give up
106 Aspirin, e.g.
107 Roger who won the Best Actor Tony for "Nicholas Nickleby"

ACROSS THE BOARD

ACROSS

1 Demanded without reason
7 Leader of Lesbos?
13 Unlikely attenders of R-rated films
19 Honor
20 Injustice
21 Feel remorse for
22 November 5, in Britain
24 Not remote
25 Thin as ___
26 Depression
28 Humans last lived there in 2000
29 Wild sheep of the western United States
36 Mocks
37 "La Gioconda" mezzo-soprano
38 Flies over the Equator
39 Salt Lake City player
40 Annual Sunday event, with "the"
43 Breezes (through)
44 Best Actor of 1991
49 Treat like a hero, maybe
52 In direct opposition
53 Gaudy jewelry, in slang
54 Broad
55 Alphabet quartet
56 Trail to follow
58 Ring figure
59 It's quite different from the high-school variety
66 Transfix
67 Eurasian ducks
68 Climactic scene in "Hamlet"

69 Parrying weapon
70 Blackmore's Lorna
72 City 70 miles SSW of Toledo
76 ___ state
77 Viking, for one
81 La Scala cheer
82 Events registered by seismometers, in brief
83 Resident: Suffix
84 Foamcore component
87 "Doctor Zhivago" role
89 Deserving a lower insurance premium
91 Army supply officer
96 Spigoted vessel
97 Italie et Allemagne
98 Single-handedly
99 Equitable way to return a favor
102 Egg roll topping, perhaps
109 Thatched
110 Perfume ingredient
111 Mrs. Woody Allen
112 It may be bilateral
113 Belgian city with an 1854 manifesto
114 Like shorelines, often

DOWN

1 Lose strength
2 Prefix with pressure
3 Standoffish
4 Give bad marks
5 Signs of a bad outlet
6 "Venice Preserved" dramatist Thomas

7 Part of U.N.L.V.
8 Natural bristle
9 Year that Michelangelo began work on "David"
10 One desiring change
11 National flower of Mexico
12 Illinois city, site of the last Lincoln-Douglas debate
13 Favorable
14 TV pooch
15 FedEx rival
16 Moon of Mars
17 Unabridged
18 Rudder locations
20 Move, to a real-estate broker
23 Kipling novel
27 Procure
29 Batting average, e.g.
30 ___ citato
31 ___ Bator
32 Quaint "not"
33 Caboose
34 Some deodorants
35 Abbr. after Cleveland or Brooklyn
36 Fair
40 Four Holy Roman emperors
41 Bazaar units
42 Iowa college
43 Go rapidly
45 Charge for cash
46 Large chamber group
47 Ancient Greek coins
48 Pickup attachment
49 Start of something big?

50 Shooting star, maybe
51 Mad magazine cartoonist Dave
54 Spoonful, say
56 Bygone blades
57 Kitten "mitten"
58 Second string
59 Bossman or bosswoman
60 Stinky, as gym clothes
61 Pizza place
62 Capri, e.g., to a Capriote
63 Magazine founded by Bob Guccione
64 ___ of Nantes, 1598
65 "Super Duper ___" (anime series)
70 "Forty Miles of Bad Road" guitarist
71 Flip over
72 Some offensive linemen: Abbr.
73 Port near Nazareth
74 Purveyor of chips
75 Open court hearing
77 ___-à-porter
78 "And ___ thou slain the Jabberwock?": Carroll
79 Spillane's "___ Jury"
80 Within striking distance
81 "It's c-c-c-cold!"
84 Pipsqueak
85 Word with page or wood
86 ___ Stadium, opened in 1923

by Barry C. Silk

87 Feeling evoked in drama
88 Basketball datum
89 Security system component
90 Playground retort
92 Prefix with economics
93 Celtic speaker
94 ___ beetle
95 "Don't even bother"
100 Sun Valley locale: Abbr.
101 Invoice amount
103 Once known as
104 Untold millennia
105 Half brother of Tom Sawyer
106 Moreover
107 Manhattan part
108 Impersonated

ACROSS

1 2003 Stanley Cup champions
7 Portrays
12 It's found in many pockets nowadays
16 Command to an overfriendly canine
20 Genus of poisonous mushrooms
22 Brewing
23 Pasta used in soups
24 Actress Polo
25 Nickname for a bodybuilder
26 Flip
27 Junior in the N.F.L.
28 Bunch
29 Popular 1970s British TV series
32 Bug
34 Fraternity letters
35 Dungeon items
37 "Now you're talking!"
38 Took the risk
45 From ___ Z
47 Radiate
51 When a second-shift employee may get home
52 City that overlooks a bay of the same name
53 Opening screen option on many an A.T.M.
56 "Think big" sloganeer
57 One inside another
59 Spot alternative
61 Fine-tunes
62 Split
63 Abbr. in a real-estate listing
64 Creator of the Tammany Hall tiger
66 Tic-tac-toe plays
68 Warner Brothers shotgun toter
69 "Whose woods these ___ think I know": Frost
71 Liberals
73 Actor Brynner
74 ___ rut
75 Keats, e.g.
76 Ilk
77 It may have two doors
79 Ralph who co-wrote "Have Yourself a Merry Little Christmas"
81 Cartoonist Keane
82 "The Praise of Folly" writer
84 Cause of unemployment
86 It might follow a slash mark
90 "Amen!"
91 Club alternative
92 Slangy street greeting
94 Ball with a yellow stripe
95 Arrangements
98 Four-star hotel amenity
99 J.F.K. info: Abbr.
101 Football defensive line position
102 Old musical high notes
103 Deuce beaters
104 Where to pick up pick-up sticks
106 Viking Ericson
108 Summer Mass. Setting
109 Bug
110 "We ___ please"
111 Nativity scene figures
114 ___ Mae
116 Stead
117 Like most apartments
119 A hyperbola has two
121 Having stars, say
122 Deliver, as a harsh criticism
124 "Star Trek" TV series, to fans
125 Exasperated teacher's cry
128 Shade of blue
130 Kids drink from them
132 Comedian Margaret
133 Part of a shark's respiratory system
137 Missing glasses' location, usually
145 Genesis son
146 Issue
148 The second "R" in J. R. R. Tolkien
149 Wrinkles
150 Fan mag
151 Pixar fish
152 Africa's ___ Mountains
153 A super's may be supersized
154 Result of pulling the plug?
155 Overflow
156 Unesco World Heritage Site in Jordan
157 Gives in return

DOWN

1 Block
2 Birds that can sprint at 30 m.p.h.
3 Extensive
4 One of a people conquered in 1533
5 French orphan of film
6 Camper's aid
7 Miss
8 "___ first . . ."
9 Arrangement of 40-Downs
10 "Ain't gonna happen"
11 Commercial prefix with foam
12 Cyclades island
13 Before: Abbr.
14 Longtime Boston Symphony conductor
15 Hollow center?
16 Barely fair, maybe
17 Sugar source
18 Read aloud
19 Exclamation of surprise
21 In itself
30 Went from second to first, say
31 Fasten with a pop
33 Will Ferrell title role
36 Erect
38 Not brought home
39 Off
40 See 9-Down
41 Awake by
42 Bootleggers' bane
43 Son-in-law of Muhammad
44 Go-ahead
46 Common hockey score
48 Proposed "fifth taste," which means "savory" in Japanese
49 Keeps
50 Put forth
54 "Do you want me to?"
55 Tasmania's highest peak
58 Z-car brand
60 International oil and gas giant, informally
62 Benedict III's predecessor
65 Misses, e.g.
67 Negative
70 Sentiment suggesting "Try this!"
72 Secured, in a way, with "on"
78 Cipher org.
80 T or F, e.g.: Abbr.
81 Construction project that gave rise to the Ted Williams Tunnel
83 Sphagnous
85 Some taters
86 Over
87 Building component?
88 Shrinking, perhaps
89 Took it easy
91 Gone bad
93 Frog legs, to some
95 Hold off
96 TV puppet
97 Precept
98 Pal of Kenny and Kyle
100 Tach reading

by Mike Nothnagel and David Quarfoot

105 Common entry point
107 Alpine sights
112 Behind
113 Happen, slangily
115 "I'll pass"
117 Plush
118 Connoisseur
120 Pawned
123 Head counts?

126 Tristram's love
127 More gloomy
129 Singer Mann
131 "That's ___!"
133 Look
134 Footnote abbr.
135 Impart
136 Player's call
138 Behind

139 "Bridal Chorus" bride
140 Bazooka Joe's working peeper
141 Ground cover
142 Early Chinese dynasty
143 Choice word
144 Email, e.g.: Abbr.
147 Cartoon feline

52   OFF WITH THEIR HEADS!

ACROSS

1 Swarm
5 Lots
10 11th-century year
14 Audibly shocked
19 Hot rod rod
20 One of the Four Seasons
21 German article
22 Glow
23 "Will the long-winded ___ ___ his sermon?"
26 Philosopher Kierkegaard
27 Puts on
28 Power brokers
29 "Let me tell you . . ."
30 Mark, Anthony and others: Abbr.
31 "Tasty!"
32 "The majority of British ___ ___ policy coming to fruition"
34 Left over
36 Shoot out
37 Took care of
40 Washington State airport
43 Amaze
44 One of five Norwegian kings
48 "I noticed you use the ___ ___ often than the tarnished one"
51 Promised
52 Ties a second knot
53 Habit
54 Human ___ Project
55 Alphabet quartet
57 "The driver's crew decided to make the ___ ___ priority"
60 "Life ___ beach"

63 Welcome at the door
65 Crossed one's i's and dotted one's t's?
66 Promgoers: Abbr.
67 "The parishioners ignored the ___ ___ meat on Friday"
71 Understands
74 Train head
75 Work hard
76 Ultimatum's end
80 It might lead to a cloud formation, for short
81 "The judges put the names of each ___ ___ for the M.C. to read"
86 Pusher catcher, for short
87 Shoe letters
88 Retinue of Pan
89 YouTube offering
90 Baloney
92 Teacher: Var.
94 "As one member of the crew ___ ___ co-worker leaned on his shovel"
101 Nigerian export
102 Any ship
105 Company bought by Chevron in 2005
106 Dig
107 Box-and-one alternative
109 Mushroom variety
110 "You won't find any ___ ___ Turner album"
112 Wilder and Hackman
113 Wash. Neighbor
114 Potato pancake
115 Race pace

116 Daisy type
117 It's frequently stolen
118 Calm
119 Tom Joad, e.g.

DOWN

1 Bad-weather gear
2 Apply
3 Dwellers in Middle-earth
4 Cross
5 Park in New York, say
6 Australia, e.g.
7 Automotive pioneer
8 It may come from a barrel
9 Take up wholeheartedly
10 Deserve
11 Deceive
12 Central
13 Like some boxes on ballots
14 Franciscan home
15 Relics of the Wild West
16 ___-ground missile
17 Derisive look
18 Copper
24 English portraitist Sir Joshua
25 1994 and 1997 U.S. Open winner
29 Green shade
32 Bucket of bolts
33 Grove in many an English churchyard
34 Pure
35 Your: Fr.
37 Lat. or Lith., once
38 Ursine : bear :: pithecan : ___
39 Amaze
41 Al's is almost 27

42 Place to hang your hat
43 Lady ___, first woman to sit in British Parliament
45 Sacks
46 Mail for a knight
47 Johnson and Johnson, e.g.
49 Kind of sale
50 "___ Nous" (1983 film)
51 Having all the money one needs
54 Bible distributor
56 Milk
57 Attach, as to a lapel
58 Cuisine choice
59 Many a pirate's appendage
60 "That is to say . . ."
61 Receiver of lists
62 Tick off
64 Actress Holmes
68 Record holder
69 About which the Bible says "Consider her ways, and be wise"
70 Confederate
72 "Hairspray" actor
73 Baseball bigwig Bud
77 Top
78 Beijing-to-Shanghai dir.
79 Ike's W.W. II domain
81 Broadcast signal
82 Compromises
83 Tore
84 Minister's deg.
85 Japanese-born Hall of Fame golfer
87 Daredevil Knievel
91 Poker call

by Peter A. Collins and Joe Krozel

93 Deseeded, as cotton
94 "Hasta ___"
95 Incorporate into a city
96 Fess Parker TV role
97 Greek marketplace
98 Folk percussion instruments
99 Old enough
100 Break down
102 Smarmy smile
103 Red River city
104 Related on the mother's side
107 ___ Hari
108 Football Hall-of-Famer Graham
110 Melodramatic response in comics
111 Jazz cornetist Adderley

ACROSS

1 Big name in baked beans
8 Neighbor of Oakland
15 Gilberto's partner on "The Girl From Ipanema," 1964
19 Earsplitting
21 Cicero or Publius
22 Light shade
23 21
25 Neighbor of a Georgian
26 Filled out
27 Exchanged vows
28 Knocker's request
30 Off-road wheels, for short
31 Vespasian's successor
33 Command ctrs.
36 One of an old film trio
37 Way out
40 Los __
43 Anna of "X-Men"
45 Humans, e.g.
47 Like a butterfingers
48 Temperaments
49 Rock's __ Folds Five
50 Cries of agony
52 Viva-voce vote
53 Pastry shop treat
54 Conductors' aids
57 Quick expression of gratitude
58 Gets better
59 Natty dresser
60 Grant-giving org.
61 Butterfly relative
63 "__ She Lovely"
64 Cereal killer
66 Rather inclined
68 Breakfast spot, briefly
71 "Vissi d'arte" singer
73 "N.Y. State of Mind" rapper
75 Yossarian's tentmate, in "Catch-22"
76 Curl performer
77 Part of some three-day weekends: Abbr.
79 Number one
82 Athos's arm
83 Ontario, par exemple
84 "Generations of healthy, happy pets" sloganeer
85 Small songbird
86 Chopsticks eschewers, informally
87 Razor handle?
89 The __ Band, with guitarist Little Steven
92 Choir supports
93 He played 2,130 consecutive games
95 "Sire"
97 The Desi of Desilu
99 Middle of summer?
100 Certain people buried in Westminster Abbey
101 Black-and-white broadcast?
104 Divine epithet
106 Cut made by a saw
107 Gilpin of "Frasier"
108 Sticks (out)
109 Ignore, as a problem
115 Assist in evil
116 Freaky
117 Dimming
118 They may be revolutionary
119 The very beginning
120 1967 pop sensation, with "the"

DOWN

1 Europe's longest river
2 Turn aside
3 Beersheba's desert
4 Sticking point
5 Unilever detergent
6 Chic, in the '60s
7 People who no what they like?
8 Emulates a reporter
9 Kona keepsake
10 Brashares who wrote "The Sisterhood of the Traveling Pants"
11 Zine
12 And others, in a list
13 Old Venetian officials
14 Self-titled album of 1980
15 St. Peter, e.g.?
16 High-school gym feature
17 Chance to play
18 Ringo's drummer son
20 Styled
24 Mr. Potato Head features
29 Infamous 1999 computer virus with a woman's name
31 Woes, to a Yiddish speaker
32 More aloof
33 Target, with "on"
34 Marmalade ingredients
35 Stop: Abbr.
37 On a par with
38 Barbecue order
39 "Watermark" vocalist
41 Brightly colored fish
42 Charon's workplace
43 Wears out the carpet?
44 Declaration of August 14, 1941
46 Activity in which people get their kicks
48 NuGrape competitor
51 Call letters on 1970s–'80s TV
54 Pet cat, in British lingo
55 "Once __ midnight dreary . . ."
56 Betray, in a way
59 Soda shop order
62 Single malt, for instance
64 Rachel Carson's sci.
65 Hissy fit
67 Joule division
69 Raspberries
70 Takes, with "for"
72 Legs
74 Their business is going downhill
76 Explodes
77 Aggressively promote
78 Put the pedal to the metal
80 Promising
81 Couple
82 Dampish

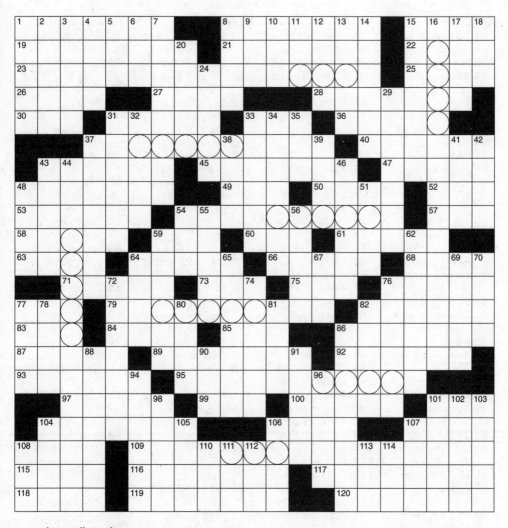

by Will Nediger

ACROSS

1 Edges at the track
5 Scores 100 on a test
11 Mother and wife of Uranus: Var.
15 Suffix with electron
18 It surrounds a lens
19 Sugar in tea, e.g.
20 Pointer on a poster
22 Seat site
24 Movie about a "Sopranos"-like actress from the Mediterranean?
26 Many a Turk
28 Simile part
29 Oscar and Tony winner Mercedes
30 Movie adaptation of "L.A. Law"?
34 The original Jefferson Airplane, e.g.
35 Rift
36 Back-to-work time: Abbr.
37 Hardware store section
39 Movie about a timeshare?
48 Add or delete, say
50 2000 title role for Richard Gere
51 English 8-Down
52 Popular movie house name
53 Middle of many German names
54 As a friend, to François
56 Comparable to a beet?
58 Crowd in Berlin?
59 Movie about the coming of difficult times?
63 Nearest the heart
65 Notes from short people?
66 Spike TV, once
67 Former Voice of America org.
68 Together
71 Movie about one of Dumbo's parents?
77 Room in la casa
78 Meat Loaf's "Rocky Horror Picture Show" role
81 Highest score achievable by a single dart in darts
82 Der Blaue Reiter artist
83 Polo alternatives
85 Recovery grps.
86 I, to Claudius
87 Advertiser's "magic word"
88 Movie about a narco's worst dream?
95 Bank quote
96 "The Matrix" role
97 Person in a tree: Abbr.
98 Bagel topping
102 Movie about a bus on Rodeo Drive?
110 Causing a ruckus
111 Job spec.
112 Canonized Norwegian king
113 Movie about the zoo's most punctual simian?
118 ___-jazz (music style)
119 Goes wild
120 Upholsterer's sample
121 Rock's end
122 Linguistic suffix
123 They connote disapproval
124 Information technology giant
125 Pull (in)

DOWN

1 Rapper with the 1996 nine-time platinum album "All Eyez on Me"
2 Trump's first
3 Kind of colony
4 Didn't make a move
5 Moving
6 George who was nicknamed "the man who owned Broadway"
7 1985 Peter Yates-directed movie
8 Latin 51-Across
9 "Make ___ double"
10 Abbr. on a business card
11 "Saturday Night Live" has a new one every week
12 Handle, in archaeology
13 Whack
14 Like a picnic
15 Cay
16 Pirate's secret
17 Young salmon
21 French waters
23 Until now
25 Mai ___
27 Canter
31 Actress Adams, star of 2007's "Enchanted"
32 Cry when going down?
33 One in Oaxaca
34 Neighbor of Nor.
38 Words of woe
39 Turner of records
40 Writer Buchanan and others
41 Strong cart
42 Screen sites
43 Angle
44 One who's out
45 "I, Claudius" role
46 Impersonates
47 "I'll do that right away!"
48 "Deliver Us From ___" (2003 film)
49 "Dumb, dumb, dumb!"
54 Bring out
55 Words before dark or black
56 Keats's "The Eve of St. ___"
57 Gossiping
60 Oil capital
61 Get into
62 Like Bruckner's Symphony No. 7
64 Actress Vardalos
67 "Oil!" author Sinclair
68 ". . . as it ___ heaven"
69 "Casablanca" extra
70 Toil
71 Nickname on "The Addams Family"
72 Schreiber of "The Manchurian Candidate"
73 W.W. II vet, e.g.
74 "Gone With the Wind" setting
75 Soldier's food, for short
76 Impersonate
79 Potty
80 Meeting planners
84 Lost Persian, e.g.
87 Toppled
89 Regatta trophy
90 P.O. delivery
91 Novelist Harper
92 Super finish?
93 Expression for the Joker
94 Buildup around the mouth
98 Take in

by Caleb Madison

99 __-pours
100 Author who wrote "Did you ever stop to think, and forget to start again?"
101 Those, in Tijuana
103 Always, poetically
104 Aspiring attys.' hurdles
105 Old TV's "__ Derringer"
106 Thrills
107 Ballot listing
108 "Oh, pretty please?"
109 Time and again
111 "Star Wars" critter
114 Tour de France units: Abbr.
115 The Wildcats of the Big 12 Conf.
116 Not lease, say
117 Vessel for Thor Heyerdahl

ACROSS

1 Dish that's often roasted
5 U.K. counterespionage agcy.
8 Belonging to
13 July holiday, with "the"
16 Spell caster
20 Declare
21 PC key
22 Silents star Bara
23 Agent Gold of "Entourage"
24 Teensy bit
25 Think the world of
27 "Now I remember"
28 Leaves in the kitchen
30 Start of instructions for what to do when this puzzle is done
33 "Moving forward" sloganeer
34 Galilee's locale
35 G.I. addresses
38 Soft-shoe, e.g.
41 "___ in cat"
43 Something to go in . . . or on
47 ___-de-sac
48 With 67- and 97-Across, second part of the instructions
57 "___ won't!"
58 Sequoyah, for one
60 Victim of Hercules' second labor
61 Given directly
63 Ones caught in a maze?
64 Little squirt, maybe
65 Lachrymose
66 "___ et manus" (M.I.T.'s motto)
67 See 48-Across
72 Brag
74 Digs
75 In and of ___
76 Most liable to sunburn
77 Call on a pitch

78 Need for the winner of a Wimbledon men's match
81 Young 'un
82 "___ Ba Yah" (campfire song)
83 It follows the initial part of a procedure
85 Beethoven's Third
88 Forecast for improved weather
92 College ___
94 Religious image: Var.
95 Seasonal activity
96 Capital of Italy
97 See 48-Across
103 Baby kangaroos
104 Start of a counting rhyme
105 BlackBerrys, e.g., for short
106 Blackthorn pickings
108 Request for Vanna
109 Staples of early education
110 "The War of the Worlds" invaders, briefly
113 How one must win in Ping-Pong
115 "Rubbish!"
116 Some corner stores
119 Orange and green fruits
123 Rock candy, essentially
126 Einstein's birthplace
127 Common hockey power play
129 Author mentioned in the Beatles' "I Am the Walrus"
130 Trillionth: Prefix
132 Study of the heavens: Abbr.
133 Bias
135 Collaborative Web document
138 Final part of instructions

145 Something you later might think better of
146 Consumer
147 "Death in Venice" and "Of Mice and Men"
148 Machine used to maneuver manure
149 Slay somebody
150 Thoreau, e.g.

DOWN

1 Head
2 With: Fr.
3 A small one helps the indecisive
4 QB Favre and others
5 Like corn bread
6 Childish retort
7 Costing a nickel
8 Rat-___
9 "Zip it"
10 Cyclops' feature
11 Experimented too much?
12 Burkina ___
13 Structure of Chekhov's "The Cherry Orchard"
14 Court figure
15 "Broom-___"
16 ___ Bay, 1898 battle site
17 Memo abbr.
18 2007 Peace Nobelist
19 Subgenre of punk rock
26 1990s Indian P.M.
29 Mugful
31 Commerce treaty starting 1947
32 "Oh, pooh!"
35 Big Ten rival: Abbr.
36 "Stupidest thing I ever heard!"
37 Poisonous shrub
39 Sound at a sauna
40 Remove with effort
41 Assume the fetal position
42 Ottoman big shot

44 Opened, as a flag
45 Skating jumps
46 Suffix with planet
48 Pro
49 Safari sight
50 Unleash upon
51 "Avast!"
52 Pantheon head
53 Respect
54 Copycats
55 Succeed effortlessly
56 Bygone TV control: Abbr.
59 62-Down carriers: Abbr.
62 Gridiron grp.
66 File on an iPod
68 Access the contents of, say
69 Mother, slangily
70 Invents
71 Let slip
73 1940s conflict: Abbr.
79 Hoity-___
80 Punjabi believers
83 "A Little Princess" heroine and others
84 Internet forum rabble-rouser
86 Iowa college
87 Brings to a boil
89 Audible pauses
90 Greeting to Gaius
91 Necessary: Abbr.
92 "___ Wedding," Alan Alda film
93 Overseas O.K.
97 Prefix with sphere
98 Sine qua non
99 Dos' followers
100 Pick up
101 Western wolf
102 Some hand-raisers
103 Alternative to a cross
107 "___ Cried" (1962 hit)
109 N.Y.C. time when it's midnight in L.A.
110 Emissions org.
111 ___ chi

by Kevin G. Der

112 Thesaurus offering: Abbr.
114 Like a team that's ahead by a safety
117 Trick-taking game
118 Girl's name that's Latin for "fame"
119 Walk
120 "I concur"

121 Behind
122 Hubbub
124 Black-eyed legume
125 Comic Charles Nelson ___
127 Highest-rated, as a hotel
128 Like the majority of Interstate highways

130 Tire (out)
131 "Like ___ not . . ."
132 Bide-___
134 Monterrey kin
136 Many-armed Hindu goddess
137 Old actresses Claire and Balin

138 Traveler's aid, for short
139 Funny
140 Kung ___ chicken
141 In accord (with)
142 Eastern Canadian prov.
143 Campers, briefly
144 Id ___

ACROSS

1 Pep rally shout
7 Sics on
13 More than a favorite
20 Program begun under Kennedy
21 Digs
22 Single advancement
23 Plea made to a chimney sweep?
25 Holding one's own
26 Topic in a golf lesson
27 Pancho's pal
29 Colonial John
30 Moving
32 ___ hole in (corrodes)
35 Graduation deliveries
37 Jobs for some underwriters, for short
38 Distribute equal amounts?
41 "The Daughter of Time" novelist, 1951
42 Friendliness
44 "___ Mucho" (1944 #1 hit)
45 1968 live folk album
47 Humorist Sedaris
48 Sub
51 Maximum extent
53 Pushover
56 Vote involved in a 15th wedding anniversary?
59 Recipient of a lettera amorosa
60 Missile Command maker
63 Floors
64 Sounds from a hot bath
65 Subject to loss on a laptop

67 Follies
69 Genetic letters
70 Have no accomplices
71 Done
72 Three times a day, on an Rx
73 Thurman of "The Avengers"
74 Title role for Streisand
75 Mire
76 Narrow-minded affairs?
80 Kitchen appliance brand
82 When doubled, an old sitcom sign-off
83 Blasts from the past, briefly
84 Payroll fig.
87 N.B.A. star Lamar ___
89 Act as a go-between
91 Main lines
93 Peter Pan rival
95 Teacher's pet?
99 Commercial prefix with jet
100 One making an impression
102 Poet who wrote "She walks in beauty, like the night"
103 Belong
104 Blacksmith, often
105 Race of Norse deities
108 Picks up
110 More like a bubble bath
112 Stop to admire one's pillaging?
117 Hams
118 World capital said to have been founded by King Midas

119 Muse of astronomy
120 "Hmmm . . ."
121 Theater annoyance
122 Manages

DOWN

1 Oomph
2 W.W. II. agcy.
3 Movie with the repeated line "To infinity, and beyond!"
4 Snobbery
5 Site of many kisses
6 Sound from a dungeon
7 Hereditary
8 Around 1,000, e.g.: Abbr.
9 Word repeated in Emily Dickinson's "___ so much joy! ___ so much joy!"
10 Winter vehicles with treads
11 Yours, in Nemours
12 Day care charges
13 State in the Sierra Madre
14 Game with Wild Draw Four cards
15 Runs the hose over again
16 Stopping place in a Carlo Levi title
17 Sexiest bell ringer?
18 Ancient Jewish ascetic
19 Lilliputian
24 Home of the world's northernmost capital: Abbr.
28 "I Never Played the Game" writer
30 Sanyo competitor
31 ___ blocker

33 "This Boy's Life" author Wolff
34 Nerve material?
36 Health org.
38 Stern cry?
39 "Very funny!"
40 Oscar winner Jannings and others
43 Again and again?
46 Spots
49 Showed hospitality at the door
50 Bygone muscle cars
52 They have substantial bills
54 Sen. Lott
55 Mountain air
56 Got started, with "up"
57 Alternative to a hotel, briefly
58 Cable channel whose first showing was "Gone With the Wind"
60 John Wayne film, with "The"
61 "Swan Lake" garb
62 Part of a Beckett play?
66 Makes an assertion
68 Tchaikovsky's Symphony No. 6 ___ minor
69 Mass, for one
70 Gallic girlfriend
72 "Pagliacci" clown
73 Guam, e.g.: Abbr.
77 Aplenty
78 Take back
79 Ministre d'___
81 You can count on them
84 Texas toppers
85 Delhi wrap
86 Bygone Dodge

by Alan Arbesfeld

88 Early 12th-century year
90 What turned-out pants pockets may signify
92 Slicker accessory
93 Toastmaster General of old comedy
94 Bury
96 Last ride?
97 Hungarian playwright known for "Liliom"
98 Like a line, briefly
101 Pauses
103 Partner in a French firm, maybe
106 Hunk
107 Actress Skye
109 Put __ in one's ear
111 Prior to, in verse
113 Select
114 We may precede this
115 Ad __
116 Box on a calendar

ACROSS

1 Goes on TV
5 Kublai Khan and others
12 Barkeep's supply
18 Transports, in a way
21 Place to make an omelet
22 Studio behind the original "Star Trek"
23 Protected
24 Program on which pundits talk about marinara and such?
26 Easily makes the hole with, in golf
27 Trapper's ware
28 Walloped, quickly
29 Hydroelectric org.
30 Venice's Bridge of ___
32 Program on which pundits say dumbfounding things?
37 You might not be able to stand this
39 Big winner at the casino
41 Home of 14-Down
42 All: Prefix
43 Bass ___
44 Possessor of many rings
45 Late bloomer
47 Suffix with viol
49 Easily concealed weapon
51 Program on which pundits talk about hangings?
56 Sulu player on "Star Trek"
57 "The Wild Duck" dramatist
59 Got dark
60 At all
62 Leave rubber, with "out"
63 Indians play it
65 Exasperated exclamations
66 Program on which pundits express indignant surprise?
71 Kwik-E-Mart clerk
73 Earring type
74 Afternoon hour
75 Personal ad abbr.
76 Kind of winds
79 Tuscan province
80 Old Dodges
84 Program on which pundits slug it out with reporters?
87 Passed out in a bad way
90 Start of a Vol. 1 heading
91 I do's
92 Whence Zeno
93 Life overseas
94 Brooding sort
96 Pollster Roper
97 Analyze
98 Wood for bows
99 Program on which pundits kvetch?
104 Buffoons
106 "Who ___?" (song from "Les Miz")
107 Mens ___ (criminal intent)
108 Works at a museum
110 Worrier's words
113 Program on which pundits deride the power of the federal government?
118 Old cash register key
119 Answer the call
120 It may be a lot
121 Waxes
122 Commentator Myers
123 Have
124 Would-be J.D.'s exam

DOWN

1 Words after hard or keep
2 ___ Thomas, the Soul Queen of New Orleans
3 Cut of beef
4 "Pardon me, Pasquale"
5 Sticker abbr.
6 Michael of "Caddyshack"
7 Nabisco ___ wafer
8 Ostentation
9 Commercial suffix with Motor
10 Med. country
11 The Cards, on scoreboards
12 Has way too much of, slangily
13 ___ double life
14 Cyclones' sch.
15 A role some people play
16 Control surface on a plane's wing
17 NPR newswoman Stamberg
19 Program on which pundits talk about Camelot?
20 Lady of Brazil
25 Just makes, with "out"
31 One who says "See you in court!"
33 In the stomach
34 Govt. gangbusters
35 Lifesaver, e.g.
36 ___ max
37 History
38 Michigan college
40 Not quite good enough for the majors, say
45 Addled
46 Nonkosher food
47 Actor Jason of the Harry Potter films
48 Volleyball action
50 Matriarch of six of the 12 Tribes of Israel
52 One of Chekhov's "Three Sisters"
53 ___ before
54 180
55 Map lines: Abbr.
58 Attention getter
61 Start of a pirate chant
63 Miler turned congressman
64 Many ski chalets
66 Sushi staple
67 Improve
68 Loamy soil
69 Program on which pundits talk for 48 straight hours?
70 "All ___" (Tomlin film)
71 State dept. figure
72 Dupin's creator
77 Strong position
78 Giant star of the 1930s and '40s
79 Big East's ___ Hall
81 Specialists in special ops
82 "Why would ___?"
83 Dither
85 Sport with a 4½-ounce ball

by Randolph Ross

86 Cine- suffix
88 "The most beautiful woman ever to visit Casablanca"
89 Years on the diamond
94 Decent
95 Isolate
96 Time online, for example
97 Harshly bright
99 Cut a cord, say
100 Present itself
101 Musical matchmaker
102 Certain caucuser
103 Beatrice, to Leonato, in "Much Ado About Nothing"
105 Subject of the book "Disaster in Dearborn"
109 Tube lineup
111 ". . . and to ___ good-night"
112 What's left
114 Covered up
115 Big load
116 "Double Fantasy" singer
117 Safety equipment

YEAR-ROUND

ACROSS

1 Portraitist of George Washington
7 Robot maid on "The Jetsons"
12 Sorority chapter
17 Leader of a flock
18 Do away with
19 Spreader of holiday cheer
21 Singer who said "At least I had that, one guy understood me"
22 Possible punishment for steroid use
23 Enhance
24 When Cannes heats up
25 Native tongue of R&B singer Rihanna
26 Bow to
27 Wise guy
28 Ear part
29 "Esq." titleholders
31 Keep an eye out for
33 Meager
34 Prefix with sphere
35 Fuming
38 Daring
39 Alvin and the Chipmunks, e.g.
40 Experts at exports
43 Genre explored by Run-D.M.C. and Aerosmith
44 Diurnally
45 "Hop ___!"
46 Mexican mouse chaser
48 Inner circle
51 Proust title character
53 Job interview topic
57 Sioux tribe member

58 State capital on the Colorado River
61 Economy-size
63 Langston Hughes poem
64 Cry at sea
66 Cancún resident, once
68 Farm call
69 Hall's partner in pop
70 "This is how it's done"
71 Worth mentioning
72 Pattern for light or sound
74 Soft hat materials
76 Actors Max and Max Jr.
78 See
79 ___ Taylor, co-host of "Make Me a Supermodel"
80 It appears when things go bad
82 Boils down
85 Thrill seeker
91 "If you ask me," online
92 The "A" of James A. Garfield
94 Some exams for joint pain sufferers
95 Litigant
96 Symptom of catarrh
97 Focused (on)
99 Brisk pace
100 Cavs, on a scoreboard
101 Nativity figure
102 "Was it ___ I saw?" (classic palindrome)
103 Samuel L. Jackson's character in "Pulp Fiction"
106 Were present?
107 It might run in the rain
109 Filled (with)

110 Part of a serial
112 Eroded
113 It's usually said with the eyes closed
114 Wig
115 Egg holders
116 Kind of skill
117 Farm machine

DOWN

1 Weightlifter's helper
2 Have a break at 4:00, say
3 Troop troupe: Abbr.
4 Basic travel path
5 First name in gossip
6 Paris was part of it
7 Equips with new clips
8 Small African antelope
9 It's darn likely
10 "My, my, old chap!"
11 Dusk, to Donne
12 Unlikely event for puritans
13 MADD member
14 Foe of Spider-Man
15 Like some modern maps
16 Coffee table item
19 Mustang rivals
20 Gene who sang "Back in the Saddle Again"
21 Cause of many uprisings
27 Members of the bar?
30 Biker's add-on
32 Early Chinese dynasty
33 Admit defeat, in a way

34 Lucratively
36 Polite disclaimer
37 ABC a.m. show, briefly
38 Last resort in poker, often
41 Doesn't waver
42 Euripides drama
43 GPS suggestion
46 Bottle opener's surprise
47 Vegas openings?
48 Untangles, in a way
49 Cyberball maker
50 Pop singer who appeared in the movie "Sgt. Pepper's Lonely Hearts Club Band"
51 It's called in a political convention roll call
52 Undercover device
53 Campaigns for
54 "Quite possibly"
55 Surface-___
56 Singles and jingles
59 Sub with sauerkraut?
60 White wine from Verona
62 W., e.g.: Abbr.
65 Professional with many contacts?
67 Lords and ladies
73 Is past?
75 Scrape (out)
77 Like some professors
79 Sask. neighbor
80 Drinks in frosted glasses
81 Married
82 Hit Sony product introduced in 1984
83 Model after

by Jeremy Newton

84 American, Swiss, etc.
85 Design feature of many a viaduct
86 Lookout, maybe
87 "OMG, that's sooo funny!"
88 Kind of bar
89 Squared away
90 First name in cosmetics
92 Now, in Nogales
93 Wages, before overtime
97 Beer serving in a pub
98 "Yippee!"
101 Jabbers
102 U.S. gas chain
104 Triple-edged sword
105 Part of a horse's genealogy
108 Cool ___
109 Genealogical grp.
111 S, on a French compass

59 IT'S A MYSTERY

ACROSS

1 Drapery material
7 Lumber supplier
14 Item marked in pounds
20 City and county of central California
21 Rushing
22 Hair color
23 School in Madison, N.J.
25 Cause of worry lines
26 Poet whose last words were "Of course [God] will forgive me; that's his business"
27 "Beau ___"
29 Coup d' ___ (quick glance)
30 Bank postings
33 Don't believe it
37 Seward-to-Fairbanks dir.
38 ___ rancheros
39 Levelheaded
40 Raw bar offering
42 Officer in "Alice's Restaurant"
43 Launches
45 Classic theater name
46 "The Divine Comedy," for Dante
49 1950s–'70s TV host
51 Petrol purchase
54 It's often punched on a keypad
55 Reader's goal
56 Online reading
58 Redeem
59 Wife, informally
61 Fraternity member
62 Difficult situation
63 Sitting with one's hand on one's chin, e.g.
66 Track-and-field event
69 Google results
70 Duds
72 Record producer who published the diary "A Year With Swollen Appendices"
73 Appetite whetter
75 Favored one side or the other
76 Kon-Tiki material
78 Turned right
79 What eds. read
82 Get divorced
83 ___ avis
84 Dropped off
87 More spooky
89 Work site?
91 German river
92 Trig angle
94 Salad morsel
95 "On Language" columnist
97 Mens ___ (guilty mind)
98 Pantry array
102 Enzyme in some yeasts
103 There's one for dance
105 Prefix with centric
106 Only U.S. vice president born in Maryland
107 San Luis ___
109 Ones in charge of a case . . . or a literal hint to the eight other longest answers in this puzzle
116 Vacation arrangement
117 Big name in auto parts
118 French subjects?
119 Alarm clock button
120 Psychiatric visit
121 Major diamond exporter

DOWN

1 Mil. authority
2 Laugh start
3 Suffix with cyan-
4 City with the world's first telephone directory (1878)
5 Loyally following
6 Nuts
7 Had work looming?
8 Combined
9 Blade in sports
10 The shakes
11 "The Da Vinci Code" scholar Sir ___ Teabing
12 Novelist who wrote "The Gravedigger's Daughter"
13 No-tell motel visit
14 Italy's Reggia di ___ (royal palace)
15 Pizza ___
16 River that rises in Cantabria
17 Beloved figure in England
18 Bearlike
19 Eve ___, "The Vagina Monologues" monologist
24 Connections
28 Quaint letter opener
30 Eating sound
31 Persian Gulf emirate
32 Cover many subjects?
33 Extremely pleasing, in slang
34 Occupied
35 Word with smart or mind
36 Upbraid
39 Biological dividing wall
41 Being debated
43 Kind of fin
44 Dumped out
45 Singer Corinne Bailey ___
47 Longtime news inits.
48 Potato choice
50 Egyptian crosses
52 Yemeni money
53 Tolkien creatures
57 Nobodies
58 Southern legume
59 Scoundrels
60 Window washer's boo-boo
62 Unlikely to be Miss America
63 Ghostlike
64 Big tournament
65 Card game played to 61
67 China's Zhou
68 Loose overcoat
71 Condense again, as an article
74 The Mormons, initially
76 High jump need
77 Certain photo caption
79 Broadcasters, e.g.
80 Predictors
81 Brief indulgence
83 "Malcolm in the Middle" boy
85 Cy Young candidates' stats
86 Liberal
88 Behind
90 Larry O'Brien Championship Trophy org.
92 Safeguards
93 Deli order

by Brendan Emmett Quigley

95 Sacred places
96 Winning hand in blackjack
99 Stewpots
100 Certain flower girl
101 "The Grapes of Wrath" family
102 T-shirt size: Abbr.

104 "___ perpetua" (Idaho's motto)
106 Lots
108 Opposite of guerra
110 Paris's Parc ___ Princes
111 Sixth-century year
112 Prefix with freak

113 Letters on a brandy bottle
114 Marine predator
115 Org. that has its benefits

60

'TWAS PUZZLING

ACROSS

1 Butcher shop purchase
6 Some foreign pen pals
10 Photo paper option
15 [How dare you!]
19 Song sung by Gwen in Broadway's "Chicago"
20 Radio host/pianist John
21 Greek market of old
22 "The Lion King" lioness
23 When jerks come out?
26 X out
27 Pertinent to the discussion
28 Kind of dialysis
29 Novice
31 "A Doll's House" wife
32 Wishes undone
33 Some people or food at parties
34 Nonkosher sandwiches
38 String around a cake box?
41 City near Tel Aviv
44 Moistens again
46 Once-in-a-lifetime exchange, maybe
47 Texas county, river or forest that's a girl's first name
49 Vinegar: Prefix
50 AOL alternative
52 Bridge
53 Men or women who pinch?
58 "New Look" designer of 1947

59 Charity's urging
60 Orbital point
62 Dope
64 Appeal to
66 Penseur's thought
67 Speck
68 Prefix with -crat
70 Hair stuff
71 Mushroom stalks
73 Dress-up costume piece
75 Month in a Faulkner title
77 One of Woody's stock at Woodstock
78 Nerd's essence?
82 Unlikely to run
87 Legal eagles' org.
88 Come up
89 Capital of South Australia
90 French Polynesia constituents
93 Lauds
94 Thrice, in prescriptions
95 Roast the other side of the marshmallow?
99 Novelist's need
100 W.W. II gun
101 "Let's just leave ___ that"
102 Teri Garr's "Young Frankenstein" role
104 Certain celebrant
107 Legislative assemblies
108 "Praise the Lord!"
112 A leveret is a young one
113 Discouraging comment to a cloner?
117 ___ Center, home of the New Jersey Nets
118 Pertaining to hair

119 "Almighty" title role for Steve Carell
120 Caustic
121 Eye part
122 Desirable places
123 Kind of difference, oxymoronically
124 "Land ___!"

DOWN

1 Monitor type, for short
2 Jolly laugh
3 Yak pack
4 Big East Conference team, for short
5 Attach, as a patch
6 Invitation information specification
7 Gathering points
8 Suffix with book
9 Like some eggs or cloth
10 They're attractive, but not necessarily to each other
11 Shocked
12 Awl, for one
13 Play about Capote
14 Salary
15 Bamboozles
16 Gyro meat
17 "Others" in a Latin phrase
18 Crown
24 Apple pocketfuls
25 Transmitter starter?
30 Fencing swords
33 The Flintstones' pet
34 Uncouth youth
35 Poland's Walesa
36 Moth, perhaps?
37 Altercation
39 Trig ratio

40 Sun Tzu's "The Art of ___"
41 Fabric that really breathes?
42 Low tie
43 Strawberry of note
45 Off-campus local
48 City near Milan
50 Outback buddy
51 Shooting sport
52 Second-century year
54 St. Louis's ___ Bridge
55 Nagpur noble
56 Fern germ
57 These, to Juan
61 Rusty on the diamond
62 Utah's lily
63 Pitcher of a perfect game, 9/9/65
64 "Vigilant ___ to steal cream": Falstaff
65 Walked with a purpose
69 Wahine's dance
72 Shooting game
74 Addams family cousin
76 Spaghetti ___
79 Hops kiln
80 Analogy phrase
81 Battery part
83 A large number
84 JPEG or text
85 Score just before victory, maybe
86 Fall mo.
90 Weeping
91 Rimes with the 1996 hit "Blue"
92 Subjects of many legal battles
93 Goad
96 Garage container

by Cathy Allis Millhauser

97 Native American home
98 Waiting at the bank, say
100 Beginnings
103 Localities
104 Dr. with advice in O magazine
105 Level
106 Monopoly game token
107 Whine
109 Place to play b-ball
110 Give orders like a drill sergeant
111 "Night" author Wiesel
114 Fact finisher
115 Hydroelectric org.
116 Mormons, initially

61

FAULT-FINDING

ACROSS

1 Seafood dishes
8 ___ the board
14 Certified
22 Socrates or Pythagoras, e.g.
23 Mangle by mastication
24 Perfunctory
25 Lower part of a duet
26 Showing concern?
27 Hanging over many a mantel
28 *Common Guernsey bull
31 Flower parts
32 West Flanders site of three W.W. I battles
33 Lid attachment
35 "Ally McBeal" co-star Lucy
36 Composer Charles
40 Ones being tested
41 *1968 film featuring a murderous cheerleader
46 *Urban farce
48 Studio supporter
49 Destination for Mary and Joseph
50 Stainless steel, for one
51 ___ ear
52 Whopper topper
56 See 47-Down
57 Hiccup
58 Life
59 Hwys.
60 Shore birds
61 *Where stars can be seen fluffing and folding
64 Kensington kiss
65 Hair line?
66 Verdant stretches
67 ___ Beach, Fla.
68 Gallic toppers
71 *What theaters play
73 One of Luther's 95
75 Look lasciviously

76 Skye of "Say Anything . . ."
77 What "matar" means on an Indian menu
78 Great Trek trekker
79 *Bean, e.g.
83 Russian diet?
84 Badge awarder: Abbr.
87 Region including Texarkana
88 Mexican waterways
89 G.I.'s
91 Serve well
92 Goes on "Wheel of Fortune"?
94 Snail variety whose name means "small gray"
95 Bygone P.M. with a palindromic name
96 "Ville d'Avray" painter
97 *Onetime regal status of Shanghai or Canton
98 *Get blankets
102 Presides over as a judge
103 Pizzeria chain, familiarly
104 "Is that ___?"
105 Apple cores?: Abbr.
106 Pulitzer-winning journalist Seymour
107 "Swept Away" director Guy
111 *Novice in an ad campaign
120 Home of the Cadillac Ranch
122 Word with aunt or voyage
123 "Heavens to Betsy!"
124 Computer information path
125 "Rama Lama Ding Dong" singers, with "the"

126 Broke out
127 Thomas Gray and others
128 Drug company once headed by Donald Rumsfeld
129 Fixed motor parts

DOWN

1 Events gone by
2 From square one
3 "___ homo"
4 Columbia athlete
5 Mardi Gras follower
6 Roy Rogers sidekick Devine
7 "Pipe down!"
8 Precision
9 Takeout option
10 Tears
11 Wilson of "The Darjeeling Limited"
12 Sport for rikishi
13 German wine made from the late harvest
14 "Killer" program
15 Showcase item
16 Some shapes in topology
17 New newts
18 Ilk
19 Ski runs, e.g.
20 Designer Pucci
21 Old car with the slogan "We are driven"
29 Sunroof and spoilers, e.g.
30 Gourmand
34 N.L. Central team: Abbr.
36 Less welcoming
37 Strongly green
38 Short jackets for boys
38 Roget offerings: Abbr.
40 Short jackets for women

41 *Bad drivers back them up
42 1 to 10, say
43 Godliness
44 Available
45 On easy street
47 Kind of examiner 56-Across was
51 Like xenon
52 Little foxes
53 Snaps back?
54 Places to develop
55 Ones who are always starting something?
57 Chilling: Var.
58 Apothecary container
62 Swells up
63 Vintage autos
64 Complete, as a Senate term
65 Pub order
68 Jacket material?
69 Start of a counting rhyme
70 Clinton's first labor secretary
71 Terse order
72 Chihuahua change
73 Small birds, in British lingo
74 Robust
76 Getaway locale
78 "Pass the Courvoisier" rapper
80 Key shade
81 Juice
82 Rap sheet listing
83 How the Great Sphinx looks
84 The fifth element
85 Gerald's predecessor
86 Staff members: Abbr.
90 Forerunner of the K.G.B.
92 Absorb, in a way
93 Takes for granted

by Byron Walden

94 Make ready for the dishwasher
96 Filch
97 2000 Jennifer Lopez thriller
98 Weekly with 30+ million circulation
99 ___ instincts
100 Shift, in volleyball
101 Monkey predator
106 Playground quarry
108 Escarpment
109 Spinner for the Spinners
110 They're no good
112 Invited
113 Alaska senator Murkowski
114 Mole, e.g.
115 1977 flick with the tagline "Terror just beneath the surface"
116 "Git!"
117 What each starred clue — and its answer — contains
118 Part of FEMA: Abbr.
119 Cabernets, e.g.
121 Little yelps

62

CHANGE OF HEART

ACROSS

1 Sudden increase
6 Jacks, e.g.
10 Wallop
14 Fancy footwear
19 Up in the air
20 Object of a mil. search
21 Deserve special perks, say
22 Georges who wrote "Life: A User's Manual"
23 Low-budget films about hearty European meals?
26 Even things
27 Conductor ___ -Pekka Salonen
28 Page with views
29 Organ repair sites, briefly
30 Some crew members
32 Hip-hop's ___ Kim
33 Where hermit painters retire?
36 "Impossible" response to the question "Are you sleeping?"
39 "I'm not quite done yet"
41 Bone: Prefix
42 Biography of Odin, e.g.?
46 Traffic directors
50 Say without saying?
51 One to one, e.g.
52 Bring (in) abundantly
54 Pinza of "South Pacific"
55 Bones that support tibiae
56 German beef?
58 Family dinner
62 Eva's half sister?
63 Fingered
64 Zinger
66 Say A is not A, say
67 College cohorts
69 Place to go for kitchenware?
73 Ivory or Coast
75 Grp. that includes Canada and Colombia
76 Hardware fastener
77 It's taken by some coll. seniors
80 It may be stroked
81 Used
84 A little extra burnishing, maybe, in brief
85 E.R. part: Abbr.
86 Ltr. holders
88 Picard's counselor on "Star Trek: T.N.G."
89 Narrow inlet
91 Supermarket section
92 Recital list
95 How beatniks raise kids?
99 Decide to take part
101 Make more tempting, as a deal
102 Worked (up)
103 Étagère with a single tiny shelf?
108 Be in a cast
109 Frequent drivers
110 Butt
111 Protester
112 Semi-attached compartment?
115 Stash
116 Where citrus trees grow in small groups?
121 Richards : Moore :: Grant : ___
122 Slate, for one
123 "The Virginian" author Wister
124 Hardly laid-back
125 Mythical enchantress
126 Explodes
127 Agent with many girls
128 White and wet

DOWN

1 Nigerian-born singer with five Top 40 hits
2 Grade elevator
3 Wee bit
4 "Original or crispy" offerer
5 Study of natural animal behavior patterns
6 Drop leaf support
7 Staggered
8 Take some off the top?
9 Skull and Bones meeting attendee
10 Rapper with a professional title
11 Mrs. Gorbachev
12 4×4, briefly
13 Infatuates
14 Less dense
15 Place to find a long-term companion, maybe
16 Oven emanation
17 Precept
18 Embarrassing outbreak
24 Like cacti
25 Chamber work
31 Fictional clue sniffer
33 California city where A & W root beer was born
34 Skater Brian
35 Chicago journalist Mike
36 Last Supper question
37 Rashad of football
38 City NW of Minneapolis
40 Lepidopterous movie monster
43 Moves quietly
44 Once around
45 Hardest to get
47 13-time Gold Glove-winning shortstop
48 Learned
49 In order (to)
53 Sharp scolding
56 Something very tough
57 Cover in a layer
59 "How can ___?"
60 Ceylon's capital?
61 French pronoun
65 Soothe, in a way, as a burn
68 "American Pie" songwriter
70 Queue before Q
71 Banker's worry
72 Ready to run later
73 When repeated, "Out of the way!"
74 Latin lambs
78 Raptor's roost
79 Date not marked on a calendar?
82 Circular gasket
83 Inundate
87 With no adverse consequences
90 Old TV's "___ Three Lives"
91 Numbers, at times
93 Subject of a 2004 F.D.A. dietary supplement ban

by Rich Norris

94 Disturbance
96 Missouri feeder
97 Done
98 Straight: Prefix
100 Marching smartly
103 Archaic Irish script
104 Hanger?
105 Kenyan grazer
106 Deep-six
107 1970s–'80s supermodel
111 "So be it"
112 Family head
113 Over
114 Celebration time, for short
117 Grp. with a co-pay
118 High ball
119 Noted war photo site, briefly
120 Reagan adviser Nofziger

ACROSS

1 Titles for some monks
5 Litter unit
8 Wind with a wide range
12 Fashion
18 Tony's cousin
19 Paul Anka's "___ Beso"
20 "Too rich for my blood"
21 Carbohydrate-binding protein
22 Be fooled
24 Is completely hamstrung
26 Cold sufferer's complaint
28 Completely cover
29 Fool
30 Contradict
31 Stream bank sliders
33 Mad workers: Abbr.
34 Old printing process, for short
35 Big bore
38 And more: Abbr.
40 Musical set in Berlin
43 Dept. head
44 Stomach section
46 Way off
50 Ballet's Markova or Alonso
51 "WarGames" org.
53 Photographer's request, maybe
56 Opposite of comico-
57 Part-time players
59 Some playground shoes
60 Cut
61 Confines
62 Cooking meas.
63 Phlegmatic
65 Public persona
67 Hospital procedure, for short
69 IV to III, maybe
71 Part of a bedroom suite
73 Pigskin pickoff: Abbr.
74 Little bits
77 Title of some 2004 Summer Olympics preview shows
81 "O.K., play!"
82 Not quite boiling
83 Security agreements
84 Spanish Harlem grocery
85 Kitties
86 Double ___
88 Have a date, say
89 It's not a silk purse source, it's said
90 Tennis center?
93 Cousin of "Voilà!"
95 Mixed bag
96 You may have a nightcap when you're in these
99 Like some salons
101 Platform introduced in 1981
103 1969 Nabokov novel
106 Certain feeds for horses
108 Atlantic City casino
112 Perjure oneself . . . or what can be found six times in this puzzle
114 Batted the ball too high, perhaps
115 Punish by fining
116 Cast iron, e.g.
117 "Yes"
118 Victim of Pizarro
119 Lessee
120 Ominous time of old
121 ___ gestae
122 Poetic adverb

DOWN

1 Inflexible teaching
2 Toes the line
3 Catcher's collection
4 Clockmaker ___ Thomas
5 Sri Lankan export
6 Wear out, potentially
7 Producer who discovered and married Loren
8 Poet known as "the Tentmaker"
9 High society
10 Make greater strides than
11 LAX listing: Abbr.
12 Eau ___
13 Opportunity to go beyond the first grade?
14 Come back
15 Suffix with form or inform
16 Like forks
17 Many Rice grads: Abbr.
20 Hosp. area
23 Kind of rice used in risotto
25 Hooray for Jorge
27 Child's attention-getting call to a parent
32 Like some customs
34 Bigot, of a sort
36 Prefix with business
37 Cast events after filming is done
39 Showed up
40 Wine vessel
41 How a ship may be turned
42 Cardinal's residence
45 Some Venetian Renaissance paintings
47 Be perfect
48 They're often drawn
49 Defendant in court: Abbr.
51 Fresh
52 Slip a Mickey to
54 Belgian treaty site
55 It doesn't really represent change
57 Left
58 Nugget holder
60 Distiller ___ Walker
64 1960s baseball All-Star Blue Moon ___
65 Cousin of equi-
66 Square ___
68 Reply to "You couldn't have!"
69 Pull up
70 Cry of exasperation
72 Loses one's shirt?
73 Ties
75 New York City racetrack, informally
76 Macy's logo
78 Surge
79 2006 N.B.A. champs
80 Put away, in a way
81 Concerned wife's question in the E.R., maybe
84 Western wear
87 Like a home that's no risk to the builder

by Joe DiPietro

89 Soap-making
   solution
91 Subtlety
92 Former late-night
   TV host
94 Blow out
96 ___ opposite
97 Longtime Philippine
   archbishop ___ Sin

98 One of the Dutch
   Masters
100 Suffix with
    vapour
102 As yet
103 Priest's urging
104 Two for some
    hand holders
105 Preacher's post

107 Offended
109 Siouan people
110 Rationale
111 Ruler of the Aesir
113 Italy's equivalent
    of the BBC

ACROSS

1 Titles are often put in it: Abbr.
5 Scarlett O'Hara, e.g.
10 Like Arnold Schoenberg's music
16 1990 Literature Nobelist Octavio __
19 Singer Winans
20 Certain bulb
21 Smooth and shiny
22 Actress Thurman
23 Switch in an orchestra section?
26 "Take the filly in the fifth," e.g.
27 Pressing need?
28 Union member since 1896
29 Wise men
31 Emmy category
34 You can make one for yourself
37 North Carolina university
38 Negative north of England
40 Pilgrim?
45 86-Across's alma mater: Abbr.
48 Got cozy together
50 Beau __
51 Scare off
52 Stumble __
53 Kipling's "Follow Me __"
54 Came about
56 Something near many a checkout line
57 Neolithic outlaws?
63 Bank offering, for short

64 Beckett's "Endgame: __ In One Act"
65 "Crazy Legs" Hirsch of the early N.F.L.
66 Parented
68 How dastards speak
71 Rabbit's home, maybe
72 Major-league manager Tony
73 Be Circe-like
74 Alfred E. Neuman visages
75 Cut
76 Sch. group
77 Invisible lost dogs?
83 Sheet music abbr.
84 Do some tune-up work on
85 First Shia imam
86 Gen. Robt. __
87 Swag
89 Some photo files, in computer lingo
92 Signifying
95 Internet initialism
96 Gets fat?
98 Org. for 86-Across
99 Composer Dohnányi
101 Blackthorn
102 Author Zora __ Hurston
104 African nation founder Jomo __
108 Inside pitch?
111 Traditional symbol of friendship
114 Devon river
115 Go-go club?
120 Turn down
121 Hero pilot

122 Result of some sandbagging
123 Whistler's whistle, maybe
124 Trough site
125 Key of Bach's best-known Mass
126 J.F.K.'s "Why England __"
127 They ring in a ring

DOWN

1 Clinches
2 Bible reading
3 Let win
4 Franz who composed "You Are My Heart's Delight"
5 French approval
6 Part of E.S.L.: Abbr.
7 Stead
8 Spoils
9 __ terrible
10 Bermuda hrs.
11 Swab
12 Milo's title partner in a 1989 film
13 El __
14 One opening up a can of worms?
15 Everyday disinfectant
16 Add new connections between floors?
17 Whitaker played him in a 2006 film
18 Nukes
24 Menotti role for a boy soprano
25 Actress Belafonte
30 Pout
32 Curly conker

33 "The Naked and the Dead" star, 1958
35 All the rage
36 Longtime D.C. delegate to Congress __ Holmes Norton
38 PX users
39 Spider-Man's __ May
41 "Delish!"
42 Graf __
43 Loaded with fat
44 "The Time Machine" people
46 Distances in Canada
47 Force in the ocean
49 Costume designer Danilo __
51 Another name for 28-Across
55 Soda fountain supply
58 Gourmet
59 Gene variant
60 Word origin: Abbr.
61 Crepes
62 Kid's comeback
67 Meadows of comedy
68 Certain Himalayan
69 Anatomical cavity
70 Dieter?
71 Needing a lift?
72 Reveal to, as a secret
74 Grouse
75 Serf
78 W.W. II Axis leader
79 Leman and others
80 American suffragist honored with a 1995 stamp

by Daniel C. Bryant

81 Desires
82 Genesis creator
88 Cowboy actor Calhoun
90 Jug capacity: Abbr.
91 A deadly sin
93 Saturn S.U.V.
94 Les __-Unis
96 Cry upon an arrest
97 Is honest (with)
100 Old Indian V.I.P.
103 Numbers game
104 Some sneakers
105 Way out
106 __ Polo of "Meet the Fockers"
107 Galway Bay's __ Islands
109 Explorer Tasman of Tasmania fame
110 Messenger of Noah
112 "Rule, Britannia" composer
113 Sleep indicators
116 "Baudolino" author
117 Thrice, in Rx's
118 "You betcha"
119 Collector's goal

65

WEB MASTER

ACROSS

1 Precipitate
7 Amplifier jack letters
10 Liveliness
16 "Sort of" ending
19 Full assembly
20 Nabokov heroine
21 Falafel sandwich sauce
22 Never, in Nürnberg
23 They work on Steinways
24 Where you might see 115-Across
27 They're hidden in a Hirschfeld sketch
28 Others, in Latin
29 Tie followers, briefly
30 Rubber that meets the road
31 Coffee order
34 Deceive
36 Consumers
38 Pumpkin bomb-throwing enemy of 115-Across, with "the"
40 Scottish cattle breed
42 "Show me!"
43 Gibson's "Ransom" co-star
44 Prominent stars in constellations
49 What's more
50 Food writer Rombauer and others
52 Related to base eight
56 Royals abroad, maybe
58 "___ see"
60 Go (for)
61 Bandleader Puente
62 Scratch cause
65 Leaves behind
68 "London Fields" author
69 Taliban leader
70 Way overseas
71 French goose
72 Mess up
73 Plant with tendrils
74 Selfish cry before and after "all"
75 Sight from the Bering Sea
77 Astrologers' work
79 Geraint's beloved
80 Vintage wheels
81 System of beliefs
83 Baby carrier brand
84 Dress lines
86 Singer Lauper
88 Legal org.
91 Plus
92 Loathing
94 Shoelace ends: Var.
97 Handel opera based on Greek myth
100 Film star who played 38-Across
105 Resemble
106 Wish granters
108 The planet Venus
110 Memo starter
111 Lux. locale
112 "___ fool . . ."
114 Identify from memory
115 Theme of this puzzle
119 Lighthearted
120 Suffix with puppet
121 Extremely
122 Pupil's spot
123 It's covered by a sleeve
124 Hosp. staff
125 Learn easily
126 Beam
127 Firewood measures

DOWN

1 10-G, e.g.: Abbr.
2 Laundry whitener
3 Actor Jeremy of "North Country"
4 Nervousness
5 Run down
6 Some intellectual property: Abbr.
7 Chewy cookie
8 Immunity ___ on "Survivor"
9 Monet painting also known as "The Woman in the Green Dress"
10 And more: Abbr.
11 Wooden shoe
12 115-Across's day job
13 They run through South America
14 Publicity
15 Peculiarity
16 Visible
17 California's High ___
18 Joan of Arc's crime
25 Visual presentation of what gave 115-Across special powers
26 Tentacled enemy of 115-Across
32 Economics fig.
33 Indian fort locale
35 ___'acte
36 High ways?
37 To boot
39 Drawers in a laundry room
41 Hardly luxurious
44 Looks good on
45 Assay
46 Largest moon of Uranus
47 Film star who played 26-Down
48 Quattro + due
51 Comfy shoe
53 Stopwatch info
54 All excited
55 Goes ballistic
57 Company leaders: Abbr.
59 Bouquet
63 Mohawk, for one
64 Film star who played 115-Across
66 White-glove affairs
67 Sp. matrons
76 Big time?
78 Modern test subj.
82 "Scenes From a ___" (Woody Allen film)
85 Home of Rapid City: Abbr.
87 Setting of the painting "Washington Crossing the Delaware"
89 Natural sweetener
90 "Don't look ___ that way!"
93 Suffix with glass
95 Dim perception
96 Old campus grp.
97 Let up
98 Stake attachment, maybe

by Elizabeth C. Gorski

"Sounds Like It's Cold in Here"

ACROSS

1 18th-century Venetian fresco painter
8 Gets with the times
14 Pellet shooters
20 It's lighter than air
21 Site of two ecumenical councils
22 "Capeesh?"
23 Question to a paralegal?
25 ___ Sea, west of New Zealand
26 Type
27 Hoods
28 Overhead shot
30 "Sugar Lips" trumpeter
31 What if, informally
33 Figure in an Edmund Spenser poem
34 Inner: Prefix
35 Ancient name for Great Britain
38 Red Sox franchise?
41 Three-time Masters winner Nick
42 Bogus
44 Symbol on the back of a dollar bill
45 Warning sign outside of Br'er Rabbit's home?
47 Classic cowboy name
49 Not on good terms (with)
54 Pigeon
55 Sire
56 Neighbor of Switz.
57 London's ___ Square
58 Brown shade
59 Affiance
62 Imagine that
63 Useful advice for a ring referee?
68 Botanical angle
69 Science of the ear
70 ___ Davis, first African-American to win a Heisman
71 How-to
73 It's more than a stretch
74 CB radios, once
75 Some batteries
78 "Don't make ___!"
79 Juilliard deg.
80 Clinician in the 'hood?
83 Canadian prov.
85 Knife
86 Ancient Egyptian kingdom
87 Silicone implant companies?
93 Man and ape
94 Start of some choice words?
95 Parting words
96 Hoops Hall-of-Famer Thomas
98 Brink
99 Low person on a staff
100 "Marshal of Cripple Creek," e.g.
102 Sure target
106 Beloved of Pyramus
108 Matzo mover?
111 Georgia's Lake ___, behind the Buford Dam
112 Underwater trap
113 Connect with
114 Timeless, in verse
115 One living month to month, say
116 Weeks in Madrid

DOWN

1 Fancy shooting marbles
2 "If you ask me," in a chat room
3 Matter of life and death: Abbr.
4 It's left on a ship
5 I
6 Boxer nicknamed "The Bear"
7 Promising words
8 Uncommon blood type, informally
9 Childish claim
10 Horizontal: Abbr.
11 Chum
12 Abounded
13 Hunt overseas
14 Incidentally
15 Wrap around the neck
16 Overdoes the accolades
17 Philly money maker
18 Almost at
19 Forwarded
24 Lemon or orange
29 Vicks nasal decongestant
32 Hero of New Orleans
33 Be outscored at the end
35 Jet locales: Abbr.
36 Doctor Zhivago's love
37 Sound on classic Pong
38 Rhythm
39 Play with machines
40 French for 44-Across
42 Score the winning point in cribbage
43 Renounce
46 "Chill!"
47 Twist
48 For initiates only
50 Bête ___
51 ___ Bing! (go-go bar on "The Sopranos")
52 Over
53 Exclamation with a handshake
56 "This is not ___" (warning label)
57 "The Lion King" character voiced by Whoopi Goldberg
58 Slightly above average
59 Invitation stipulation
60 Brain scan letters
61 Homeland of Orpheus
63 ___ Sutra
64 Bar ___
65 Die Zeit article
66 "Essays of ___"
67 Periods between Winter and Summer Olympics
72 Egyptian symbols of royalty
74 U.S.N. officers
75 French cleric
76 Duller than dull
77 With the intent
79 Botch
80 Architect ___ van der Rohe
81 Musket end?
82 Bliss
84 Stand for things
85 Lice and mice, e.g.

by Paula Gamache

87 Automotive comeback of 1998
88 Cardinal's topper
89 Power source
90 Cry with a salute
91 French engineer Gustave
92 Sobieski who played Joan of Arc
93 Duffer's accomplishment
96 Suffix with social
97 Butt abutters
100 Wind in a pit
101 Uffizi Gallery hanging
103 Singing partner of Brooks
104 Numerical prefix
105 Old theaters once owned by Howard Hughes
107 Jerry's partner
109 Festoons with Charmin, informally
110 Pro ___

ACROSS

1 Doodled, e.g.
5 Elvis film "___ Scarum"
10 Attorney's favorite sweets?
16 Reign
17 "Loverboy" actress who made the cast sick?
20 It's love, in Lille
21 Séance-loving crime writer?
23 Adjustment means on a radio
24 Yards, e.g.
25 Obi-Wan Kenobi, for one
26 Uris hero ___ Ben Canaan
27 Market closing?
28 Longtime abbr. after Ted Kennedy's name
29 Kind of tape
31 Earthquake
33 Meshed foundation in lace
35 Exclamation from a blockhead
36 Show too much feeling?
39 "O.S.S." star, 1946
40 Hall of Fame golfer who invented the all-plastic club?
45 Alla ___ (pasta style)
48 Planned site of the Geo. W. Bush Presidential Library
49 Piece that gets riveted
50 Young wife (age 18) of Charlie Chaplin (age 54)
51 Restraints
52 Egg ___ yung

53 All-telling gossip queen who repeats everything she hears?
55 Letters of commerce
56 Laying-on of hands?
59 "You're such ___ for helping"
60 Ronny & the Daytonas hit
61 Eccentric
62 Acapulco gold
63 Long (for)
65 Letters of sizes
67 Yul Brynner died the same day as ___ Welles (odd fact)
69 Relatives of TV host Tom
71 Everest setting
72 Avant-garde composer who sat around a lot?
76 Linger in the hot sun
77 Loses on purpose?
78 Y-axis, for one
79 Handy places to shop
80 Army type, for short
81 Prima donna Norman
82 Passionate tennis star?
85 Yaw relative, on an aircraft
86 Some etiquette rules
87 Online address
88 "Rats!"
91 Regular writing
94 York, e.g.: Abbr.
95 Hollywood's Téa
97 Eye the bull's-eye
99 Trip-planning org.
100 Option for a sandwich
103 Lower than: It.

104 Disney pirate, 1953
105 Moscow V.I.P. who liked to cook on a ship?
110 Eban of Israel
111 "I have no face cards" actress?
112 Near Eastern port
113 Easter ___ (period up to Pentecost Sunday)
114 European resort Monte ___
115 Driving alternative in S.F.

DOWN

1 Explorer Francis
2 Destroyer
3 Author Leonard
4 Hall of Fame coach Ewbank
5 U.S. president after Grant
6 Noriega's weapons
7 Delgado's rivers
8 Rear admiral's org.
9 Extremely upset
10 Detestable one
11 Former Dodge
12 Operated
13 Reason for overtime
14 Top Chinese Zhou
15 Your future is their business
17 Freeboot
18 Old I.B.M. offering
19 Useful article
21 Red Roof rival
22 Lip
28 Entertainer Martin and others
29 Teutonic name part
30 Tenor, perhaps
31 Enos Slaughter's team for 13 yrs.
32 Roo's donkey friend
34 Slope
35 "Wagon Master" actress Joanne

36 Heaven on earth
37 Assigner of G's and R's: Abbr.
38 Tuba sounds
40 Wild
41 Action on Wall St.
42 Swamps
43 Monstrousness
44 "You dirty ___!"
45 Patrick Macnee's 1960s TV co-star Diana
46 Opus with singing
47 Interstate sight
48 Nonmatching item, maybe
52 Toy store ___ Schwarz
54 Add-on for Gator
56 Guy who digs fossils, slangily
57 American Beauty pest
58 Inspiration for Keats
61 Nails but good
63 Old aviation magazine ___ Digest
64 Have a bawl
66 Reshape a cornea, say
68 Items for knitters
70 Gallantry-in-war medals: Abbr.
71 House of Representatives divider
72 Tree with serrate leaves
73 Big name in tea
74 Ocho minus cinco
75 US Airways datum: Abbr.
77 Vacation destination for sandwich lovers?
80 It's void in Vichy
81 English duke ___ Gaunt

by Merl Reagle

PICTURE THIS

When this puzzle is done, read the circled letters in the top half of the puzzle clockwise starting with the last letter of 66-Across; and read the shaded letters in the bottom half of the puzzle clockwise starting with the second letter of 77-Across.

ACROSS

1 Dr. Seuss character with a red hat
7 Train stop?
12 Not useless, as clothing
20 British noble, for short
21 Football Hall-of-Fame coach Greasy ___
22 Earmarked (for)
23 Leader of the Fauvist movement
25 Title of a work by 23-Across
26 Publicity
27 Fictional spread
28 Hip in the '60s
29 Hideout
30 Agcy. overseeing reactor safety
31 It's deep
33 Winter protection
35 Metric weight
36 Vegetable with yellow pods
38 Nurse
39 Intense aversions
44 Somewhat reduced
47 Academic area
50 Debate (with)
51 Whirling
53 Nabokov novel
54 Flying grp. since 1918
56 ___ Accords of 1993
57 Workout target
58 "On&On" singer Erykah ___
61 Special ___
63 Say "Final answer," say
65 Will be now?
66 Double-layer breads
67 First name in spydom
69 Paris's ___ la Paix
70 Suppliers of greetings
73 What Ramona wore in a 1966 Chuck Berry song
76 Year Super Bowl XXXVII was played
77 Ziegfeld Follies designer
79 Scuffles
80 Morning deposit
81 Individual
83 Al Kaline, in uniform
84 Son, at the Sorbonne
85 It's cultivated in the Andes
86 Stone in a 2008 Olympic medal
87 Rejections
89 Invoice amount
91 Carted off
93 Auspices: Var.
94 Cushion user?
98 Brags about
99 More cool
102 Canterbury can
103 Boardinghouse boarders
105 Florence attraction
107 Musical for which Ben Vereen won a Tony
108 Those, to Muñoz
112 See 106-Down
115 Nobelist Pavlov
116 Big D player
117 Visiting the U.S. capital
119 Sportage maker
120 25-Across, e.g.
122 23-Across, e.g.
125 Factor in a restaurant rating
126 Skylit areas
127 Like the return of swallows to Capistrano
128 Cupid, e.g.
129 Fiber-yielding plant
130 Volleyball position

DOWN

1 Old term of respect
2 Concert venue
3 Otter cousins
4 Home of the Ramon Crater: Abbr.
5 Scuffling
6 N.Y.C. cultural event
7 Brightest star in Scorpius
8 Tiki bar offering
9 Devil's home?
10 Onetime political columnist Joseph
11 Sax player's need
12 Cleanup hitter, e.g.
13 Like the earliest Olympic festivals
14 Animal oddity
15 Had a big laugh
16 Long-distance letters
17 Revolutionary 1930s bomber
18 Duke of Cornwall's father-in-law, in Shakespeare
19 Part of H.E.W.: Abbr.
24 Show horse
32 Like the mathematician Euler
34 Fond du ___, Wis.
35 Personal quirk
37 Horned viper
38 Reply to irritably
40 Compound variant
41 How 25-Across appeared at a 6-Down in 1961
42 Kipling short story, with "The"
43 Low-cost accommodations, briefly
44 Reddish purple
45 Angrily crusading
46 Styles of 25-Across and the like
48 Ancient land near the Dead Sea
49 Pouch
52 Spain joined it in 1982
55 How long 25-Across was 41-Down before being noticed and fixed
59 Be bold enough
60 Web browsers
62 Unreasonable, pricewise
64 Oozy mixtures
66 Fraternity letters
68 Prefix with chemical
71 Most urgent
72 Well-oiled
74 Concert venue
75 Brings around
78 Brad and 86-Down, e.g.
82 San Francisco's ___ Hill
85 Touch off
86 See 78-Down
88 "The Laughing Man" author
90 Prospering ones

by David J. Kahn

92 ___ es Salaam
95 Make a slip
96 "Alley ___"
97 Current
100 Worked on a Life sentence?
101 Coulee
104 Ho Chi ___

106 With 112-Across, Okla. military area
107 First installment
109 Get around
110 Bridal path
111 Butterfly variety
112 On ___ with (equal to)

113 Celebrity
114 Andersson of "Wild Strawberries"
116 Some 6-Down curators: Abbr.
118 Canadian natives

121 "Ladders to Fire" writer
123 Long in films
124 Make lace

69

UH-OH

ACROSS

1 Like tests and dirt roads
7 Web programmer's medium
11 Deadens
16 Adolphe ___, musical instrument inventor
19 "Honestly, man!"
20 It may be gray
21 Economist Janeway
22 Open someone else's emails, maybe
23 Not accented
24 Will's opposite
25 Poker player's wear
26 Brynner of stage and screen
27 Sale sweeteners
29 Helpful comment to a judge?
32 "Stripes" actor, 1981
34 Imago, e.g.
35 Brunch time
36 Maine, e.g.: Abbr.
39 "Also Sprach Zarathustra" hitmaker, 1973
41 A cadet might be asked to pick it up
43 Insurance paperwork
46 Snowy ___
47 Fruit flies?
52 Dirty radio sitcom?
55 Given to showy affectation
56 Put to use
57 Monastery office
58 Polonius's hiding place
60 Bank holding
61 Do some grapplin'
65 Makes a muffler, e.g.
66 Weapon in the Charge of the Light Brigade
67 Jokey question to a Verizon technician?
71 Summer swarm
72 With regard to
73 Beauty spots
74 Line at a track
75 Cowgirl Dale
76 Chinese brew
80 Output of une législature
81 Bull: Prefix
82 Darius the Scamp?
88 Pot-smoking cleric?
91 Raccoon relative
92 Endor inhabitants
93 The story of the aftermath of Oceanic Flight 815
94 Read the riot act to
96 The Tigers, on scoreboards
97 Donnybrook
100 Engine problem
101 One who may give you a shot in the arm
105 Result of excessive rowing?
109 Makes clear
113 Hairy TV cousin
114 Shade of pink
115 ___ Torrence, American sprinter who won three gold medals at the 1992 and 1996 Olympics
117 Make merry
118 Casbah wear
119 Set of keys?
120 Suffix for a collection
121 Henry Fielding novel and heroine
122 Fix, as fritters
123 Form beginning
124 Cell suffix
125 Beth, for one

DOWN

1 Sound like an angry dog
2 Saying again and again
3 "Get ___" (doo-wop classic)
4 Libyan money
5 1979 Broadway hit with the song "On This Night of a Thousand Stars"
6 X
7 Turn to the left
8 Home-run run
9 Herringlike fish
10 Point near the deadline
11 Evolve
12 Celebs as a group
13 Drops in the air
14 "Fiddlesticks!"
15 Like spandex
16 Watch furtively
17 One of the ABC Islands
18 Plant circulatory tissue
28 Joined forces (with)
30 Line at a track
31 Scuba venue
33 Genesis creator
36 "True blue" and gold team
37 No neatnik
38 Volvo rival
40 Scepter topper
41 Tropical drink embellishment
42 Variety show lineup
44 Turkish inns
45 Cousins of cockatiels
48 Singer Kitt
49 Voice a view
50 Send to the Hill, say
51 Lang follower
53 Big Board: Abbr.
54 Tolled
59 Criticizes in no uncertain terms
60 Knocks down
62 Spring Jewish holiday
63 Historical Scottish county
64 On a plane?
65 Chess piece: Abbr.
66 Poe poem that ends "From grief and groan to a golden throne beside the King of Heaven"
67 Compound conjunction
68 r's, in math
69 P.D. rank
70 When shadows are shortest
71 Green activity
75 Grub
77 Hymn start
78 Microwave
79 Adventurous deed
81 Kind of storm
83 Environment-related
84 Bed on wheels
85 In the dumps
86 Inventory unit
87 Backed up
89 Mathematician Turing
90 Miss Havisham's ward in "Great Expectations"

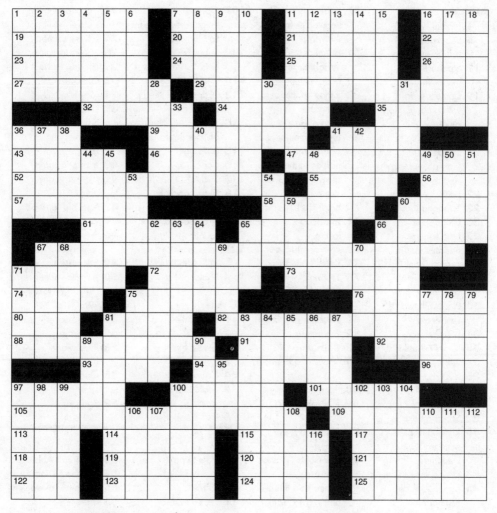

by Richard Silvestri

ACROSS

1 Nailed
5 ___ diagram
9 Is in the Vatican
12 Stubborn response
19 Contact sport with a purification ritual
20 Jobs offering of 1998
21 Start of the seventh century
22 Paws
23 *Distinguishes
26 Languished
27 Little fingers
28 Brightest star in Auriga, from the Latin for "little she-goat"
30 Plant with two seed leaves
31 Literary wrap-up
33 *Does a hostler's work
36 ___ onto
37 Bar product
38 Make a choice
39 Sharp rebuke
40 "Taking Heat" memoirist Fleischer
43 Played out
45 San ___, locale just north of Tijuana, Mexico
47 "The Story-Teller" storyteller
48 *Participates in a bear market
51 Word of dissent
52 English actor Sir ___ Jacobi
53 Suffix with disk
54 Burn cause
55 Card's insignia
56 Formal
57 Like many root vegetables for the winter
61 Home of the Wright Brothers Natl. Memorial
63 It may be illegal to hang one
64 Start of an announcement . . . or a hint to what's hidden in the answers to the six starred clues
70 Empty (of)
71 Landscaper's locale
72 Free of mistakes
74 Dutch artist Theo
78 TV pooch with a temper
79 Alley-___ pass
81 Ancestor of a banjo
82 President-___
83 Cross shape
84 *Plays at a pond, in a way
88 Speak carelessly
89 Ellen of "Grey's Anatomy"
91 "Dune" director David
92 Emerson's "jealous mistress"
93 When said three times, a 1970 film
94 "___ Mutual Friend"
95 Seasonal time, in store signs
97 Provokes
99 *Engages in some mutual gossip
102 Loser of a footrace with Hippomenes
106 "Christopher Robin went down with ___": Milne
107 Queens neighborhood near La Guardia
109 Subjects of many bets
110 Clique
112 *Commits knitting boo-boos
114 Actress Annabella of "The Sopranos"
115 Brit's oath
116 Conceited
117 Sticker?
118 Most grinchlike
119 Merino mother
120 Worrisome engine sound
121 "___, how love can trifle with itself!": Shak.

DOWN

1 The Beatles' "___ Why"
2 Give a hint
3 Correct
4 Olympics no-no
5 Scoreboard side
6 911 respondent
7 Busters?
8 Sweet 16 org.
9 How to put a coin in a coin slot
10 Lugs
11 "A Visit From St. Nicholas," e.g.
12 "___ a living"
13 Entertains, as a child at bedtime
14 Accept a bad defeat, in slang
15 Chicken dish
16 Medium of OPEC transactions
17 Some landlocked bodies of water
18 Vacation time in Valois
24 Silvery salmon
25 ___ facto
29 Lacking limbs
32 Give off
34 Moving easily
35 Like Bart Simpson's hair
37 Cabinet head: Abbr.
40 Summer drinks
41 Like some dirt paths
42 "___ old for this!"
44 Residential sign
46 "He-e-ere's Johnny!," e.g.
49 Equatorial land
50 Pulitzer winner for "Russia Leaves the War"
52 Load bearer?
55 Caved in
56 Proofreader's mark
58 Québec traffic sign
59 Barbara of "Mission: Impossible"
60 Co. name ender
62 Midpoint: Abbr.
63 Bygone TV inits.
65 Examine covetously
66 Brisk
67 Guthrie with a guitar
68 Sweater's place
69 Make a record of
73 Try
74 Isn't serious
75 Stipend
76 Pain along the course of a nerve
77 Junkyard junk
78 Strict disciplinarian
80 Bribes

by Jim Page

83 Ballyhoo
84 Seconds, say
85 Temper tantrum
86 Removing, as paint
87 Everything
89 Frauds
90 Plane seating
   specification
96 Right away
98 Retreats
100 Make it home safely
101 Fingerprint feature
102 Very, in music
103 Nothing
104 "Lady T" singer
   ___ Marie
105 Lunkheads
108 Answer, shortly
110 Doctrine
111 Overly rehearsed
113 ___ soldier

71

NAME THAT PHRASE

ACROSS

1 Small amount of power
5 Where opposite sides meet
11 Fireplace tool
16 Be bold enough
20 Eponym of a North Carolina "-ville"
21 Skeptical response
22 Use TurboTax, perhaps
23 Particular
24 Mother of Cronus
25 Like Rudner's audiences after a good joke?
28 "Stormy" seabird
30 Zool. or ecol.
31 Drama that uses masks
32 Supremely macho
33 Treat for Damone?
37 Northern star?
39 Drool catchers
40 Volkswagen coupe convertible
41 Runners may round them
42 Like fries, typically
43 Sunlit ledge
44 Google search result
45 Delhi-to-Madras dir.
47 Author Dinesen
49 Exist
50 Attack vigorously
52 Where Paul stays when performing in New York City?
58 Carol ending?
59 Hindu honorific
61 Once known as
62 "Heroes" actress Larter
63 It's said for stress
67 Chewed out
69 Comes in dramatically, like West?
72 Baghdad's ___ City

73 More furtive
75 Threshold
76 Needing air freshener
77 Better-suited
79 Funny frame
80 Largest U.S. movie theater chain
83 "___ Millions" (Eugene O'Neill play)
86 The rite place?
89 Black, in a way
91 "The Neverending Story" author
95 McAn's favorite novel?
99 Astronomical collision results
101 Tyrrhenian Sea port
102 Dict. tag on "tzar"
103 It may be radical
104 Duped
105 Op. ___
106 Odds of Alda winning an Oscar?
110 Take on
112 Piece of software, for short
115 Patron saint of goldsmiths
116 Sign of a champ
117 Unwrap, in verse
119 Sound
120 Knave
123 ___ a customer
126 Gilbert and Sullivan princess
127 Tinnitus causes
128 Kiss on the cheek, perhaps
129 Putting in a row, like Sampras's rackets?
133 More affordable
135 Conductance unit
136 Suffix with fail
137 Person of learning
139 Court case where Ripken is one of many plaintiffs?
143 Trickle
145 ___ tape

146 Don't fold or call
147 Banishes to Elba, e.g.
148 Light brown
149 Spotted
150 Nautical measure
151 Recipients
152 Having similar genetics

DOWN

1 Boxer's approval
2 "Quickly," quickly
3 Horror film enjoyed by Turner?
4 It holds a service
5 More whimsical
6 Fish with toxic blood
7 Trees with soft wood
8 ___ curiae (friends of the court)
9 Mixer
10 Official lang. of Mauritius
11 Roy Orbison and Marvin Gaye, e.g.
12 Musical that inspired Redding?
13 Agcy. with the Office of Disease Prevention
14 Scintillate
15 It's on the back of the $1 bill
16 Bleak
17 Home of the world's largest aquarium
18 What a stamped hand may allow you to do
19 Typography units
21 Cologne trio
26 Viracocha worshiper
27 Rick's love, in film
29 Bedside workers, often: Abbr.
34 Relax
35 Hairstylist José
36 P.D.A. part: Abbr.
38 Humorist George

39 Woman in "Othello"
42 Sidestep
43 Cheese with eyes
44 Turmoil
45 Say "#@%!"
46 Try to unearth
48 Spelling clarification
51 -like, alternatively
53 "Take a Chance ___" (ABBA song)
54 Tripod, sometimes
55 Banned chemical
56 Skin layer
57 Shoulder frill
60 Going nowhere
64 Half 19-Down
65 Fill in (for)
66 "The Daughter of Time" author
68 Choking spot
70 ". . . if ___ saw one!"
71 Tulip chair designer Saarinen
74 "Dies ___"
78 Standard partner
79 Accord rival
81 Clearly impress
82 Take turns?
83 Parts of a range: Abbr.
84 "The light has dawned!"
85 Seminary subj.
87 Flower typically given to Neeson?
88 Brand of nonstick cookware
89 "W." director
90 "This can't be!"
92 How Goldin and her rivals finish in photography competitions?
93 Boring things
94 Cosmetics magnate Lauder
96 Available, in a way
97 Dirty
98 Levitate
100 Mathematician Lovelace

by Trip Payne

107 The Gang's leader
108 ___ lady
109 Sarah Palin's husband
111 Taiwan's setting
112 Mean: Abbr.
113 One just out
114 Georgia or Virginia, e.g.
118 Dupes
121 Teacher's teaching
122 Airport monitor info, for short
124 Comes back the same
125 Common noun ending
126 Really existing
127 Part of R&D: Abbr.
129 State tree of Texas
130 Organic fertilizer
131 Physicist Schrödinger
132 Trotter fodder
134 Brownish songbird
138 Actress Polo
139 Contents of jewel cases
140 Uncle, in Uruguay
141 Played a heart, say
142 Little: Suffix
144 86-Across, e.g.

72

LAUGHING ALL THE WAY

ACROSS

1 Hog lovers
7 Cheesy snack
11 Bad sport
20 Kind of valve in the heart
21 Potato source
22 Begin
23 Like some chocolat
24 Prefix with -logy
25 Witnesses giving written testimony
26 Barbecue sound
27 Wrap up by
29 Round dances
31 Bother no end
32 Symbol of strength
34 Repeat calls?
36 N.F.L. coach with a perfect 17-0 record in 1972
38 Like preowned cars
40 Spin-producing tennis shot
41 Like Silly Putty
44 Neat as __
46 Oslo's land: Abbr.
47 Wave off
49 Fulminate (against)
50 Gets ready to go out in the cold
53 Book in which the destruction of Samaria is foreseen
54 Gang brawl
56 Violent behavior, in British slang
57 It means a lot to Jorge
59 Oktoberfest souvenir
61 Candied holiday serving
62 Former Toyota
64 Pacific salmon

66 Invited to one's penthouse, say
68 "Hooked on Classics" record company
69 Cry when a surprise guest arrives
73 Stuck, after "in"
77 Having bristles
79 View from a beach house
80 Elizabeth Ann and others
82 With 83-Down, early learning aid
85 Greases
87 Egypt's Mubarak
89 Like some fireplaces
90 Warm blanket material
92 Virile
94 Answered the phone
97 G.M. or G.E.
98 Top-Sider, e.g.
101 1501, on a monument
102 TV's Science Guy and others
103 Abscond
105 Sound: Prefix
106 Memorable parties
108 Cracks up
109 Regis Philbin, e.g.
111 Stretchy
114 Admit
116 Bug-B-Gon maker
117 Beginning
119 Code-cracking org.
120 Without delay
123 Venerable
125 Georges Braque, for one
127 Fruitcake flavorings
128 Wanderers
129 Throat soother

130 Boot camp pals
131 Landing spot for 74-Down
132 Plumbers' drain openers

DOWN

1 Banquo in Verdi's "Macbeth," e.g.
2 2008 documentary about the national debt
3 December 25 answer to 69-Across?
4 U.F.O. fliers
5 Choir supports
6 Act opener
7 Basketry palm
8 "We've got __!"
9 Rum Tum Tugger, for one
10 Greeting from 74-Down
11 Tabs in the fridge?
12 Buried treasures
13 Open indelicately
14 Maniacal leader?
15 Schedule of TV programs
16 Mild chili designation
17 Song whose subject is encouraged to "hurry down the chimney tonight"
18 Singer James
19 What remains
28 Apollo's birthplace
30 Towers' attachments
33 Grape graspers
35 Includes in an emailing
36 __ Na Na
37 Rustic excursions
39 Bongo, e.g.

41 Wrap fully
42 Country singer McCann
43 K–6 sch. designation
44 By surprise
45 Sound of the Northwest
48 D.D.E. opponent
51 __ cit. (footnote abbr.)
52 One reaching a goal?
55 "Burma Looks Ahead" author
58 Bossy types?
60 Listener
63 Mass production figure?
65 C.I.S. members, once
67 Whom psychiatrists see
70 Stick in the water?
71 Pops
72 Three French __
74 December 25 answer to 69-Across?
75 Anoint with sacred oil, old-style
76 Early PC interface
78 QB Manning
81 Archaic verb ending
82 Javelins and Hornets, e.g.
83 See 82-Across
84 Father __
86 Succeeded at musical chairs
88 Poet's foot
91 Paintbrushes and such
93 It's worth 100 smackers
95 Lays off
96 Manners of speaking

by Elizabeth C. Gorski

ACROSS

1 Harry's pal at Hogwarts
4 Hit 2004 film with many sequels
7 What this puzzle's eight concentric rings (light and dark) represent
13 Wooden peg
18 Pressed for time
20 1968 N.B.A. All-Star Dick
22 ___ Adler of Conan Doyle's "A Scandal in Bohemia"
23 Georgia's Fort ___, site of an 1862 surrender
24 Malevolent look
25 Rubber gasket
26 Gratis
27 Lincoln Town Car, for one
28 Patriots' Day mo.
30 Big ox
31 Prefix with political
32 ___ dance
33 Six-Day War combatants
35 Entrance
38 Actress ___ Dawn Chong
40 "Nascar Now" channel
42 Medevac worker
43 Way to go
44 Dog biscuits and such
47 Formulator of the Three Principles of the People
52 Gopher-wood construction
53 Submarine egress
54 Ruination
55 Infra's opposite
56 King famous for frightening people
59 Like some campaign ads
62 Pomeranian's bark
63 Sic ___ (bibliographical term)
64 Elementary particle
65 Actress/model Connie
68 On land
70 Appropriate center for this puzzle
71 Frozen food company
72 Exterior decorator?
74 Beautify
76 Let one's anger show
79 Email address ender
80 Treasure sought in "Titanic"
82 Heavy metal band?
83 Stuck in the mud
86 Storm
87 No longer working
89 Cuff feature
90 Satisfies, as baser instincts
92 Husband, in Hidalgo
93 "___ 911!" (comedy series)
94 Fed. purchasing org.
95 Long-range weapon, briefly
97 According to
98 The Auld Sod
99 Childhood skin affliction
103 Goes around
106 Where a pin may be made
108 Greenwich Village campus, for short
109 Poorly
110 Volkswagen model
111 BBC panel show regular Phill
115 Brand of basketball
117 Something it's not always wise to share
119 Generally
120 Grace ___ ("Jane Eyre" character)
121 1960 Bobby Rydell hit
122 Electricians
123 Ready to play, you might say
124 One of these can be found reading counterclockwise somewhere in each concentric ring
125 Behave
126 Go down

DOWN

1 Philbin's "Live" co-host
2 Responsibility
3 Simba's mate in "The Lion King"
4 The Everly Brothers' "Wake Up Little ___"
5 Make impossible demands
6 Little bit
7 Scale-busting
8 "Gaspard de la Nuit" composer
9 Tack room items
10 Veneer patterns
11 First-time driver, often
12 Porker's pen
13 Museum displays
14 Yossarian's tentmate in "Catch-22"
15 "Mack the Knife" songwriter
16 Lassitude
17 Pantyhose brand
19 Worn out
21 Bigelow beverages
29 Rodent, to a raptor
32 Red food dye source
33 All together
34 Roman rebuke
35 Comprehend
36 Trunk in your trunk
37 Plays
39 Ireland's ___ Islands
41 Exam for H.S. jrs.
45 Retin-A treats it
46 Region near Mount Olympus
48 "In a pig's eye!"
49 Controversial 1987 exposé by ex-MI5 agent Peter Wright
50 Cartman's first name on "South Park"
51 Bay Area county
54 Oatcakes popular in Scotland
57 Discreet attention-getter
58 Exclamation in "The Farmer in the Dell"
60 Semisoft cheese from Holland
61 Tunes that might make you want to get out on the floor?
64 Romeo's reckless friend
66 Legal claim on property
67 Writer Ferber
69 Hull scrapers
72 Desk-borrowing worker
73 Top 10 hit for Sarah McLachlan
75 Harvest
77 Nicholas Gage memoir
78 Possessor?
81 Ray aka the Hamburger King
82 Poet's inspiration
84 Sharpness
85 Preordained
88 Bursts open
91 Pedestrian safety feature
92 What Mr. Spock suppressed
93 Leave one's post, possibly
96 Lee with the 1960 #1 hit "I'm Sorry"
99 Bungling
100 "Skip to ___"
101 Hoax

by Patrick Berry

102 ___ stick (trick-or-treater's accessory)
104 Make up (for)
105 Painter of a Zola portrait
107 In different places
110 Jack's partner in rhyme

111 Cloak-wearing "Star Wars" race
112 Rolaids rival
113 Big-screen beekeeper
114 Propelled
116 ___ Miss
118 Domino dot

ACROSS

1 Chickens, e.g.
6 Workers with hammers
12 Punch relative
15 Captain of fiction
19 Enthusiastically accepted
20 Facing
21 Coffeehouse fixture
22 Take ___ (go swimming)
23 Not secure
24 How organized philosophers deal with ideas?
27 Like about 20% of the world's land area
28 Gillette product
29 Bronchodilator user
30 Highway S-curve?
34 Vex
35 Composer Charles
36 Playbook figures
39 Pulled off
42 Reinforcing bracket
45 Bygone copy
48 Suffix with Ecuador
49 Software basis
50 Spanish article
51 Countess bankrupts St. Louis N.H.L. team?
55 Some 35mm cameras
57 Actor Wilson
58 Digital communication?: Abbr.
59 Words on an "Animal House" cake float
60 Legendary Onondaga chief
63 Alien craft

66 Cackler
67 Warning before driving past the town dump?
73 Some Windows systems
74 Start of a selection process
75 Break up
77 Down time
80 100%
82 Marvel Comics hero
84 Denials
85 Wayne Gretzky?
91 Soph. and jr.
92 Holder of a runoff?
93 French river or department
94 Reliever
95 Must
97 Fr. holy title
98 Ancient Cretan writing system
100 ___ Pictures
101 Readily recite, with "off"
103 Being too large to fall?
110 Onetime Robin Williams co-star
114 So-called Mother of Presidents
115 "Shucks!"
116 Singles bar pickup strategy?
119 Flying monster of film
120 "Baywatch" actress ___ Lee Nolin
121 Rocket from China
122 Notice
123 Bit of Weather Channel news
124 By all ___
125 Kind of card
126 Chucks
127 Pick up

DOWN

1 Israel's Ehud
2 Grammatically proper identification
3 Nail polish ingredient
4 Loser of 1988
5 "Casino Royale," for one
6 Animals with black-tipped tails
7 One of a dozen
8 "If ___ you . . ."
9 Subject of Genghis Khan
10 Princely abbr.
11 Arms race inits.
12 Diving seabirds
13 "Nuts!"
14 Make a queen, e.g.
15 Present at birth
16 Deleted
17 Maurice Chevalier song
18 Ecuador and Venezuela are in it
25 Zilch
26 Friends of François
31 Crumbly cheese
32 Symbols of strength
33 Dilbert co-worker
37 Safari equipment
38 "Matilda" author, 1988
40 As above, in a footnote
41 Not those, in Brooklyn
42 Ooh and aah
43 Dark
44 Hebrew matriarch
45 Classic song that begins "And now the end is near"
46 Sussex suffix
47 Jiffy
49 Ike or Billy at the O.K. Corral
52 Qatar's capital

53 Prince Albert's home: Abbr.
54 Root crop
56 Con
61 N.L. Central player
62 Co. IDs
64 Flipper
65 Biblical breastplate stones
66 Part of 10-Down, maybe
68 Mirror image?
69 Old ballad "Robin ___"
70 Philatelist George, founder of the largest weekly newspaper for stamp collectors
71 Frank ___, two-time Oscar-winning director
72 Turn outward
76 Onetime Texaco competitor
77 GPS options: Abbr.
78 Answer to the old riddle "What lies flat when empty, sits up when full?"
79 "Forget I said anything"
80 Score right before a win, maybe
81 Unique
83 G.I.'s food
86 Train systems
87 Actress Hatcher
88 Den ___, Nederland
89 Cluster
90 Wives in São Paulo
96 Mask feature
98 Puddle producer, perhaps
99 Incantation opener

by Yaakov Bendavid

100 Hybrid clothing for women
102 Actresses Best and Purviance
104 Marina sights
105 "Now I see"
106 Kathleen Kennedy Townsend, to J.F.K.
107 City south of Brigham City
108 Raises
109 "Fiddler on the Roof" role
110 When doubled, a Samoan port
111 Wowed
112 Start of some congregation names
113 Land in Genesis
117 Summer hours in L.A.
118 Auto monogram

75

PULLET

ACROSS

1 Bushed
5 Entrance to many a plaza
9 Rimsky-Korsakov's "The Tale of ___ Saltan"
13 Exactly right
19 Free
21 ___ avis
22 Attempted something
23 *Boardwalk offering
25 Thought out loud
26 It might make you snort
27 Home of the World Health Organization
28 Stickers?
30 ___ Day, May 1 celebration in Hawaii
31 Must-have
33 Soft ball brand
35 "___ mine!"
36 One on the way out
38 *Diamond substitute
44 1987 disaster movie?
46 Rest spot
47 Place for a pickup?
48 Word with exit or express
49 Something that's drawn
50 Whiz
51 Any hit by Little Richard
53 Many a Bob Marley fan
54 Mideast title
56 Seaport on the Adriatic
58 Turned away from sin
60 Earth
61 Outstanding
63 Lawn tools
64 *Handy things for a toy?
68 ###
72 Free
73 Itching
78 Took a corner on two wheels
81 Fix, as brakes
82 Vituperation, e.g.
83 Wake Island, e.g.
84 "Nothing ___!"
86 Transplant, in a way
87 "Up in the Air" actress Kendrick
88 Do followers
89 Navel buildup
90 Former flier, for short
91 Slugger
93 *Staple of "Candid Camera"
97 Xerox product
98 Baseball's Master Melvin
99 Loughlin of "Full House"
100 Nincompoop
101 Conditions
104 Killjoy
109 Comparatively statuesque
111 Point of view
113 Enfeeble
114 *Radio Flyer, e.g.
117 Like a winter wind
118 1997 Peter Fonda title role
119 Hoax
120 Old-fashioned
121 TV's Foxx
122 Brake
123 "Superman II" villainess

DOWN

1 Kind of metabolism
2 Military camp
3 *Certain study session
4 Head of Haiti
5 ___ formality
6 Actor Hauer
7 Believe in it
8 Not his'n
9 Ad-packed Sunday newspaper section
10 A giraffe might be seen on one
11 Pound sound
12 You may catch them on a boat, in two different ways
13 Shrimp
14 Old Church of England foe
15 Role in 2011's "Thor"
16 Chinese dynasty of 1,200 years ago
17 Curved molding
18 Drops (off)
20 Start of a childish plaint
24 Believe in it
29 "Goody goody gumdrops!"
32 At any time, to a bard
34 Ward (off)
37 Survey choice, sometimes
38 Less cramped
39 Like some maidens
40 Trolley sound
41 Expedition
42 Keyboard key
43 Shows, as a thermometer does a temperature
44 "Uh-huh, sure it is"
45 The very ___
46 Hinder
50 Test ___
51 *Something to stand on
52 Piece over a door or window
53 It had a major part in the Bible
55 Descent of a sort
57 Many a summer worker
59 Solitaire puzzle piece
62 Wander
65 Blue Angels' org.
66 Ain't fixed?
67 Classic brand of hair remover
68 Line of cliffs
69 Intolerant sort
70 Bouquet
71 ___ of the past
74 Taper off
75 *It may be found near a barrel
76 Feudal serf
77 Fanny
79 Decrees
80 Lady of Spain
85 "___ do"
89 Service arrangement
90 Know-how
91 Boo follower
92 They're often acquired at a wedding
94 Drunk's activity

by C. W. Stewart

95 Scribbled
96 Got up on one's soapbox
97 One waving a red flag
100 Wild
102 Dentist's advice
103 Actress Berger

104 Bros, e.g.
105 Pass over
106 ___ no good
107 SC Johnson brand
108 "Dirty rotten scoundrel," e.g.
110 Old NASA landers

112 Half of a sitcom farewell
115 Project closing?
116 It might get your feet wet

76

SAY WHAT?!

ACROSS

1 Nursery sounds
6 Bates's "Misery" co-star
10 Compadre
15 Having more than one band
19 Weapon, e.g., in military-speak
20 Regarding
21 Something well-preserved?
22 ___ avis
23 "I've heard enough, retail outlet!"
25 "I agree completely, dog-eared bit of paper!"
27 What you might get by moving a head?
28 "Stop right where you are, picture holder!"
30 "One if by land, two if by sea" and others
31 Extinguished, with "out"
33 Spots before your eyes?
34 Alaska Purchase negotiator
35 Symbol of royalty in old Egypt
36 Skunk, e.g.
38 Big-screen canine
40 Jeans brand
41 The majority
44 "You're in danger, tall hill!"
49 Surname in a Poe tale
51 Check out
52 Like racehorses
53 Objectivist Rand
54 "The chair doesn't recognize you, steakhouse and chophouse!"
59 Before, to Byron
60 Scorecard blemish
61 Lift provider
62 Vessels with spouts
65 Light TV fare
67 Sticky seedcase
68 Explorer Richard Byrd's plane
70 Writing surface
71 Make nonsensical notes?
73 Roast V.I.P.
75 Work in the field
76 "I'd be miserable without you, tapestry!"
80 D.C.-based news source
82 Australia's Lake ___ National Park
83 See 93-Across
84 Inasmuch as
85 "Goodbye, place I used to live!"
89 Philip with a 1975 best seller on C.I.A. secrets
90 Sistine Chapel ceiling figure
91 Like many sunscreens
92 Cessation
93 Is 83-Across
95 Big name in California wine
97 Endorser's need
99 Another name for Buddha
103 Speak for everyone in the room
104 "Just keep doing what you're doing, suitcases!"
109 One of the Bobbsey twins
110 "I read you loud and clear, breakfast meat!"
112 "It was all my fault, gun attachment!"
114 Over again
115 Pop singer Lopez
116 Addition to café
117 Keys in a chain
118 Amount that's settled for
119 Caddie's offering
120 "This looks like trouble!"
121 Manicurist's aid

DOWN

1 Some nest builders
2 Lacking color
3 Diesel engine manufacturer
4 Rented out
5 Packs
6 Checked out before robbing
7 Athlete who wrote "Off the Court"
8 Complete
9 "You're mistaken"
10 Certificate on a wall, maybe
11 "___ Pearl" (Jackson 5 hit)
12 Gossip subject
13 One that's passed along
14 Brute of fantasy
15 Sign symbol
16 Kipling poem about Burma
17 Lack of constraints
18 James of "X-Men" films
24 Lay the groundwork
26 Great body
29 Old West gambling game
32 Inevitable
34 "Rugrats" father
36 ___ artist (film crew member)
37 Soprano pineapple and others, briefly
38 Con ___ (tenderly)
39 Something that shouldn't be flat
41 Patrons of the arts
42 Green-skinned god
43 Old Jewish community
44 Pines
45 "Puss in Boots" figure
46 Former carrier name
47 Land heavily
48 Acronymic weapon
50 "Mr. ___" (1983 Styx hit)
55 19th Amendment beneficiaries
56 Cable network with the motto "Not reality. Actuality."
57 Panhellenic Games site
58 Elementary school grads, typically
63 Ascendant
64 Torch bearer
66 Key group
67 Objected to a shearing, possibly
68 Pines
69 "Shucks!"
71 With deviousness
72 Michael of "Juno"
73 Lodge
74 Diner of 1970s–'80s TV
77 Giveaway at the poker table
78 Make
79 Not just big
80 Fictional island in two Alistair MacLean novels
81 Augurs
85 Situated at the thigh
86 Bearer of a dozen roses, maybe
87 A, in Arnstadt
88 Turn down

by Patrick Berry

93 Showing deviousness
94 Person of Perth
96 Nurses old grudges, say
97 Runcible spoon feature
98 Banks known as Mr. Cub
99 Wayne's pal in "Wayne's World"
100 Fish
101 TV host with "New Rules"
102 Unable to relax
104 Serious attention
105 Lemon juice, e.g.
106 Home of Hallvard's ruined cathedral
107 Life saver?
108 Vivacity
111 "Incidentally," in chat rooms
113 Philosophy suffix

ACROSS

1 1988 Grammy winner for "Crying"
7 Tweak
13 Bosses
20 Cry from a balcony
21 ___ pork
22 Many a Nevada resident
23 Dance seen in a Lincoln Center performance of "Don Giovanni"?
25 Penn State campus site
26 Also-___ (losers)
27 Prefix with caching
28 Baja's opposite
30 Author
31 "Hang on ___!"
32 Locale for a cattail
33 "None of the leading sales people came in today"?
36 Grandparents, typically
38 With a wink, say
39 Berkeley campus nickname
40 Celebration after a 1964 heavyweight championship?
42 "You don't need to remind me"
48 Not so big
49 Tampa paper, briefly, with "the"
50 Blackmore heroine
51 Washed (down)
54 Female co-star in "Love Crazy," 1941
55 Stirrup?
57 Tolkien creatures
58 41-Down was named after one: Abbr.
59 Scarlett O'Hara's real first name
60 Voiced
61 Summer sign
62 Little dipper?
63 Claimed
64 Chop
65 The Mavericks, on scoreboards
66 Up for grabs, as convention delegates
68 Shriners' headwear: Var.
69 Gob
70 Ending with soft or spy
71 Decide to sleep in the nude?
73 Drink with one's pinkie up, say
74 Some cats blow on them
75 Sodium ___
76 "Around the Horn" cable channel
77 Summer treats
79 1983 #1 hit with the lyric "Put on your red shoes"
81 What whitewashers apply?
84 ___ Friday's
85 Interlocks
86 ___ acid
88 Response to the query "Does Ms. Garbo fist-bump?"?
94 Summer mo.
95 "Rock 'n' Roll Is King" band, 1983
96 Make it
97 Actress Polo
98 See 33-Down
99 Polynesian potable
100 They're often said to be fair
102 Love before war?
106 Looms
107 Shocking, in a way
108 Leonard of literature
109 Sting, e.g.
110 Team that once played at Enron Field
111 Bob Evans rival

DOWN

1 Former German chancellor Adenauer
2 Imagine
3 One hit by a tuba
4 Singer Grant and others
5 Prefix with -lithic
6 Stuffs oneself with
7 Shot, e.g.
8 Question that may be answered "And how!"
9 Garfield's owner
10 For the most part
11 Country star ___ Lynne
12 "Così Fan ___"
13 Agcy. with a list of prohibited items
14 Tree whose two-word name, when switched around, identifies its product
15 A Fonda
16 Plane over Yemen, maybe
17 College town just off Interstate 95
18 Thief, in Yiddish
19 Wolf (down)
24 When doubled, a number puzzle
29 Credit
32 "Totem and Taboo" writer
33 With 98-Across, showy play
34 Story teller
35 Judo-like exercises
37 French beings
38 Offspring
41 Town on the Hudson R.
42 Filmmaker Allen
43 Pipe shape
44 Apollo target
45 Bygone hand weapon
46 Catch
47 Crib items
49 Lugs
51 Like a corkscrew
52 What Cher Bono, e.g., goes by
53 Ceases
55 Soap units
56 River to the North Sea
58 Artist Francisco
59 Director of the major film debuts of James Dean and Warren Beatty
62 Not live
63 Home to Sun Devil Stadium
64 Tickled
67 Old Fords
68 Like Mussolini
69 Ranks
70 Didn't miss
72 Game whose name is derived from Swahili
73 Sean Connery and others
74 Turn brown, maybe
77 Jazz singer Anderson
78 Busy
80 Doesn't miss
81 Most murky
82 It's worst when it's high
83 High and softly resonant
85 Alex of "Webster"
87 Sweet-talks

by David Levinson Wilk

88 Southwest Africa's
___ Desert
89 Commercial name
suffix
90 Handles
91 Lifts
92 "___ could have
told you that!"
93 Seven: Prefix

94 Speck
98 Assns.
99 Alphabet string
101 Retired flier
103 It landed in the
Pacific Ocean on
3/23/01
104 Yucatán year
105 Drink with a head

78

MY TREAT

When this puzzle is done, the circles will contain five different letters of the alphabet. Connect each set of circles containing the same letter, without crossing your line, to make a simple closed shape. The resulting five closed shapes together will form a picture of a 117-Across. The five letters can be arranged to name a good place to get a 117-Across.

ACROSS

1 Essence
5 Start of a nursery rhyme
9 "I won't bore you with the rest"
12 Actress Davis
17 They're often deep-fried
19 1964 title role for Tony Randall
21 ___-jongg
22 Indy 500 legend
23 1950s NBC icon
24 Spanish for "rope"
25 Some versions of a 117-Across
27 Ingredient in a 117-Across
30 "How is this possible?"
31 Repeat
32 Green lights
34 "___, danke"
35 Reversal of sorts
36 "Top Chef" host Lakshmi
40 Trouble's partner, in Shakespeare
41 Kimchi-loving land
42 "___ honor"
44 Some cuts
46 "___ straight!"
48 DKNY competitor
49 1960s campus grp.
51 "In case you weren't listening . . ."
53 Amazon's business, e.g.
55 Whence spiderlings emerge
59 Ingredient in a 117-Across
64 Suffix with meth-
65 Island visited by Captain Cook in 1778
67 Year Columbus died
68 French kings' coronation city
69 Imprudent
71 David of television
73 Brawl
75 Thin Japanese noodle
76 Salsa seller
78 Ready, with "up"
80 Broadway lights
82 Word with black or stream
83 Utensil for a 117-Across
86 Sugary drinks
88 ___ nothing
89 Like the buildings at Machu Picchu
91 Watched
92 ___ Fields
95 Filmmaker Riefenstahl
96 Senator Hatch
98 ___ nova (1960s dance)
102 Characters in "The Hobbit"
104 "Web ___" (ESPN segment showing great fielding plays)
107 Sniggled
109 A stake, metaphorically
110 Holly genus
111 Attack fervently
113 Doing some cartoon work
115 Cruise, say
117 Something delicious to drink
121 Version of a 117-Across
123 What a graph may show
124 Baltimore and Philadelphia
126 Come to ___
127 "Catch-22" bomber pilot
128 "Later, alligator!"
129 Versatile utensil
130 Whizzes at quizzes?
131 Name connector
132 Pizzazz
133 Influence

DOWN

1 Fellas in "Goodfellas," e.g.
2 Barely manages
3 Bad thing to be in
4 Container for a 117-Across
5 Cortisol-secreting gland
6 Family member, in dialect
7 Construction crane attachment
8 It's crunched
9 Baby baby?
10 Besmirch
11 Like many a 117-Across
12 Private eye Peter of old TV
13 "___ Man" (1992 movie)
14 Obscure things
15 Neophytes
16 Manchester United rival
18 Bristle
20 Wild ones may be sown
26 Lived and breathed
28 Pizzazz
29 Gobble up
31 Meas. of screen resolution
33 Valuable iron ore
37 Possible response to "You've got spinach between your teeth"
38 Fails
39 Excessively orderly, informally
41 Jewish deli order
43 State straddling two time zones: Abbr.
45 Thailand, once
47 West Coast evergreens
50 Like mountains and computer images
52 Burned things
54 Caustic cleaners
55 ___ corn
56 Twisty tree feature
57 "Beau ___"
58 ___ sponte (of its own accord)
60 Pots and pans for baking
61 Spanish wine
62 It may be burnt
63 Hurdles for high-school jrs.
66 Main lines
70 Six: Prefix
72 Mountain sighting, maybe
74 Mountain
77 Breathing aids
79 Movie villain who sought to disrupt a space launch
81 Union opponent
84 Utensil for a 117-Across
85 Field unit
87 Quantity of a key ingredient in a 117-Across
90 Scoreless score
92 Inside look?
93 The primary instruction
94 Bit of gymwear
97 Winnemucca resident, e.g.
99 Low-rent district

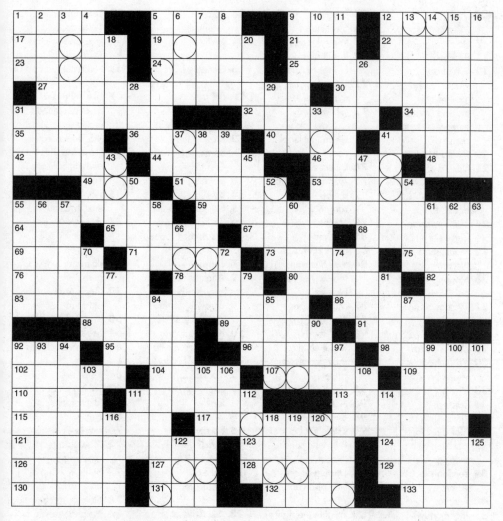

by Pete Muller

79

BODY ENHANCEMENT

ACROSS

1 Meaningless
7 Dolt
11 Reached
19 Symphony whose second movement is marked "Marcia funebre. Adagio assai"
20 Ring bearer
21 Dew, e.g.
22 What a poltergeist investigator does?
24 1862 invasion battle site
25 Mount for the god Neptune
26 Monopoly purchases: Abbr.
27 TV show whose name precedes a colon
28 See 49-Across
30 What the tired waiter provided?
33 Worry
34 Totals
36 "Interesting . . ."
37 Noted explorer traveling with a monkey
39 London's locale: Abbr.
40 Fruit for lagomorphs?
46 Shows worry, in a way
49 Old French 28-Across
50 Some people have funny ones
51 Lighten (up)
53 Mauna ___
54 Livens (up)
56 Disorderly poultry workers?
62 Opera
65 Practices
66 Sweetheart
67 Wistful remark
70 Result of a bad swing, maybe
71 There may be many in a family
72 Got around
73 ___ law (old Germanic legal code)
74 Detectives' aids
75 Attempts to climb a mountain range?
78 "Monk" org.
82 Noshed
83 Snick and ___
84 Van Susteren formerly of Fox News
87 Mass of eggs
88 10,000 61-Down
90 Sad sports headline in a Providence paper?
95 Verdi's "___ tu"
96 Actress Gershon
98 Sweetheart
99 Estate total
101 Billy who sang "Rebel Yell"
103 Dusting on the side of a cut gem?
109 Point in the right direction?
110 Friend of Eeyore
111 Bronze, e.g.
112 Like some sabbaticals
114 Point to
116 Churchgoers, sometimes?
120 Didn't just spit
121 Senders of some Christmas gifts
122 Excels
123 Roasters, essentially
124 "Why don't we?!"
125 Get dark?

DOWN

1 "___ Ramsey" (1970s western)
2 Prize at the Barcelona Olympics
3 Botching
4 Bedding
5 Numerical prefix
6 Basketful, maybe
7 Like some air and dollar bills
8 Snaps
9 A famous one begins "Thou still unravish'd bride of quietness"
10 Buns, e.g.
11 One instrumental in music history?
12 Vodka ___
13 Like a lord or lady
14 Undisturbed
15 Follower of Israel?
16 Hinged implements
17 Take off
18 Abdicate
20 Mold
23 "___ will not"
26 Eye layer
28 Peeping Tom, e.g.
29 Little bit
31 Help in making a prediction, maybe
32 Riddle-me-___
33 Monk's title
35 Numerical prefix
38 Unrestricted, as a mutual fund
41 Tom Sawyer's crush
42 Scornful replies
43 "Woe ___" (grammar guide)
44 TKO callers
45 Paolantonio of ESPN
47 Like things that go bump in the night
48 MS. enclosures
52 "Love Me Do" vis-à-vis "P.S. I Love You"
55 Actress Lena Olin, e.g., by birth
57 Easter Island is part of it
58 "Born on the Fourth of July" hero Ron
59 Great-grandfather of Noah
60 Web
61 See 88-Across
63 Certain Black Sea dweller
64 It's a gas
67 Taking place in
68 Ellipsoidal
69 Fulfills
70 Morse T
71 "The Balcony" playwright
73 Suffix with hip or tip
74 Stale Italian bread?
76 Neighbor of Colo.
77 Golden ___
79 One who's been released?
80 Wires may connect to them
81 Voltaire or Adam Smith
85 Maintaining one's composure, say
86 T or F: Abbr.
89 Rapper ___ Wayne
91 Follow

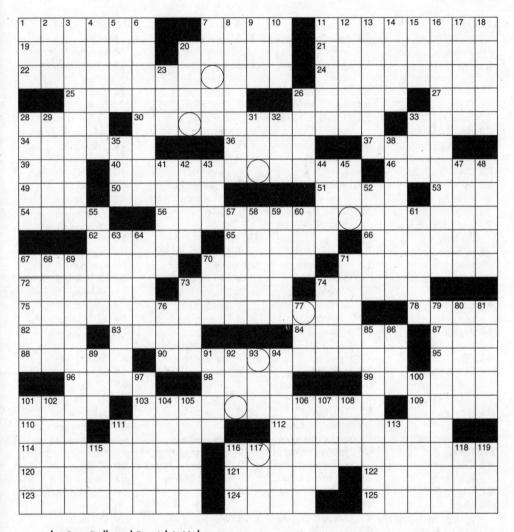

by Ben Pall and David J. Kahn

THE END IS IN SIGHT

ACROSS

1 Punch
4 Birthstones whose name starts with the same letter as their month
9 Senescence
15 Puzzle
20 Advantage
21 "Chasing Pirates" singer Jones
22 "Stop that!"
23 Matt in the morning
24 It means nothing
25 Parting words from the busy type
28 Whom a guy might hang with when he's not with the guys
30 Isn't shy with an opinion
31 Area in a 1969 Elvis Presley hit
32 "The Chosen" author Chaim
34 Cabinet dept. since 1965
35 Pottery base
36 Hans Christian Andersen story
43 Kind of shot
46 Critter with foot-long teeth
47 Dipped sticks?
48 Island known for having "the wettest spot on Earth" (450+" of rain per year)
49 French Revolution figure
51 Adrien of cosmetics
52 Iraq war subj.
53 Hardly breaking a sweat
55 Goldenrod, e.g.
56 Article for Lil Wayne

57 Eastern sect
58 Appears gradually on the screen
59 One of 15, once: Abbr.
60 Major upset, say
62 See 72-Across
65 Monster of Norse myth
66 End of a command at the Battle of Bunker Hill
69 Symbol of strength, to the Maya
72 With 62-Across, Whoopi's "Ghost" role
73 Granter of an honorary degree to George Washington in 1776
74 Farmer's ___
77 Where K-I-S-S-I-N-G happens
79 Hydroxide, e.g.
80 C.I.A. forerunner
81 Palm variety
82 "Godspeed!"
86 Water ___ (dental product company)
87 How some stock is purchased
88 City on the Ruhr
89 Pianist Albéniz
90 TV part
91 Gymnast Comaneci
92 Place with snorts
93 End of a Benjamin Franklin aphorism
96 Bring to a ___
98 9/
99 Pacifist's protest
100 The Jackson 5's first major label
103 Most clueless
108 Papal legate
111 2009 fantasy film based on a best-selling book

114 Goof
115 Former U.N. leader Kofi
116 Key of the "Odense" Symphony
117 "Swan Lake" maiden
118 Arm of a starfish
119 Has over
120 Tree with fan-shaped leaves
121 Grill brand
122 Cause for a TV-MA rating

DOWN

1 Contemporary of Freud
2 See 96-Down
3 Vegetable on a vine
4 Cruising the beat
5 Hoi ___
6 Coach Parseghian
7 Varnish resins
8 Jesus, to Christians
9 Quarterfinal groups, e.g.
10 "The way I see it . . ."
11 See 15-Down
12 Jesús, for one
13 Notre Dame football legend
14 Time to enjoy le soleil
15 With 11-Down, leaders
16 Chicago mayor before Emanuel
17 Number with two
18 Riga resident
19 Switch ending
26 Creator of Thidwick the Big-Hearted Moose
27 Watch on the beach, maybe
29 Like bubble gum and questions

33 Skills
35 Main
36 Détentes
37 Classic root beer brand
38 1980s lightweight boxing champ
39 Of the same sort
40 D.C. baseballer
41 "Ya think?!"
42 Stuff in a pit
43 Give a body check
44 "C'est ___"
45 Vols' school
49 Where Julio Iglesias was born
50 Rampaging, after "on"
53 Had been
54 They moved from Minnesota to Los Angeles in 1960
56 1994 Denis Leary/Kevin Spacey flick
57 Sorority letter
60 Stone in Hollywood
61 Word repeated in "I ___! I ___!"
62 Bellyache
63 Home of the 46-Across: Abbr.
64 "Ta-da!"
66 "Così Fan ___"
67 "Buzz off!"
68 Eddie on "Leave It to Beaver"
69 Dovetails
70 Emily Dickinson poem "For Every Bird ___"
71 Bombastic
74 Some clickers
75 Over
76 Military group headquartered in Colo. Spgs.
78 Architect Saarinen
79 Hankering
81 "___ Alive"
83 Today preceder

by Daniel A. Finan

84 "Silent" one
85 Krazy ___
86 Something to watch when there's nothing on?
87 Big name in brewing
90 Modern update
93 Clue
94 San ___, Calif.
95 Little thrill
96 2006 comedy title character from western 2-Down
97 Buck in the Country Music Hall of Fame
100 [Kiss]
101 "Yikes!"
102 Perfect specimens
103 Half: Prefix
104 Cry after hitting a jackpot
105 "Peter Pan" fairy, for short
106 Struggle (through)
107 Surfer's concern
109 "Dies ___"
110 Serengeti antelope
112 Witch
113 Point of writing?

ACROSS

1 Crackerjack
4 Org. fighting pirates?
9 Pink shade
14 Wyle and Webster
19 Man of mystery
20 Stylish
21 Mountain ridge
22 Hit TV show that ended in 2011
23 Cuts in a cardboard container?
25 American-born Japanese
26 Prefix with meter or methylene
27 Tax lawyer's find
28 Heel
29 7'1" former N.B.A. star
30 Feminine suffix
31 Yelled initially?
34 Nursery noise
36 Empty
37 26 of the 45 U.S. presidents: Abbr.
38 Instruction part
40 Beach site, maybe
42 It might be skipped
44 So-so formal dance?
46 Went far too slowly during the 10K?
54 State symbols of North Dakota and Massachusetts
55 Leader who said "All reactionaries are paper tigers"
56 Slight
57 "Use the Force, ___"
58 Arizona is the only state to have one
59 Attach to
61 "Rocks"
62 Certain helicopter
63 Piece of black-market playground equipment?
69 Cousin of kerplunk
71 ___ for life
72 Purple shade
73 Press
76 It comes out in the wash
77 Northernmost borough of London
81 Freud's one
82 Antlered animal
83 Wool or cotton purchase request?
85 Disgusting advice?
87 Way out
88 24 hrs. ago
90 Isle of the Inner Hebrides
91 Brown-___
94 New York's historic ___ Library
97 Top of a ladder?: Abbr.
98 Whiskey bottle dregs?
103 Courtroom entry
107 Corporate shake-up, for short
108 Beyond ___
109 People whose jobs include giving tours
111 To have, in Le Havre
112 "I don't give ___!"
113 Nobleman after a banquet?
114 Rita Hayworth's femme fatale title role of 1946
115 Effects of many waterfalls
116 Felt bad
117 Bind
118 Toothpaste brand once advertised as having the secret ingredient GL-70
119 Not settled
120 Hits and runs
121 Rev.'s address

DOWN

1 Mosey
2 Perform Hawaiian music, say
3 Shell alternative
4 "Uncle Moses" novelist Sholem
5 Smack
6 Former French first lady ___ Bruni-Sarkozy
7 Staggering
8 Game tally: Abbr.
9 It was invaded in the War of 1812
10 Prayer
11 Airlift, maybe
12 Really bugged
13 Orphan girl in Byron's "Don Juan"
14 Seldom
15 Urging at a birthday party
16 I-5 through Los Angeles, e.g.
17 Heckle, e.g.
18 Thou follower?
24 Some volcanoes
28 Doesn't stop, in a way
32 Pitcher part
33 Animal with a snout
35 Urgent transmission, for short
38 Result of a pitch, perhaps
39 Schedule opening
40 Trolley sound
41 Distant
42 Side in checkers
43 Metered praise
44 Tasseled topper
45 Leader exiled in 1979
47 Not much
48 Nobelist Walesa
49 Queen's request, maybe
50 Skin cream ingredient
51 Adds insult to injury, say
52 Land on the Sea of Azov: Abbr.
53 Cultural org.
59 Stomach area
60 Deferential denial
62 Junk bond rating
64 Something on a hog?
65 Stalk by a stream
66 Feudal lands
67 Ex-governor Spitzer of New York
68 When repeated, a TV sign-off
69 Kind of story
70 Hi-tech organizer
74 Sonoma neighbor
75 Metric wts.
77 Vast, in verse
78 Vietnam's ___ Dinh Diem
79 "What ___?"
80 Towel
82 Reach at a lower level
84 Emoticon, e.g.
86 See 102-Down
89 "___ tu" (Verdi aria)
91 Words following see, hear and speak
92 1972 Best Actor nominee for "The Ruling Class"
93 Winning length in a horse race

by Kurt Mueller

94 Finally
95 Side in a pickup game
96 Minute
97 Swiss quarters?
98 Confederate general who won at Chickamauga

99 Noted 1991 Harvard Law grad
100 Supplied, as data
101 Slot machine symbols, often
102 With 86-Down, what Washington purportedly could not do

104 Boors
105 Banks who was known as Mr. Cub
106 Late bloomer
110 Some notebook screens, for short
113 Fourth notes

SEPARATE CHECKS

ACROSS

1 When repeated, advantageous to both sides
4 71 answers in this puzzle
9 Get used to it
14 Several CBS dramas
18 "___ Story: A Journey of Hope" (Jenna Bush best seller)
20 Expect
21 French toast piece?
22 It might be pulled
23 Pompeii, e.g.
24 Bride in "The Gondoliers"
25 "What the Butler Saw" playwright, 1969
26 Noted diamond family name
27 See circled letters in 76-/109-Down
30 Restless walker
32 Title character in a 2009 Sandra Bullock crossword film
33 "Well, I'll be!"
34 "Told ya so!" looks
36 "Fear is pain rising from the anticipation of ___": Aristotle
39 Wampum, e.g.
41 Endangered
44 . . . in 119-/120-Across
48 Sweetheart
50 Sweetheart
51 Part of a pack?
52 Panamanians and Peruvians
53 1960 Olympics host
54 Duel tool
55 Radii, e.g.
57 Cut
58 Some drink garnishes
59 Place for some animal baiting
60 Sharpness
62 Bit of physics
63 Hostess's ___ Balls
64 . . . in 116-/117-Across
67 Summer letters
70 Enter, for one
72 Give a hard time
73 Check, as one's numbers
76 Huntee in a game
79 Mounted
80 Authorizes
81 "Of thee" follower
82 Michael Jordan, e.g.
83 Conservative side
85 Comparison's middle
86 T. S. of literature
87 Neither more nor less, in France
88 . . . in 39-/60-Down
90 Item in a restaurant basket
92 Virus named for a river
94 French CD holder
95 Enemy of a Medici
97 Composition of many a cask
98 Techie's hangout
102 It may have sand in it
103 . . . in 17-/43-Down
109 User-edited website
110 Words on a sandwich board
112 Emerson's "___ Beauty"
113 "The Neverending Story" writer
114 Upper class?
115 First woman to teach at the Sorbonne
116 "Think" or "Think different"
117 They're stranded, briefly
118 Times past
119 Best ___
120 Rear's rear?
121 Radiator sound

DOWN

1 Hospital wings
2 Language akin to Kalaallisut
3 Like Gomer Pyle
4 See
5 Had a balance
6 Dry's partner
7 Not yet final, at law
8 Leaves a crooked trail
9 Owned up to
10 ___ Marquez, Nickelodeon cartoon girl
11 ___-at-law: Abbr.
12 Master
13 Game with a setter
14 . . . in 1-/4-Across
15 Pitcher's place
16 "___ out?" (poker query)
17 Merchandise ID
19 Cowardly sound
28 Unfold
29 Miami squad
31 Dada figure
35 Tightfisted sort
37 Silliness
38 Missing, as the start of a party
39 The U.N.'s ___ Ki-moon
40 Definitely not Felix Unger types
42 "___ Pastore" (Mozart opera)
43 Honorary law degs.
44 Inches for pinches
45 Buenos ___
46 Lake ___, Switzerland/France separator
47 Some tails, for short
49 Add to, perhaps
53 Uncle ___
54 Brief word of caution
56 . . . in 12-/35-Down
57 Pulitzer-winning Sheehan
60 France from France
61 "Do You Hear What I Hear?," e.g.
62 "In case you didn't hear me . . ."
65 1970s TV spinoff
66 Wrap for a queen
68 Big bargain
69 Ankle supports
71 Piece of work?
74 Even chances
75 A perfect score on it is 180: Abbr.
76 Daily weather datum
77 Aoki of the World Golf Hall of Fame
78 Off-road specialist
79 2003 Affleck/Lopez flick
80 Century 21 competitor
83 "I'm listening"

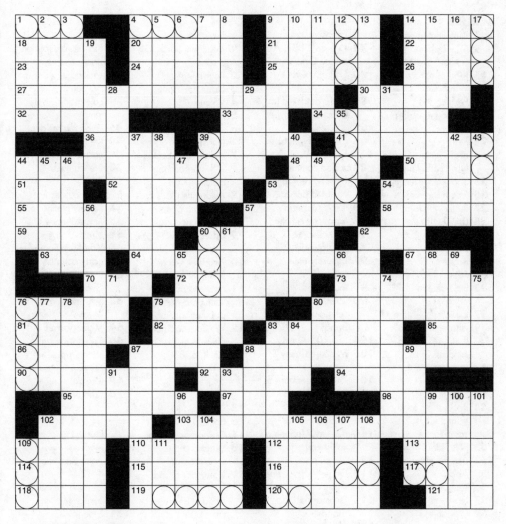

by Pamela Klawitter

84 ___ leash
87 "View of Toledo" artist
88 U.K. carrier, once
89 Word with cherry or cotton
91 Rush igniter
93 Offshore accommodations

96 Actors' grp.
99 Sally ___ (teacakes)
100 Show-biz father and son
101 Graceful word?
102 Program coordinator?
104 Vituperate

105 Japanese noodle
106 Part of AARP: Abbr.
107 Small: Suffix
108 Outlet
109 Mode
111 Strauss's "Ariadne ___ Naxos"

ACROSS

1 Airplane amenities
9 "The Dublin Trilogy" dramatist
15 Kind of attraction
20 Windward
21 Fashion frill
22 Add-on meaning "galore"
23 Start-press order for a New York daily?
25 Shaded shelter
26 Sleuth Lupin
27 Suffix with form
28 Dresden's river
30 St. Pete-to-Savannah dir.
31 Flaps
32 Make out
35 Big name in potatoes
37 Explorer's writing
39 Flippered animal that runs a maid service?
43 Legal assistants
46 Mart start
47 Sparks
48 Request for candy from a kid at camp?
52 Nutritional abbr.
53 Like the yin side: Abbr.
56 Author Sinclair
57 Start
59 Dewlapped creature
62 When to call, in some ads
64 "Rocky III" co-star
65 Gnarly
67 Ohio university
68 Congratulatory phrase at a "Peanuts" bar mitzvah?
74 "Sounds like ___!"
75 Western Indian
76 High lines
77 Romeo's predecessor?
78 Keir of "2001: A Space Odyssey"
80 End of a Greek run
82 Ones gathered for a reading, maybe
85 ___ result
86 One of the Bobbsey twins
88 Jaded comment from a constantly updated person?
93 1981 German-language hit film
96 Part of some itineraries?
97 Leisurely time to arrive at the office
98 1970s, to a schmaltzy wedding band?
104 See 106-Across
105 Musée d'Orsay artist
106 Things determined by 104-Across
107 Everybody, to Erich
110 "___ me" (phone comment)
111 Match part
114 Geneviève, for one: Abbr.
115 Denmark's ___ Islands
118 "Scooby-Doo" girl
120 Amnesiac's vague recollection of having a hobby?
125 Construct
126 Environment
127 TV character who worked for Steinbrenner
128 Six-pack holder?
129 Certain newspaper advertisement
130 Washed

DOWN

1 Substitute for forgotten words in a song
2 Pour thing?
3 Stops panicking
4 Valued
5 Prefix with -centric
6 "I can't believe it!"
7 Holiday celebrated with bánh chung cakes
8 Asian title that's an anagram of an English one
9 Unsettling last words
10 Two-time Oscar nominee Joan
11 Home to about 15% of the world's population: Abbr.
12 W. Coast air hub
13 Fashion magazine
14 "2, 4, 6, 8 — Who do we appreciate?," e.g.
15 ___ egg
16 Back
17 College-area local
18 What a chair should cover?
19 Cosmetics brand with the classic slogan "Because I'm worth it"
24 Swiss mix
29 Often-trimmed tree
32 Designed for two
33 Takes in
34 "___ out!"
36 Serpentine shape
37 "Beatles '65" and others
38 Hanauma Bay locale
40 Antipollution mascot Woodsy ___
41 AOL's website, e.g.
42 Birth control option, briefly
44 Lacking a surrounding colonnade, as a temple
45 Ljubljana resident
49 Ready to be called
50 French meat
51 Active
53 Casino offering
54 Poetic "plenty"
55 Singer Aimee
58 Muffs
60 What a pajama party often is
61 It's NW of Georgia
63 Sch. that plays Texas A&M
64 Memory: Prefix
66 Calendario unit
68 When tripled, et cetera
69 Musical number
70 "The Producers" character who sings "When You Got It, Flaunt It"
71 Mucho
72 Actor Rickman
73 K–12
79 "Broken Arrow" co-star Michael
81 Type in
83 Portrayal
84 Zeus' disguise when fathering Helen of Troy
87 Blood-typing system
89 Modern party planning aids
90 Sports column
91 Go south, as sales
92 Scot's "wee"
93 In excelsis ___

by Tony Orbach and Janie Smulyan

94 Japanese "thanks"
95 Frequent, in verse
98 Stand on short feet
99 Straight
100 Eve who wrote "The Vagina Monologues"
101 ___ egg
102 Beat it
103 Best in crash-test ratings
108 Order to a barista
109 "Zigeunerliebe" composer
112 "La Bohème" soprano
113 Key of Brahms's Symphony No. 4: Abbr.
116 Eleven, to Éloïse
117 Edwardian expletive
119 Ones putting on a show, for short
121 They: Fr.
122 German rejection
123 Cause of some repetitive behavior, in brief
124 A Stooge

ACROSS

1 Animal with a huge yawn
6 Garden support
10 ___ of roses
15 "Swans Reflecting Elephants" artist
19 Formula One driver Prost
20 Bandleader Puente
21 Religion founded in Iran
22 Dash
23 Reduces significantly
25 "Your Movie Sucks" writer
26 Billion: Prefix
27 "A penny saved is . . ."
30 "___ me anything"
32 Winery wood
33 Needle case
34 Like a black hole
35 "Where there's a will, there's . . ."
42 Mama Cass
43 Partner of 74-Across
44 Spread out
45 Email alternative
48 Effrontery
49 Entertainment providers at a sports bar
52 Pop's ___ Tuesday
53 Fill
54 Perfect service
55 Certain commando
56 "Where there's smoke, there's . . ."
60 Founder of United We Stand America
62 Despicable
64 John who searched for the Northwest Passage
65 Buddhist teaching
66 "People who live in glass houses . . ."
71 Rhododendron cousin
74 Partner of 43-Across
75 Chinese "path"
76 Stinks to high heaven
80 "He who laughs last . . ."
84 Russian council
86 Land in a river
87 Some are queens
88 Part of a cul-de-sac address, maybe: Abbr.
89 Neighborhood east of SoHo
91 "This ___ You're Talking To" (Trisha Yearwood song)
92 "Riddle me, riddle me ___"
93 Public respect
96 Managed
97 2, 3, 4 or 6, for 12
99 "If at first you don't succeed . . ."
102 Revenue line
105 It can make a 10 a 9
106 Alley ___
107 Sante Fe-to-Denver dir.
108 "Don't bite the hand . . ."
115 Legend of the Himalayas
116 Oldest von Trapp child in "The Sound of Music"
117 Protein building blocks
120 Reposed
121 Looped handles
122 Bone-dry
123 Sacred city of Lamaism
124 Mrs. Garrett on "The Facts of Life"
125 Places to live in the sticks?
126 Struck out
127 Stupid, in Sonora

DOWN

1 Is sick with
2 Sick
3 Analgesic
4 Boulevard where Fox Studios and the Los Angeles Convention Center are located
5 "Almost finished!"
6 Wasted
7 Former Yankee Martinez
8 Departing words?
9 Synthesizer designer Robert
10 Helped in a job
11 Middle Eastern salad
12 Area of Venice with a famous bridge
13 It has banks in Switzerland
14 Director Martin
15 Step
16 It's out of this world
17 Port on the Gulf of Guinea
18 Silly
24 Western terminus of I-90
28 ___ Majesty
29 Contraction with two apostrophes
30 Relationship disparity, perhaps
31 Console
36 Naught
37 Rapscallion
38 New newt
39 Part of T.A.E.
40 Comet part
41 "That's good enough"
45 C-worthy
46 Scintilla
47 TV warrior for good
50 It's north of Baja, informally
51 Prime cut
53 A star may represent it
55 ___ blue
57 College cheer
58 Bog buildup
59 "Star Trek" role
61 Cooking pots
63 Baylor's city
67 Applied some powder to
68 Wasted
69 Title girl in a 1964 Chuck Berry hit
70 Toe woe
71 Come from ___
72 Fanboy's reading
73 Stud money
77 Javanese or Malay
78 Ban ___ (Kofi Annan's successor)
79 Laurence who wrote "Tristram Shandy"
81 "Good grief!"
82 Surly manner
83 Material for a suit?
85 Party of the underworld
90 ___-di-dah
91 Suffix with robot
93 Hebrew letter after koph
94 Fights with
95 Permits

by Paula Gamache

98 It might be on the road
99 One behind the lens
100 Farm mate
101 Didn't suffer in silence
102 Flair
103 Forward
104 Exempli gratia, e.g.
109 Economist Greenspan
110 It has a period of 2π
111 No pressure
112 Its highest point is Wheeler Peak: Abbr.
113 Current carrier
114 Nymph spurned by Narcissus
118 August hrs.
119 ___ Tomé

85

UNDERWATER SEARCH

When this puzzle is done, look for a name (hinted at by 37-Down) hidden 17 times in the grid, each reading forward, backward, down, up or diagonally, word search-style.

ACROSS

1 One going into an outlet
6 Sonata movement
11 Org. for Lt. Columbo
15 33⅓ and others
19 Buzz
20 Huge quantity
21 Cross letters
22 "___ la Douce"
23 Again
25 "I before E except after C" and others
27 Tampa-to-Orlando dir.
28 Swelling of the head
30 Carry illicitly
31 Modern: Ger.
33 Old Turkish V.I.P.'s
34 "Now you ___ . . ."
35 Skippy alternative
38 Attachment points under the hood
42 Finnish city near the Arctic Circle
46 Oodles
48 Street on old TV
49 Racketeer's activity?
51 "Ideas for life" sloganeer
53 Skips on water
55 "The Canterbury Tales" pilgrim
56 Sight near a drain
57 Also
61 Dues payer: Abbr.
62 Mark Twain, e.g., religiously speaking
64 Sp. miss
65 Human, e.g., foodwise
67 Salad orderer's request
70 Mercedes competitor
73 Bothered
74 Attractive
77 Mother of Horus, in Egyptian myth
79 "Mona Lisa" feature
82 Prince Valiant's son
83 Part of the Hindu Godhead
88 Summer hangout
89 Italian 10
91 Organic compound
92 Rights of passage
94 1936 Loretta Young title role
96 Pioneering computer
99 Back end of a time estimate
100 Carolina university
101 Terminology
104 ___ Banos, Calif.
105 Skipping syllables
107 Edible Andean tubers
108 Cousin on "The Addams Family"
110 Prepared for YouTube, say
113 Tyson nickname
116 Suffix with planet
119 "Just a sec"
121 Hillary Clinton and Nancy Pelosi
124 "Fargo" director
125 "This ___!"
126 Inner tube-shaped
127 Perplexed
128 Objectives
129 Firm part: Abbr.
130 Bag of chips, maybe
131 Unlocked?

DOWN

1 Maven
2 Bit of Viking writing
3 Sign
4 Ladies' club restriction
5 Miracle-___
6 Nicolas who directed "The Man Who Fell to Earth"
7 Twice tetra-
8 Big name in upscale retail
9 Cracked or torn
10 What Rihanna or Adele uses
11 City of the Kings
12 Former Texas governor Richards
13 Like the alarm on many alarm clocks
14 Least hopeful
15 Notes to pick up on?
16 Self-righteous sort
17 Mid 22nd-century year
18 Ed.'s convenience
24 French island WSW of Mauritius
26 Non's opposite
29 Tryster with Tristan
32 Slippery ones
34 Awake suddenly
35 Teased
36 "Have ___ myself clear?"
37 2003 Pixar film
39 "___ further . . ."
40 U.S.A. or U.K.
41 ___ Bator, Mongolia
43 Stoic
44 Occasional ingredient in turkey dressing
45 1972 Bill Withers hit
47 Applies, as paint
50 Banks and Pyle
52 PC key
54 Lower layer of the earth's crust
58 Suffix with Capri
59 Magazine with an annual Hot 100
60 Neighbor of Que.
63 Stood like a pigeon
66 Improvised musically
68 "Lord, is ___?"
69 In concert
71 Hope grp.
72 Spot
74 One concerned with el niño
75 Sans-serif typeface
76 Field of stars?
78 Will of the Bible
80 Pick 6, e.g.
81 Someone ___
84 Zero
85 "Sense and Sensibility" sister

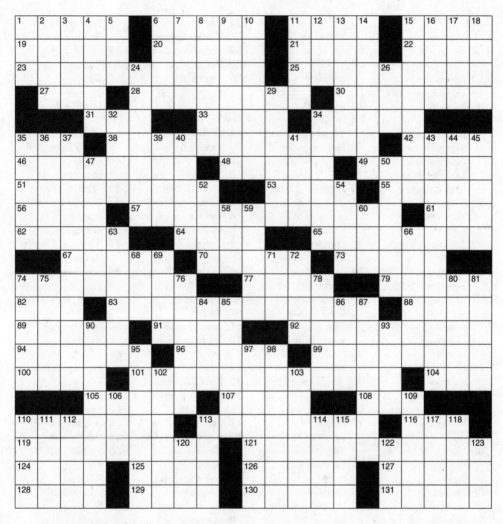

by Alan Arbesfeld

86

PARDON "E" INTERRUPTION

ACROSS

1 Director
6 Stereo syst. component
10 Recipe abbr.
14 Number crunchers, for short
18 State capital whose name comes from the French for "wooded area"
19 Mississippi River's largest tributary
20 The Hermit Kingdom, once
21 Lie a lot
22 Island from which Tiberius ruled
23 Lively dance performed as a six-pack is being laid to rest?
26 Canine king's regime?
28 Small chain component
29 Baker of jazz
30 Dominant theme
31 West African monetary unit
32 Ones crunched during crunch time?
35 Tanned skin
38 Hostile feelings
41 Eco-warriors?
48 Grammatical topic
49 Earth tone
50 Smoke
51 Web address component
54 Beat soundly
56 Encounter with an Alaskan bear?
59 Beneficiary of a 2008 bailout
63 Expected
64 Very unpleasant

65 Red Scare prosecutor Roy
67 Mr. of old cartoons
68 1813–14 vice president
70 Fan club focus
71 Stockpile
73 Hundred Acre Wood young 'un
74 Not permanent
76 Set of shot glasses for Christmas?
80 A man or a mouse
83 ___ equivalent (measure of explosive strength)
84 Eggs served raw
85 W.W. II title
88 Native New Zealander
89 Sharpshooter Oakley when she was a charming young musician?
93 Have an emotional impact
96 "Or ___ what?"
97 Interject
98 Canning seal
99 Paterson's successor as New York governor
104 Newborn on a ranch
107 Sneaky trick
108 Interstellar valet's job?
113 Ship info kept for the Spanish Armada?
115 Foo Fighters frontman Dave
117 Golf rarities
118 Drew on a screen
119 A.L. M.V.P. in 2005 and 2007, informally
120 House that won't catch fire

121 Old Harper's Weekly cartoonist
122 Wheelless vehicle
123 Desires
124 Bygone communication

DOWN

1 1970 # 1 hit for the Jackson 5
2 Waterfall sound
3 Sufficiently aged
4 "Hamlet" courtier
5 Consider carefully
6 Stiffly awkward, as movement
7 One doing course work
8 ___ Minh (1940s independence movement)
9 "Miss Julie" composer Ned
10 Shinto shrine entrance
11 Filled in
12 Cook so as to lock in the flavor, say
13 Comrade
14 Bogeymen's hiding places
15 Hoi ___
16 Compound also called an olefin
17 Puts on the ballot
20 Mathematician Gödel
24 Comrade
25 Continuing to criticize unnecessarily
27 Pop name
32 Border
33 "What nonsense!"
34 Plan for the evening?
36 Start of a Wagner title

37 Biblical priest at Shiloh
39 Stable sounds
40 Hurt badly
42 Opposing
43 Snug retreat
44 "Wall Street" character Gordon ___
45 ___ Chicago Grill
46 Far-away connector
47 Notorious investor
51 Brabantio's fair daughter
52 Not deceived by
53 "Gotta go," in chat rooms
55 "Last Time I Saw ___" (Diana Ross song)
57 Seer's perception
58 Blue uniform wearer
60 All-Star Dick of the 1960s–'70s Knicks
61 Dumbfounded
62 Knuckle-headed action?
65 U.S.N. rank
66 It's due south of Iran
68 "C'mon, sleepyhead!"
69 Starchy staple of Africa
72 Bloodmobile supply
75 Tuscaloosa university, for short
77 Smidgen
78 Workers' rights agcy.
79 W.P.A. initiator
81 Like the climate of 66-Down
82 "So I ___"
86 "Evita" narrator
87 Predatory fish

by Patrick Berry

89 Like the day of the summer solstice
90 Smiley's creator
91 Is caught up in the Rapture, e.g.
92 "Cool"
93 Dennis of the court
94 Orchestral work premiered in 1805
95 Moves laterally
100 Tried to convince
101 "That's fine"
102 Thousand thou
103 Certain dental repair
105 Aboveboard
106 Valley ___
108 Ring
109 Richard of "Bee Season"
110 Outhouse door symbol
111 Take turns?
112 One going on foot?
114 HP products
116 Salty fillet

ACROSS

1 Word with liberal or visual
5 Foliose
13 Hero of a John Irving best seller
19 Beverage whose logo was once the bottom half of a woman's legs
20 Actress who co-starred in "Havana," 1990
21 Protect
22 Heads-up in Ireland?
24 Danish cheese
25 "Gerontion" poet
26 "Yikes!"
27 Australia's Great ___ Basin
28 Dorm police, for short
29 Superman's attire, e.g.?
34 Head of London?
35 Venezuela's Chávez
36 Security interest
37 Metric liquid meas.
38 Achievement
40 Farm pails?
47 City raided in "Godzilla Raids Again"
49 Cloud producer, informally
50 ___ Highway (route from Dawson Creek)
54 Willing to do
56 Fluid
57 Boxer on season four of "Dancing With the Stars"
60 Aggregate
61 Like items at a supermarket checkout
64 "I feel the earth move under my feet," e.g.?
65 Q.E.D. part
67 Paris's Musée ___
68 Benjamin
69 W.W. I German admiral
70 Fancy garb for Caesar?
72 Characterized by
74 Suffix with absorb
75 Exploited
76 Sugar providers
77 Flower also known as love-in-idleness
79 French school
80 "___ my case!"
81 "Button your lip!"
83 Antisthenes, notably?
88 Veronese masterpiece "The Feast in the House of ___"
91 ___ Canals
94 Birthplace of the Rep. Party
95 First tribe met by Lewis and Clark
97 Hard butter
98 Something talked about on "Today"?
105 Surrealist who avoided the draft by writing the day's date in every space on his induction paperwork
106 Victuals
107 Michael of "Juno"
108 "Who ya ___ call?"
110 Unnatural
111 Extremely occult?
115 Happy
116 Set sail
117 Tick off
118 Deeper blue?
119 O.K.
120 "The War Is Over" writer/singer

DOWN

1 Ticked off
2 Beer served without artificial carbonation
3 Vacation spot that's crazily busy?
4 Round storehouse
5 Cousin of Inc.
6 "Ick!"
7 Tennis's Ivanovic
8 Cabbies' clients
9 End of July by the sound?
10 Pelvis-related
11 Somewhat informal?
12 Grade school subj.
13 Pointer's words
14 Start of all Oklahoma ZIP codes
15 Tumbler
16 Architectural space
17 Regular price
18 Set for a detective, maybe
21 "Eek!," e.g.
23 Yearn (for)
27 Suffix with problem
30 Watch from the sidelines
31 Río makeup
32 Kind of pad
33 Certain triple-decker
39 U.K. decoration: Abbr.
41 Bitter, in a way
42 "Ghosts" playwright
43 What Bryn Mawr College is not
44 N.Y.C. subway inits.
45 Skyscraping
46 Wows
48 Married couple?
51 Prank involving a hammer and nails?
52 1986 film shot partly in a decommissioned power plant
53 Mint on a hotel pillow, e.g.
54 Good for something
55 What karats measure
56 Reversed
57 Columbia athletes
58 Bread on the table, maybe
59 "___ that a lot"
62 Salsa singer Celia
63 U.S. visa type issued to visiting diplomats
64 Labyrinthine
66 Complete: Prefix
68 Gradual increase in vol.
71 Row
72 Strip
73 Yes, to no: Abbr.
76 Woman's support
78 Bother
80 Word derived from the Latin "uncia," meaning "one-twelfth"
81 Baked ___

by Dana Delany and Matt Ginsberg

82 Uncle Sam, for one
84 "Hmmm . . ."
85 Quick
86 Followers: Suffix
87 French vote
89 Nail polish, e.g.
90 Collisions
91 Sticky roll?

92 "C'est si bon!"
93 Put in one's two cents' worth
96 Like custard
99 "This has got me fuming!"
100 Die out
101 Creamy shades

102 Dashes may be part of them
103 Speak to the masses
104 Betray
109 Capital near the 60th parallel
111 No. typically between 2.0 and 4.0

112 Omaha Beach craft, for short
113 One of these days
114 Kind of jacket

88

CORNERED

ACROSS

1 *Nitty-gritty, as of negotiations
6 *Boater
11 Sponge (up)
14 *Title figure in an Aesop fable
19 Royal African capital
20 Something plighted
21 Co. once owned by Howard Hughes
22 "L'shanah ___!" (Rosh Hashana greeting)
23 Amtrak train
24 Emulated the phoenix
26 New Mexico county
27 Roughly plan
29 Effects
31 Losing casino roll
32 Not included
34 James ___, duettist on the 1982 #1 hit "Baby, Come to Me"
36 It might be French, Swiss or Italian
37 Insipid writing
40 Globular
42 Fight (off)
43 "Well, that's odd"
44 Go ___ great length
46 More placid
48 Boss
50 Corporate owner
52 Passé
54 Term of address in Dixie
55 Susan of NPR
58 *Work on at a desk, say
60 Shot up
64 Death, in Dresden
65 Thief
67 Take no action regarding
69 Bale binder
70 Settled down
72 Grunts may come out of them
74 Author Shute of "On the Beach"
76 Throw out
77 *Bracket shape
79 Mini-tantrums
81 Barrio babies
83 Eavesdrop, maybe
84 Exactly like
86 Log holder
88 What Chesapeake dogs are trained to do
90 Golden rule word
92 Leader of Abraham?
94 Time of lament
95 Ayn Rand protagonist
99 "I have been half in love with ___ Death": "Ode to a Nightingale"
102 Locus
103 "Il était ___ fois . . ." (French fairy-tale starter)
104 Ancient kingdom in Asia Minor
106 Incredibly stupid
108 Newsman Baxter on "The Mary Tyler Moore Show"
109 Kitten's cry
110 Fishermen with pots
112 Onetime weight-loss drug
114 Exclamation after a workout
116 Convertible
118 The dot on the "i" in the Culligan logo
122 ___ acid

124 Alabama speedway locale
126 2011 revolution locale
127 Crazy
128 Britney Spears's "___ Slave 4 U"
129 More judicious
130 Stimulant
131 Really feel for?
132 Ia. neighbor
133 Stellate : star :: xiphoid : ___
134 Artery opener

DOWN

1 Some intimates
2 Billiards need
3 Have ___ in one's bonnet
4 See 87-Down
5 Library area
6 Poetic stanza
7 Many a vaudevillian
8 Listed
9 Polished off
10 Question from one in another room
11 Bad marks
12 Because of
13 Roast go-with
14 The "it" in the lyric "turn it on, wind it up, blow it out"
15 Campus drillers
16 C
17 Frozen food brand
18 Ad-filled weekly
25 4 on a phone
28 Cool sorts
30 Computer option for a document
33 Singer Washington
35 *Ernest and Julio Gallo product
37 Regulars on VH1
38 Asia Minor

39 Model
41 The Whale constellation
45 Pro ___
47 Enzyme regulating blood fluid and pressure
49 Cabbage dishes
51 Original "Wagon Train" network
53 Classic McDonnell Douglas aircraft
56 Goes bad
57 *Usual amount to pay
59 Act like a protective mother
61 Hit one out of the park, say
62 Sap
63 Innocent
66 Actress Knightley
68 "The ___ Tailors," Dorothy L. Sayers mystery
71 N.Y.C. landmark
73 Trite
75 Ignore, in a way
78 Fishing line fiasco
80 Tick off
82 Monterrey Mrs.
85 One with endurance
87 With 4-Down, $MgSO_4 \cdot 7H_2O$
89 Fingers, for short
91 Source of many English words that come to us via French
93 "Strap yourselves in, kids . . ."
95 *Part of a boxer's training
96 Time it takes to develop a set of photos, maybe

by Kay Anderson

97 Scrupulously followed, as the party line
98 No-win situation?
100 One living off the land, maybe
101 One-piece garment
105 Where kids get creative in school
107 *It's pitched for a large audience
111 Fifth of eight
113 Learn to get along
115 Bit of smoke
117 *Common secret
119 Smelly
120 Israeli conductor Daniel
121 After-dinner drink
123 Iowa college
125 Margery of rhyme

89

DON'T!

ACROSS

1 Group working on a plot
6 Seurat painted in one
10 "Look what ___!"
14 One of Santa's team
19 Old Olds
20 Biblical shepherd
21 Alma mater of football great Roger Staubach
22 Opt for the window instead of the aisle?
23 Don't . . . !
26 Ottoman relative
27 Lover of Bianca in "Othello"
28 See 3-Down
29 Plea to the unwelcome
31 Loo
33 Bug-eyed primates
35 "Dream on"
37 Priestly robe
38 Don't . . . !
40 Us, e.g.
42 Attack like a bear
44 First person in Germany?
45 Stir up
46 "___ is life . . ."
47 Like some wrestlers' bodies
48 "___ for Cookie" ("Sesame Street" song)
50 It's not good when it's flat
51 Word processing command
52 Don't . . . !
56 Skirt chaser
57 Good news for a worker
58 It's passed down through the ages

59 Like some old-fashioned studies
60 Homeric cry?
63 Apothecary weight
64 More, in scores
65 Bass in a barbershop quartet, e.g.
66 Old Tokyo
67 Do-it-yourselfer
69 Filing aid
70 Open
72 Established facts
73 Don't . . . !
78 Person with a code name, maybe
79 Puts words in the mouth of?
80 A trucker may have one: Abbr.
81 Hurricane of 2011
82 Advanced sandcastle feature
83 Target of some pH tests
84 Org. for some guards
86 Famous Georgian born in 1879
87 Camera operator's org.
88 Don't . . . !
92 30, for $1/_5$ and $1/_6$, e.g.: Abbr.
93 Start without permission?
95 Possible result of a defensive error in soccer
96 Rogers on a ship
97 Sharpens
98 Email from a Nigerian prince, usually
99 Now or never

101 Indulge
103 Don't . . . !
108 Distanced
109 Biblical twin
110 Filmmaker van Gogh
111 One of the Allman Brothers
112 Harry Potter's girlfriend
113 Trick out, as a car
114 In view
115 Palais du Luxembourg body

DOWN

1 Trade's partner
2 ___-American
3 One may be seen on a 28-Across's nose
4 Indo-European
5 Stats on weather reports
6 Sunbathing sites
7 Can't stand
8 "Automatic for the People" group
9 iPod type
10 Liquid, say
11 "Matilda" author
12 "___ had it!"
13 Poor character analysis?
14 Building material for Solomon's Temple
15 Shade of green
16 Don't . . . !
17 UV index monitor, for short
18 Total hottie
24 Shipwreck spot, maybe
25 Ones with crowns
30 End of a series: Abbr.
31 Biblical twin

32 Basic skateboarding trick
34 "If only!"
35 It has a crystal inside
36 Brand for people with milk sugar intolerance
38 Got started
39 Figure of speech
41 Not the ritziest area of town
43 Small dam
46 "Ditto"
48 France's equivalent to an Oscar
49 Two who smooch, say
50 Mawkish
51 Gilbert Stuart works
53 Hacking tool
54 Spanish newspaper whose name means "The Country"
55 Bring up
56 Done in
59 Packer of old
60 He was named viceroy of Portuguese India in 1524
61 "Heavens!"
62 Don't . . . !
65 Look down
68 A big flap may be made about this
69 Possible change in Russia
71 Banks on a runway
73 Briton's rejoinder
74 Long-armed simian, for short
75 Element in a guessing contest

by Josh Knapp

76 Chilling, say
77 Concern when coming up, with "the"
79 Archetypal abandonment site
83 Corporate type
84 Inexperienced with
85 Witticisms
86 Aníbal Cavaco ___, Portuguese president beginning in 2006
88 Kind of keyboard
89 Model used for study or testing
90 Without flaw
91 Large ___ Collider (CERN particle accelerator)
94 Bramble feature
96 Lock horns (with)
98 Dis
100 Some linemen
101 Definitely not a hottie
102 Reuters alternative
104 "Just ___ suspected!"
105 "What ___ said"
106 Uracil's place
107 Volleyball action

ENTWISTED

ACROSS

1 Bryn ___ College
5 Often-parched gully
9 Goal of phishing
13 Where the Baha'i faith originated
17 It entered circulation in 2002
18 "My heavens!"
19 1997 best seller subtitled "Her True Story"
20 Lifted
21 Result of being badly beaned?
23 Scraping kitchen gadget with nothing in it?
25 Big name in root beer
26 Drill attachment with teeth
28 Offered a shoulder to cry on, say
29 Cry after a series of numbers
32 ___ Meir Tower, Israel's first skyscraper
34 CBS's "The ___ Today"
35 "Author! Author!" star, 1982
39 Broadly speaking
41 Leonine movie star of old
45 Pale yellow-shelled sea creature?
47 Differ
49 Contraction before boy or girl
50 October haul
51 Year the Paris Métro opened
52 Front-wheel alignment
53 Vlasic pickles mascot
55 That babies come from a 53-Across, e.g.
56 Gather
57 English weight
58 Return address info
60 View the effects of a big lunch in court?
63 Promise of a sort
65 Person with a headset, maybe
66 A bit slow
67 Fluorescent candy?
75 Materialize
80 Register, to a Brit
81 It's an imposition
82 Show shock, in a way
84 Land of King George Tupou V
85 Memorable mission
86 ___ in ink
87 Jewelry setting
89 Alternative to Ole or Edvard
90 "R" card in Uno, in effect
92 "Cheers" spinoff mania?
94 Stanch
95 Eases the misgivings of
97 Star-struck entourage
98 Funny Poehler
100 Allies have one
102 Post-solstice celebration
103 Kind of tape
107 Arrives
109 Crew
113 Hapless Roman ruler?
115 Taser for children?
118 Campfire treat
119 Hit ___ note
120 Tiny-scissors holder
121 Cone former
122 Desire, with "the"
123 "Buddenbrooks" novelist
124 Trickle
125 They can be prying or crying

DOWN

1 Very, informally
2 Charismatic effect
3 St. Paul's architect
4 Downed power lines, e.g.
5 Bonded
6 Turkish V.I.P.
7 Häagen-___
8 Things to think about
9 Almost matching
10 Polyphemus, to Odysseus
11 Kind of colony
12 Giant who made "The Catch," 1954
13 "No worries"
14 Mil. educators
15 Sheltered
16 Quiz bowl lover, say
19 Corrupts
20 Mirror image
22 Over again
24 Daydreams, with "out"
27 "Why not!"
30 Black Watch soldier's garb
31 Vast, old-style
33 Scavenging Southern food fish
35 Stockpile
36 Foamy mugful
37 Climbing aid
38 Falls into line
40 Clear
42 "The only rule is that there ___ rules"
43 Pittsburgh-based food giant
44 Soprano Fleming
46 Glut
48 Take a whack at
51 My, in Bretagne
54 Garrulous Garrison
56 Entrees sometimes prepared in crockpots
59 Charles, e.g.
61 Tipping point?
62 Subj. of the 2005 Pulitzer-winning book "Ghost Wars"
64 Hags, e.g.
67 Picks up
68 Possible lagoon entrance
69 Serious
70 Unemployed persons with full-time jobs
71 California's ___ Castle
72 O.T.B. conveniences
73 Slender fish
74 1983 Woody Allen film
76 Less fortunate
77 China's Zhou ___
78 Visually transfixed
79 Reviewers' comments on book jackets, typically
83 Distrustful
87 God, with "the"
88 Cut-off pants?
91 Not consent
92 Like some chickens
93 Mea ___

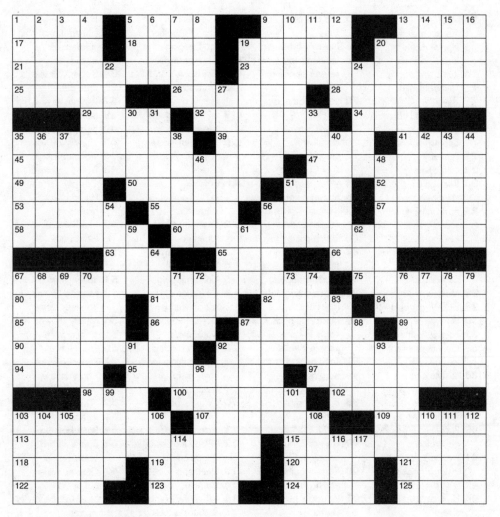

by Paul Hunsberger

MASQUERADE

Ten famous people are attending a costume party in this crossword. After the grid is filled, change the two circled letters in each theme answer to "unmask" a celebrity.

ACROSS

1 Tierra en el agua
5 Horror movie locale, in brief
10 Run ___ of
15 "Whoa! Calm down!"
19 Be featured (in)
20 Words on a Spanish valentine
21 Temerity
22 Choir part
23 Rods on a cowboy's truck
25 Environmentally sound keyboard
27 Prepare the soil for planting, perhaps
28 Multicapable
29 DLXXVI doubled
30 Lily type
32 Foreign visitors?
33 Only nonsentient zodiac symbol
36 In style
37 Voting to pass
38 Empathetic words
40 Password preceder, generally
41 Example, for instance: Abbr.
42 007 strategy
44 High card up one's sleeve
46 Baltimore daily, with "the"
47 ___ voce
48 French river or department
49 Web programs
53 Property claims
55 Some sexy nightwear
60 Clingy wrap
61 Ties up
63 Memo abbr.
65 "To Live and Die ___"
66 Narrow overhang
68 Government resister standing ready
70 It might be in a belt
71 More than attentive
72 Immature egg
73 East Coast rte.
74 Was sincere
76 Strong point
78 It often involves a Snellen chart
80 ___ about
82 All, in old-time stage directions
84 Modern address
85 Shock a fairy-tale monster
89 Nocturnal birds liable to keep people awake
91 Take most of
94 Burglar discouragers
95 Billiards shot
97 Fannie ___
98 "Pastorals" poet
99 Former Portuguese colony in China
100 Certain game-ending cry
101 Industrial hub of Germany
103 1983 domestic comedy
104 Like invalid ballots
107 Fries, e.g.
109 Soup spoon designed for shellfish
111 Last costume at a costume party
113 Requiem hymn word
114 Visibly stunned
115 Michael and Sonny's brother in "The Godfather"
116 Cleaner target
117 Five-spots
118 Transport, as across a river
119 1999 Broadway revue
120 Seasonal worker, say

DOWN

1 U.N. member since '49
2 Like some newly laundered shirts
3 Ointment base
4 Bitterly cold
5 Californie, e.g.
6 Collection of specialized words
7 Green-headed water birds
8 What wavy lines may indicate in a comic strip
9 Lean-___
10 Celestial being, in France
11 Actor José
12 Trilogy that includes "Agamemnon"
13 Eye layers
14 Carnival follower
15 When the events in flashbacks took place
16 Field with unknowns
17 RR stop
18 "___ knight doth sit too melancholy": "Pericles"
24 Part of "the many," in Greek
26 Canola, for one
28 Clears out of, as a hotel room
29 Hosts, briefly
31 Cheerful and spirited, as a voice
34 Singer Ocasek
35 Fruit drink
37 It might have serifs
39 Before long
40 Straight
42 ___ Vista (Disney video distributor)
43 Boiled cornmeal
45 Cashew, for one
46 Hit hard, as brakes
49 Northeastern Indian state
50 ___ d'Or (film award)
51 Italian "first"
52 Many a "Damn Yankees" role
54 Mutely showed respect
56 Truck fuel
57 Paper collector
58 Kagan of the Supreme Court
59 "The Crucible" locale
62 Pooh-bah
64 Business card abbr.
67 Gets the water out of
68 Many Monopoly spaces
69 They might atone
72 Moved like water into plant roots
75 Very, very funny
77 Short answers?
79 Festive time
81 Note to self
83 "___ in the kitchen with Dinah" (old song lyric)
85 Bad situation

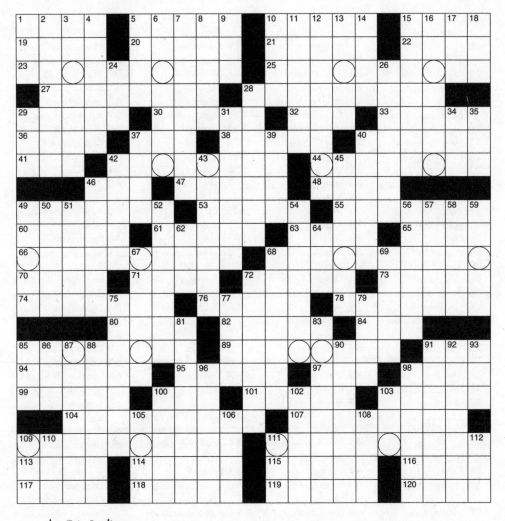

by Eric Berlin

86 Suffix with Cray-
87 Unfilled spaces
88 Mesmerized states
90 Newspaper section that competes with Craigslist
91 Hockey team's advantage
92 Smallish marsupial
93 Prize
96 Elk's weapon
98 "The Prisoner" author
100 "A Free Man of Color" playwright
102 Veep Agnew
103 Part of a business sched.
105 Count ___ (Lemony Snicket villain)
106 Snakelike
108 Palliative plant
109 Org. in "Burn After Reading"
110 Round body
111 Opposite of ppp, on scores
112 Hirohito's title: Abbr.

GRIN AND PARROT

ACROSS

1 Dancing misstep
5 Time's 1981 Man of the Year
11 Churchill item
16 Chattering bird
19 Subject of a blurry photo, maybe
20 Some terminals
21 Mild 11-Across
22 Ice climber's tool
23 Ride
24 Détente as a means of self-preservation?
26 World Factbook publisher, in brief
27 Floored by
29 Some extra bills, maybe
30 Symbols of a budding romance
32 Big name in office supplies
33 "The ___ Bride" (Rimsky-Korsakov opera)
36 Take ___ (rest)
37 Like most churches
40 Make a homie's turf unfit for habitation?
44 Adjust
45 "Today" rival, for short
47 Veep Agnew
48 Off
49 Thai money
50 Dissertation
53 Where the 34th Infantry Division fought: Abbr.
54 Joint legislative assemblies
55 Israel's Weizman
56 Seven, for one
58 Songs for one
60 Eye part
61 Diminutive of a common Russian man's name
63 Antiulcer pill
65 Juice component
67 Lay out some newspaper copy the old-fashioned way?
71 Debating two options, say
72 Whine
73 Barrel part
75 Match closers, for short
78 Tucson sch.
80 Quickly
82 "While you ___ out . . ."
84 Go off
86 They're laid by aves
88 Shiny, hollow paperweight
89 Prefix with venous
90 Star men?
91 Churchgoers
93 Electoral map shade
94 Blender maker
95 Rhombus on an award?
99 Taking drugs
100 Dead letter?
101 Concert for ___ (2007 event)
102 Highflier's home?
104 Derailleur settings
106 Cartoon character whose last name is Höek
107 Dressing place
111 P
112 What a mysterious restaurant critic has?
116 1968 live folk record
117 Company with Patch Media
118 Sourpusses
119 Precipitation prediction
120 Something special
121 Many a shampoo
122 Court nobleman in "Hamlet"
123 Bottoms
124 "Mr. Roboto" band, 1983

DOWN

1 Banks raking in the money?
2 Criticize severely, with "out"
3 Chichén ___ (Mayan ruins)
4 Getaway where Italian pies are consumed?
5 Crumpled (up)
6 Close to, in poetry
7 Skyscraping
8 Dutch city
9 Mailed
10 Setting of the castle Rocca Maggiore
11 Early third-century year
12 France's Belle-___-en-Mer
13 Vacancies
14 Foe of the Pawnee
15 Cyrano de Bergerac wooed her
16 Strength required to lift a car?
17 Revolutionary line
18 What a raised hand may mean
25 "Can't beat that contract"
28 Duke ___, Rocky's manager/trainer
31 1986 Indy 500 winner
34 Weapon in Clue
35 Ticked-off states
37 "Quién ___?" ("Who knows?")
38 Shopping center
39 What PC gurus provide
40 Some New Guineans
41 Army units
42 "Yes ___?"
43 Couple
45 Scholastic measure: Abbr.
46 Seder serving
51 Title character in love with Elvira
52 Snitch's activity
54 Light on the stove
56 Drag-racing fuel
57 Grubs, e.g.
59 Ukrainian city
62 Obliterates
64 Last thing a fellow actor says, maybe
66 Awards won by shrimps?
68 Surround
69 Drop a letter or two
70 Actress Mimieux
74 Dropped the ball
75 Dole's running mate of 1996
76 Like some contraception
77 Where your opinion on "One lump or two?" counts?
79 Skirt
81 Nascar Hall-of-Famer Jarrett
83 Spots for hammers and anvils
85 Sharp irritation

by Brendan Emmett Quigley

87 Berry in some energy boosters
89 Slice of old Turkey?
91 Bird hangouts
92 Target competitor
96 Intl. humanities group
97 Bowler's target
98 Refrain bit
99 End of a pricing phrase
102 Japanese beer
103 Fire-___ (carnival performer)
104 Home for a certain old woman
105 Tattoo removal reminder
108 Like some sparkling wines
109 Side (with)
110 Sauce thickener
111 Car wash need
113 A single may get you one, briefly
114 PC key
115 Like some flat-screen panels, for short

93

GETTING IN SHAPE

ACROSS

1 Small amount
6 Nab, as a base runner
13 Well-known maze traveler
19 Slings
20 "I kid you not!"
22 "Things Fall Apart" author Chinua ___
23 Full-length
24 See highlighted letters intersected by this answer
26 Game hunters
28 Business card abbr.
29 Friend of Fifi
30 Fleur-de-___
31 Frozen beverage brand
32 One in debt
34 Author ___ Hubbard
35 Guess on a tarmac: Abbr.
36 Geological feature on a Utah license plate
38 Polite
40 Some batteries
41 Speak horsely?
43 ___ hall
44 Tennis's Berdych
45 Type
46 Golfer nicknamed "The King"
47 Year Michelangelo began work on "David"
48 As ___ (usually)
49 Charades participant, e.g.
52 Newsroom workers, for short
53 "Unfortunately, that's the case"
55 "Hurry!"
57 Obedient
58 Umpire's ruling
60 "I ___ the day . . ."

61 Priestly garment
64 Folkie Guthrie
65 Repeated musical phrases
67 Mazda model
69 Facility often closed in the winter
71 Home state for 86-Across: Abbr.
72 Soviet space station
73 Zig or zag
74 Home to the Venus de Milo
76 "Easy as pie"
80 Majority figure?
82 Texans' org.
85 Palindromic vehicle
86 Cheney's successor
87 82-Across stats
88 Launch
90 Jack or jenny
91 Beginning of un año
92 Eggs in a sushi restaurant
93 Freshen, as a stamp pad
94 Isn't wrong?
96 Popular pie flavor
97 Ends
98 PC key
99 1977 thriller set at sea
100 Comedy Central's "___.0"
101 Prefix with -gon
103 Pointed tool
104 ". . . . ___ saw Elba"
105 Co. that owns Moviefone
106 Commonly called
109 See highlighted letters intersected by this answer
114 Child's pet
115 Phenomenon associated with the Southern Oscillation
116 Message seen after 13-Across dies

117 Setting for van Gogh's "Cafe Terrace at Night"
118 Phillies div.
119 Drama has it
120 Shooting sport

DOWN

1 So
2 Character in "The Hobbit"
3 See highlighted letters intersected by this answer
4 Critical situation
5 Cosmetician Lauder
6 They have mtgs. in schools
7 Not std.
8 Share
9 Harvey of "Reservoir Dogs"
10 Two-for-one, e.g.
11 Flunk
12 Media watchdog org.
13 "Going Rogue" author
14 Rheumatism symptom
15 1969 film with an exclamation point in its title
16 When the table is set
17 Missing parts
18 Realizes
21 Jewel holder
25 Book after Joel
27 Cousin of an oboe
32 See highlighted letters intersected by this answer
33 Sassy
34 Site of a key battle in the War of 1812
35 Flotsam or Jetsam in "The Little Mermaid"
36 Fleet

37 He played the candidate in "The Candidate," 1972
39 "___ in the Morning"
40 '10 or '11 person, now
41 Buster
42 Shop posting: Abbr.
44 Follow
45 Aviation pioneer Sikorsky
46 Designer of the pyramid at the 74-Across
50 See highlighted letters intersected by this answer
51 It's for the birds
54 Garlicky mayonnaise
55 "___ for Cookie" ("Sesame Street" song)
56 Totaled
59 Ashanti wood carvings, e.g.
62 See highlighted letters intersected by this answer
63 Reason to doodle
66 Apple debut of 1998
67 "I'm less than impressed"
68 Mouse in a classic Daniel Keyes book
70 Contact ___
73 RCA products
75 "I didn't mean to do that!"
77 Quite a schlep
78 "Do the Right Thing" pizzeria owner
79 Thomas who lampooned Boss Tweed
81 "You have no ___"

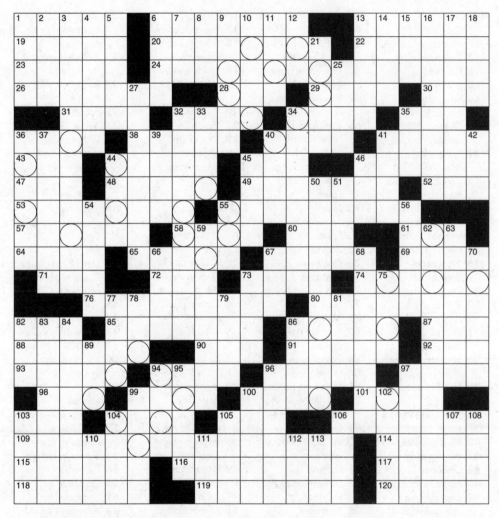

by Joel Fagliano

94

TAKE IT FROM THE TOP

ACROSS

1 Onetime propaganda source
5 Portmanteau
8 Obstruct
13 Brings in
18 Funny Johnson
19 See 6-Down
20 Queen City of the Rockies
21 Prefix with light or sound
22 Holiday purchase, informally
24 Tone setters for conductors
26 Item in a certain email folder
28 A couple of Spaniards?
29 Email alternatives
30 Source of the Amazon
31 South Carolina's state bird
32 Neurotic Martin Short character
35 Not discounted
36 Give up
38 Start of a 1957 hit song
40 Press and fold, say
41 Pecking order?
42 Oxidized
43 Agree (with)
44 Cousin who's "altogether ooky"
45 Vague early afternoon time
47 Like certain investments
49 Soaked
53 To the point, to lawyers
55 Times ___
57 Succeed
59 Bridge expert Culbertson
60 Go back and forth
62 Some are cohesive
64 Territory
65 1985 film based on "King Lear"
66 How some games finish
67 How some cars screech
69 Plant known as "seer's sage" because of its hallucinatory effect
71 Loser
72 Skinny
74 Screenwriter Ephron
75 Somme place
76 Prefix with magnetic
77 Old fishing tool
79 An instant
81 Blowup, of a sort
82 ". . . but possibly untrue"
84 Peeper protector
86 Wield
88 Uncorking noise
90 His debut album was "Rhyme Pays"
91 Grating
92 W. Hemisphere grp.
95 Queen's land
97 Like average folks, in Britain
98 Enthralled
99 ___ Park, classic Coney Island amusement locale
100 V formation?
102 Shop chopper
104 Bounce (off)
105 Mil. officers
106 Avg. level
107 Change quickly
110 Incredibly nice
115 Matter in statistical mechanics
116 Bulldog
117 Dispatch boats
118 Neighbor of Oman: Abbr.
119 "Pride and Prejudice" actress Jennifer
120 9-Down holder
121 Pickup line?
122 One of the Chaplins
123 Underworld route

DOWN

1 Transference of property to pay assessments
2 Asian republic
3 Gets up for the debate?
4 Certain poetic output
5 Reveal
6 With 19-Across, far back
7 Beats it and won't explain why?
8 Proof that a "Jersey Shore" character has an incontinence problem?
9 Heady stuff
10 Entire "Reservoir Dogs" cast, e.g.
11 Athlete's attire, informally
12 Pampers maker informally
13 Arrests an entire crime syndicate?
14 Inits. in '70s and '80s rock
15 Slayer of his brother Bleda
16 Like some majors
17 Impudent
20 Longtime ESPN football analyst Merril ___
23 Protected images, for short
25 Russian novelist Maxim
27 Fancified, say
32 Singer Gorme
33 Eschews Mensa material when going to parties?
34 "Drag ___ Hell" (2009 movie)
36 "Star Wars" character ___-Gon Jinn
37 SALT party
39 Dashboard choice
42 Contents of Lenin's Tomb, e.g.?
46 Settle in
47 Aquatic nymph
48 The Wildcats of the N.C.A.A.
50 Merits at least a 20% tip?
51 "Airplane!" woman
52 King or queen
53 Hard Italian cheese
54 Slower to pick up
56 Phone button trio
58 ___ Minor
61 Break down
63 A bar may offer it
68 One-dimensional: Abbr.
70 Flat flooring
73 Minute
78 Scout's mission
80 Assertive comeback
83 118-Across is in it
85 Super Bowl IV M.V.P. Dawson
87 Scoring stat for N.B.A.'ers

by Joe DiPietro

89 Wallop

91 Motorola phone line

93 Departure from the norm

94 Untraditional, as some marriages

95 Charges

96 Give a hard time

99 Soup kitchen implements

100 They're shown by X's, O's and arrows

101 Luggage attachment

103 Some annual bills

104 Major org. representing entertainers and athletes

108 Anita of jazz

109 Desideratum

111 ___ Fit

112 Brooklyn's Flatbush, e.g.: Abbr.

113 Go unused

114 Symbol for electric flux

ACROSS

1 "Right back at cha!"
9 Unclear
15 Sandcastle engineering equipment
20 Took one step too many, maybe
21 She was beheaded by Perseus
22 "Dallas" Miss
23 One of St. Peter's heavenly duties?
25 "The Untouchables" villain
26 "How's it ___?"
27 Ship part
28 Roast slightly
29 Mujeres con esposos
31 Place for un béret
33 Conquer
36 Kitty, in Segovia
37 Singer Cassidy
40 One side of a quad, maybe
42 "Snakes on a Plane," e.g.?
46 Brand of tea
48 Term on a tide table
50 Subject of a Magritte painting
51 Doc workers' org.?
52 What a lazy mover prefers to carry?
56 Projections on some globes: Abbr.
57 Your, in Tours
58 Blues instrument
59 Harsh cry
60 Cheap and flimsy, as metal
62 Big bump
63 Poet Mark
64 "___ Fan Tutte"
65 Bob, for one
67 Workout class on a pleasure cruise?
74 William Morris workers
75 Cousin of an ampule
76 Things rings lack
77 Egg foo ___
78 Makeshift Frisbee
81 Film special effects, briefly
82 Rangers' venue, for short
85 Ax
86 Number of X's in this puzzle's answer
88 Unbelievable court infraction?
91 Game with 108 cards
92 Mouselike animal
94 Fictional Jane
95 Biblical dancer
96 Cabby's nonstop patter?
100 Key with four sharps: Abbr.
102 Curt
103 "Family Guy" wife
104 Melodic passages
106 Provide a gun for, maybe
108 "Shakespeare in Love" star
111 Anthem contraction
112 Crystal on the dinner table?
114 Bloke
118 Dickens's Drood
119 Guests at a Hatfield/McCoy marriage ceremony?
123 Appropriate
124 Playground retort
125 Classic Freudian diagnosis
126 Stinger
127 Stonewallers?
128 Looks down on

DOWN

1 Single partygoer
2 Classical Italian typeface
3 Christmas party
4 Occurring someday
5 Daughter of Loki
6 Horror film locale: Abbr.
7 Garnered
8 "The Simpsons" teacher Krabappel
9 Letters of surprise, in text messages
10 Classmates, e.g.
11 Lets in
12 City that was the site of three battles in the Seven Years' War
13 Org. with a sub division
14 Has a beef?
15 Mark Twain and George Sand, e.g.
16 1960s–'70s San Francisco mayor
17 Opera whose second act is called "The Gypsy"
18 Singer Ford
19 Cinco follower
24 Limb perch
30 "Raiders of the Lost Ark" locale
32 College in Beverly, Mass.
34 Fine fiddle
35 Rat-a-tat
37 Orly birds, once
38 "You're so funny," sarcastically
39 "Family Ties" son
41 It's west of 12-Down: Abbr.
43 "You put the ___ in the coconut . . ."
44 Marcos of the Philippines
45 "Morning Train" singer, 1981
47 Ancient May birthstones
49 Thing that may break people up
53 Rtes.
54 Polar hazard
55 Money-related: Abbr.
61 Automaker since 1974
62 Triangular sails
63 "Shoot!"
65 1997 winner of Wimbledon and the U.S. Open
66 Step down, in a way
67 Union concession
68 Creature whose tail makes up half its body's length
69 World heavyweight champion who was once an Olympic boxing gold medalist
70 Egg: Prefix
71 Feudal estate
72 "Et violà!"
73 Geom. figure
78 ___ sci
79 Peeper problems
80 Doing injury to
82 Othello, for one
83 Basic arithmetic
84 Lottery winner's feeling
86 Easy eats

by Andrea Carla Michaels & Patrick Blindauer

87 Poorer
89 Word with level or devil
90 Arrow maker
93 Mendes of "Hitch"
97 Charge, in a way
98 Chips away at
99 Given false facts
101 Co-star of Kate and Farrah, in 1970s TV
105 Belted one
107 Ho-hum
108 Celebration
109 Theory
110 Did laps
113 Cries in Cologne
115 One of a pair of towel markings
116 17-Down piece
117 Challenge for jrs.
120 Ballpark fig.
121 Turndowns
122 Jeanne d'Arc, for one: Abbr.

96

BAKER'S DOZEN

ACROSS

1 Number of coins in la Fontana di Trevi?
4 Singer Bryan
9 Formal occasion
13 Power option
17 Roasted: Fr.
19 Invader of 1066
21 Logan of "60 Minutes"
22 ___ fide
23 Muscat's land
24 Focus of Gandhi's philosophy
26 Sweet's partner
27 Radioactivity figure
29 Plans to lose
30 S'pose
32 Uppity sort
33 Degs. from Yale and Harvard
35 TMC competitor
36 Fried chicken choice
37 "Odyssey" temptress
39 Infinite
42 Chem. unit
43 Turkish title
45 Mediterranean isl.
46 Makes a scene
49 "Humbug!"
50 Feminine suffix
51 And others
53 Credit card bill nos.
55 Wearing a wig and shades, say
57 Marriage site
60 Baseball's Bando
61 "The Boy Who Cried Wolf" storyteller
62 Classic jetliner
64 Old hi-fi records
66 Accurse
68 Big grocery store chain
69 Tagalong
70 On the double
72 "Pinwheel and Flow" artist
74 "Fee, fi, fo, ___"
75 Ratchet bar
77 "Cheers!"
78 How you might get change for a twenty
79 Perfumery rootstock
81 PJ-clad mansion owner
83 Henry ___ Lodge
85 "Paper Moon" girl
86 It means nothing to the French
87 Musician who won a 2011 Presidential Medal of Freedom
89 Shake, rattle or roll
91 Poetic preposition
92 Brightly colored lizards
94 Museum hanging
95 It has banks in St. Petersburg
96 Bugs, e.g.
97 Peak leaf-peeping time in Pennsylvania
100 Certain antibody
102 Raise, as a topic
105 Part of a Q&A: Abbr.
106 Hurt
108 "Be silent," in music
111 Cheesemaker's supply
112 Empty spaces
114 Subdued
116 Have ___ for (desire)
117 Police protection
120 Dust Bowl witness
121 English general in the American Revolution
122 About
123 Personal contacts?
124 Dangerous speed
125 Bygone spray
126 Gets in the pool, say
127 Like bell-bottoms or go-go pants
128 Barbecue sound

DOWN

1 Not having quite enough money
2 Circus Maximus patron
3 Schokolade
4 Years, to Tiberius
5 Manna, according to the Bible
6 Synthetic fiber brand
7 Year of Super Bowl XXXIX
8 Declared
9 Huge amounts
10 Pirate's demand
11 "The Lord of the Rings" menace
12 The "mode" of "à la mode"?
13 Math coordinates
14 Bakers, e.g.
15 Canine shelter
16 Certain huckster
18 How Hershey's Kisses are wrapped
20 "There is ___ in team"
25 Anne Rice vampire
28 P.O. box item
31 In the past, once
34 Corp. alias abbr.
38 No-___-do
40 Wooded area near the Rhine Valley
41 One of the Alis
42 Area known to the Chinese as Dongbei
44 ___ Building, New York landmark north of Grand Central
47 Pastry chef creations . . . and a hint to 12 other answers in this puzzle
48 Children and more children
49 Tries to get at auction
50 Squishy dish cleaner
52 Woman of one's heart
54 Less abundant
56 Suffix with human
58 Drag
59 Córdoba cordial
61 Word before republic or seat
63 ___ Beach, Hawaii
65 Spartan walkway
67 Former call letters?
71 Photo developer
73 Inc., abroad
76 "___ loves believes the impossible": Elizabeth Barrett Browning
80 So to speak
82 Followers of some asterisks
84 Girl's holiday party dress fabric
87 Cause for bringing out candles
88 Constriction of pupils
90 High beam?
93 Cheese fanciers
95 Atomic energy oversight agcy.

by Elizabeth C. Gorski

96 MTV's owner
98 Gambol
99 Not so tough
101 Orchestra section: Abbr.
102 "Moon Over Parador" actress
103 Coat of paint
104 Russia's ___ Bay, arm of the White Sea
107 "The Planets" composer
109 Sends forth
110 Bed cover
113 FedEx rival
115 Former U.S. gas brand
118 Follower of Ernest or Benedict?
119 Austin-to-N.Y.C. path

97

EITHER WAY

ACROSS

1 Followers of William the Conqueror
8 ___ Pepper
11 African menace
14 Part of a sentence: Abbr.
17 Tracing paper, e.g.
18 Twosomes
19 Partner of raised
21 Who said "Learn from the masses, and then teach them"
22 Students err?
24 Bonus reel fodder
26 Punk offshoot
27 Pistil complement
28 "10" in a bikini
29 Oklahoma city
31 Medusa killer takes his agent to court?
33 Feel that one's had enough, say
37 Temptation
38 Singsong syllable
39 Part of N.C.A.A.: Abbr.
40 Rig
41 Foreign tender?
44 Open hearings in courts
46 Reinforced ice cream container?
51 What Eng. majors pursue
52 Kay of "Rich Man, Poor Man"
53 "That's it!"
54 Info on modern business cards
56 Just sort, supposedly
58 Inferior tour vehicle for Snoop Dogg?

63 One side in a bullfight
66 Em and Bee, e.g.
67 Up
68 Recollection from a winter tourist in Poland?
71 Cut, in a way
73 It serves a duel purpose
74 Flip of a flop
75 Bit of progress
76 One encountered in a close encounter
79 Disparaging Argentine leader badly injured?
87 Ads
88 Perks
89 "Shucks!"
90 Actress Thurman
93 With 65-Down, stuck
94 The old man
95 "We totally should!"
97 One-on-one job for a ladies' man?
102 Spin meas.
103 Place to buy stage props
104 Stanza alternative
106 Former J.F.K. line
109 Rug type
110 "Son of Darius, please confirm my dog is male"?
113 Hip-hop's ___ Def
114 Rein in
115 Denizens: Suffix
116 Risk
117 Approx.
118 Guitar great Paul
119 Emergency broadcast
120 "Do it"

DOWN

1 "Don't think so!"
2 Ooplasm locale
3 Take back
4 Picture of health, for short?
5 Best effort
6 Long Island county west of Suffolk
7 Part of GPS: Abbr.
8 1970 #1 R&B hit for James Brown
9 Not be spoken aloud
10 Rx qty.
11 French clergymen
12 Way passé
13 One who gets things
14 1998 Masters champion Mark
15 It may be settled over beers
16 Nativity figure
18 Stopping point?
20 A lack of compassion
23 Come full circle?
25 "Reading Rainbow" network
28 "That . . . can't be . . ."
29 Busy
30 Send out press releases, e.g.
32 The Auld Sod
33 Former N.B.A. star Spud
34 A pastel
35 "Shoot!"
36 It's stunning
42 Pres. Carter's alma mater
43 Candy company whose first flavor was Pfefferminz
44 Federal org. with inspectors

45 Cry with a forehead slap, maybe
47 Pipe fitting
48 Drains
49 Cities, informally
50 Down in the dumps
55 Dashed fig.
56 They may be sore after a game
57 Nest egg option, briefly
58 Big ___
59 Italian article
60 Start of an aside, to tweeters
61 Jah worshiper
62 Total
63 Hampshire mother
64 SoCal squad
65 See 93-Across
66 Italian vineyard region
69 "Too bad!"
70 River islands
71 Whom Han Solo calls "Your Worship"
72 Constantly shifting
75 TiVo, for one
76 Press
77 They may be metric . . . or not
78 Dedicated offerings
80 Deluxe
81 Completely flip
82 Scaloppine, usually
83 Show, as something new
84 Curio displayers
85 Sound dumbfounded
86 Their necks can turn 270 degrees
90 Repulsive

by Jeremy Newton and Tony Orbach

91 Skirts smaller than minis
92 Having a policy of reverse seniority?
94 Top 40 fare
96 Lead's counterpart
98 Wedded
99 Producers of scuff marks
100 "New Sensation" band, 1988
101 Former telco giant
105 Get back to
106 "That's a fact"
107 "#1" follows it
108 Given the heave-ho
110 Sorority letters
111 Roxy Music co-founder
112 A street drug, for short

Note: In some squares of this crossword (as indicated by slashes), the Across and Down answers do not actually cross. Write both parts in the squares. Then use the central Across answer to interpret them properly to spell an appropriate final word.

ACROSS

1 ___ World Tour (sports circuit)
4 Stew
8 Comedian Nora
12 School hall feature
18 Rank in kendo
19 Article's start, to a journalist
20 Former New York governor Cuomo
21 Like some moving estimates
22 Justice Fortas
23 Computer animation option
25 Some harvesters
26 Calculator symbol
28 The "B" of B&N
29 Lincoln ___ (L.A. neighborhood)
31 "___ You Glad You're You?"
32 Fill-in
33 Teeing off
34 Mountain in Deuteronomy
36 X-ray units
37 Settee settings
39 Gourmet's treat
41 Paid, with "up"
42 Within the grace period?
45 Thuggish sorts
49 Armored truck company
50 Is persistent at an auction
51 Alternately
52 Ill-gotten gains
53 Signs
54 Dieter's unit: Abbr.
55 The Great Commoner
56 Front of a coin: Abbr.
59 Aunt ___ ("Star Wars" character)
60 Lead-in to 1812 or attrition
62 Stat that may be "adjusted"
63 How to get this puzzle's final word
69 Suffix with malt
70 You can believe it
71 Way off
72 Furthermore
73 Burned out
75 You go by one in Québec
76 Strike down
77 Season Pass offerer
81 Some ninths
83 Rattlesnake, at times
84 Singer Morissette
86 2011 International Tennis Hall of Fame inductee
87 Bob Marley's group, with "the"
88 Vodka source
89 Not ethereal
91 County northwest of San Francisco
92 Traumatize
95 Men in the middle of the peerage
96 Takes a bit off
99 La Città Eterna
101 Trojan War figure
103 "I'd never have suspected!"
104 Veep before Spiro
105 Gurus' titles
106 Oscar winner for "Cocoon," 1985
108 "My sources say no" source
111 Years, to Yves
112 Word with note or case
113 Like some accents
114 Item to thrust
115 "Details forthcoming": Abbr.
116 Pants
117 Prudential Center team
118 –
119 "___ questions?"

DOWN

1 Make fit
2 Dinner date request
3 Zithromax treats it
4 Sitcom waitress
5 Cardinals
6 Awards with a "Best Fact Crime" category
7 Will's ex-wife on "Glee"
8 Morse bits
9 Swiss canton
10 Seasonal saint
11 Hole in the head
12 Cap
13 Fit to be called up
14 Fruit-flavored soft drink
15 Emperor Taejo united it
16 Correct
17 Is quiet
20 Video file format
24 "Dear ___ Landers"
27 Watching without being watched
30 Jiffy
34 Minds
35 Sci-fi series set in the 23rd century
38 "Yikes!"
39 It was first broken in 1954
40 Monitor inits.
41 "Independent Lens" network
42 Puzzler
43 Come back from adjournment
44 "Awake in the Dark" author
46 Wasn't lackadaisical
47 ___ nous
48 Chi Cygni, for one
51 Italian province or seaport
54 Desk chair features
57 Short while
58 One step up from a four-cylinder
60 King, for example
61 Rock's ___ Fighters
63 Politicians' supporters, sometimes
64 Incorporating
65 Singer Marie
66 Grandson of Adam
67 Send away
68 Certain muscles
74 Oscar-nominated sci-fi film of 2009
76 Besmirches
78 Ladylove
79 Thiamine
80 Spanish bear
82 Intel interpreter, for short
83 TV award discontinued in 1997
84 Ardent adherents
85 Actor Chaney
87 Electrical worker
90 Conversation stopper

by Trip Payne

91 Over-the-shoulder garment
92 Sends millions of unwanted messages, say
93 Animal crackers animal
94 Georgia Dome, e.g.
96 Color whose name is French for "flea"
97 Blood type system
98 Rise up
100 Appraise
102 Most-quoted author in the O.E.D.: Abbr.
104 #1's, e.g.
107 Chicago trains
109 Kind of course
110 Moonves formerly of CBS

YIN/YANG

ACROSS

1 Test-drive
5 Scintillate
10 Who wrote "By their own follies they perished, the fools"
15 Name of nine Thai kings
19 Name of five Norwegian kings
20 Dogpatch yokel
21 Name on a B-29
22 "What ___?"
23 Pirates of the Caribbean, e.g.
24 Full of strong feelings
26 Instinctive desire
27 Villainous role for Montalbán
28 Bedelia of children's literature
29 Fearsome creature with plates on its back
31 Something to enjoy on a beach
34 More foamy
35 "Let's make ___ true Daily Double, Alex"
36 Two on a line
39 Razz
40 Sleaze
43 Mata ___ (spy)
47 Contented sighs
49 Start of many Portuguese place names
50 Family ___
51 Gloomy
53 Irving Berlin's "___ Be Surprised"
55 Area 51 holdings, supposedly
58 Flavor enhancer
59 Representatives in a foreign country
60 Italian woman
62 Amount past due?
63 N.C.A.A. part: Abbr.
64 Absorbed, in a way
65 Breach
66 Qatari bank note
67 It has a crown
68 Turner who led a rebellion
69 Musician's asset
71 Where the vice president presides
72 Grp. with the 1973 gold album "Brain Salad Surgery"
73 Windy City rail inits.
74 Dud
75 Green hue
76 Perfection, for some
77 Opus ___
78 Rams, but not dams
79 Rice ___
80 All together
82 Dismiss
83 Abbr. on a B-52
85 Dance partner?
86 Early online forum
87 Gillette brand name
88 Gift in "The Gift of the Magi"
90 Classic soft drink brand
92 Land o' blarney
93 Words on an information desk
94 Crow with a powerful voice
97 Guidelines: Abbr.
99 Moo ___ pork
100 Seaside
102 He might put chills up your spine
110 Perfectly
113 Edith's cranky husband
114 Not straight
115 Dept. of Labor arm
116 Started sneezing and sniffling, say
118 Sorvino of "Mighty Aphrodite"
119 Opponents of us
120 Architect Jones
121 Singer Susan with the 2009 #1 album "I Dreamed a Dream"
122 Wood alternative
123 "No problem!"
124 Fancy car starter?
125 Family of Slammin' Sammy
126 Some shooters, for short

DOWN

1 Uncool set
2 Root of politics
3 Lady's address
4 Digit protector
5 Bygone Las Vegas hotel/casino with a roller coaster
6 Certain W.M.D.
7 Lay to rest
8 Writer Zora ___ Hurston
9 Singer Tennessee ___ Ford
10 Sly laugh sound
11 Low dice roll
12 Castle guard
13 Some cobblers of lore
14 Sci-fi zapper
15 "The Social Contract" philosopher
16 Suffering from nyctophobia
17 Author Cervantes
18 On the ground, in ballet
25 Flabbergast
30 Some of Keats's feats
32 Neighbor of Sudan: Abbr.
33 "Bambi" character
37 Walter Mitty, e.g.
38 Lock
40 Master criminal of books and film
41 Establishes
42 Weighing hardly anything
43 Time in Hawaii, maybe
44 MGM motto starter
45 Question asked to one with a hangover
46 Malcolm X adopted it
48 Kuomintang co-founder
51 Is protective of
52 Particularly: Abbr.
54 "CSI" procedure
56 Grilling procedure
57 Bit of stage scenery
59 "Cheers" waitress
61 Coeur d'___, Idaho
70 British weights
71 One of a standard group of five
75 Little bit of French?
81 Singer DiFranco
84 "Bad!"
87 Ring of Fire perils
89 Eight bits
91 It may precede a kiss
93 Yellowfin tuna
94 Skedaddles

by Jeff Chen

95 Island south of Tsugaru Strait
96 Italian automaker since 1906
98 Adirondack chair element
99 Hosts of the 1912 Olympics
101 Some shark products
103 Bits
104 Marilyn who hosted 1980s TV's "Solid Gold"
105 Mates' cries
106 Nabisco brand
107 Pirouette
108 Boot, in baseball, e.g.
109 "___ Hope"
111 Corporate bigwig
112 Frozen food brand
117 Sweetie

ACROSS

1 Secretaries, e.g.
6 Modern record holder?
10 Bucks
15 Take ___ (doze)
19 Dow Jones industrial with the N.Y.S.E. symbol "AA"
20 Cataract site
21 "The Ten Commandments" role
22 ___ contendere (court plea)
23 Anaïs Nin, e.g.?
25 Seizure at Sing Sing?
27 Title girl in a 1979 Fleetwood Mac hit
28 Reverse
29 Cause for a kid's grounding
30 Heavenly: Prefix
31 Tech marvel of the 1940s
33 "Adam-12" call, briefly
34 Pioneering
37 Rice may be served in it
39 Heavenly voice of conscience?
43 Figure in Raphael's "School of Athens"
45 Going to hell
46 Verbally attack, with "at"
51 Old switch attachment?
52 Wrong
54 Due
56 House of ___ (European dynasty)
57 Sailors' spars
59 Specialty of a couples therapist?

62 "___ see it my way" (Beatles lyric)
63 Razzed
64 Adams and Falco
65 Israel's Dayan
68 Dear
71 Capital and largest city of Ghana
72 Gathering of spies
73 Fjord, e.g.
74 Very good, in slang
76 Courtroom jacket?
79 Work in a chamber, say
83 Scrutinizer
84 Prone to acne, say
85 Food item prized in French cuisine
86 De Matteo of "Desperate Housewives"
87 Put right
89 "Yeah, r-i-i-ight!"
92 Hypnotist Franz
94 Circus performer in makeup?
97 Fashion inits.
98 Starts, as a big meal
102 Business partner, often
103 Reciprocal function in trig
105 Very sore
106 Island hopper?
108 No voter
110 Herr's her
113 Storyteller for Satan?
116 Improvement of a Standardbred's gait?
118 "The ___ lama, he's a priest": Nash
119 Biology lab stain
120 Dense
121 Rend

122 Moolah
123 Prefix with history
124 Gorilla skilled in sign language
125 Kicks back

DOWN

1 Many Little League coaches
2 "Popular Fallacies" writer
3 One starting a stampede, maybe?
4 Much-read collection of verses
5 Suppose
6 Rub with ointment, as in a religious ceremony
7 Skewbald
8 Bread spread
9 Burrow, for some
10 Qualified
11 "___ and the Real Girl" (2007 movie)
12 Up
13 Criminal patterns, briefly
14 Hostess ___ Balls
15 Up in arms
16 "WarGames" grp.
17 "The George & ___ Show" (old talk series)
18 Submarine
24 Dilemma
26 Sets to zero
29 Name sung over and over in a Monty Python skit
32 The last Pope Julius
33 Década divisions
35 Decorative tip on a lace
36 ___-thon (literary event)
37 English channel, familiarly, with "the"

38 Mark's replacement
40 Counterpart of advertising
41 Antarctica's ___ Ice Shelf
42 Votary
44 Became discouraged
47 NyQuil targets
48 "Hamlet" courtier
49 Downright
50 Nickname for Theresa
53 "Leather," in baseball
55 Generous leeway
58 Onetime Procter & Gamble shampoo
59 Churl
60 Be contiguous to
61 Pages (through)
63 Kind of force
65 Corner joint
66 How some sandwiches are made
67 Wallowing sites
69 Cause of a breakdown
70 ___ of Venice
75 Movie genre
77 Element used for shielding nuclear reactors
78 Rank below capt.
79 Möbius strip, e.g.
80 Troops' harvest?
81 Athletic supporters?
82 Title below marquis
85 Big name in faucets
88 Balcony window
90 "What's it gonna be?"
91 Whip
93 Some "Men in Black" characters, for short
95 Card game akin to Authors

by Kelsey Blakley

96 Time for the balcony scene in "Romeo and Juliet"
98 Managed
99 "The Faerie Queene" character
100 It may punctuate a court order
101 Fence straddler
104 Annual advertising award
107 It may come in buckets
108 First name at Woodstock
109 Barnes & Noble electronic reader
111 Stuck in ___
112 Tag callers?
114 "Get it?"
115 Bunch
116 Reproachful cluck
117 Mess up

Looking for more Sunday Crosswords?

The New York Times

The #1 Name in Crosswords

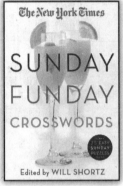
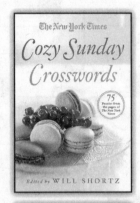

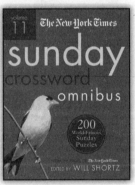

Available at your local bookstore or online at
us.macmillan.com/author/thenewyorktimes

 ST. MARTIN'S GRIFFIN

1

```
P O S T H O C   B E A A R T H U R   R O B
O A T M E A L   E V A P O R A T E   E R R
S T R I P T E A S E A R T I S T S   P D A
S E A   H E F T S       P E T E R I
E S P Y S   S R O   W T O   R U N O N S
    E A S E O F F T H E G A S P E D A L
R A S S L E     O V E R D O     U N E
U N W I S E I N V E S T M E N T   E C C E
M T I D A   C O E     S N E A K P E E K
P O L O   C E R E A L S     P I A
S N L   N O E M P T Y T H R E A T   M E L
    F R Y     T E N U O U S   S A L E
G I V E A L I F T     T O R   S E Z M E
A C I D   Y O U A R E O U T O F O R D E R
I A N   W R I E S T       B L E A R Y
U N E N V I A B L E P O S I T I O N
S T R A I N   Y S L     I S H   S A U T E
  G I S E L E       L E P E W   N O D
C O P   W I T H O U T A N Y W A R N I N G
H O E   E N T E R T A I N   I N V I T E E
I N N   D E A R S A N T A   Z E S T E R S
```

2

```
M C S   S A M B A   L E I C A     W O R M
C H E   A L A R M   A N N U M   F I X U P
G R A F F I T I P R O O F B U I L D I N G
R O S I E   S O L O     I S S U E D
A M O R     C E L S   O C E L O   I R T
W A N T S   T H R E E B L A D E R A Z O R
  O H I S E E     A R A L   E N E M Y
A S P   D E C   S O R R Y   B I S T R O
S P E L L C H E C K E R   H E N C E
C I N D E R   R A I D   L O R D E   J I B
A C E S   E L U D E   F O R G E   M O N A
P E R   T T O P S   K L E E   T O O B A D
    R H E T T   S N O W B O A R D I N G
  S P E E D S   S T I E S   V I A   N E E
S P U D S   W A I F   B A L L O T
A U T O M A T I C R E D I A L   B R E W S
G N U   U S E R S   S U C H   T R E O
  P E R O N I     M E A L   C I V I L
A L J A F F E E O F M A D M A G A Z I N E
L O O T S   T S A R S   A A R O N   E E L
E B B S   S T R A T   M S D O S   W R Y
```

3

E	S	S	A	Y		S	C	O	T		B	I	B	L	E		G	R	A	B
P	I	P	P	A		A	U	T	O		A	F	F	I	X		O	H	M	E
S	L	E	E	P	I	N	T	H	E	B	U	F	F	E	T		D	E	U	S
O	V	E	R		O	K	I	E		R	B	I			R	A	S	S	L	E
M	A	D	C	O	W		T	R	A	I	L	E	R	P	A	R	Q	U	E	T
		U	A	E				L	E	E	R	A	T		M	U	S	T		
N	B	A		T	Y	P	E	A	B			S	A	L	S	A			
C	O	L	D	H	A	R	D	C	A	C	H	E	T		A	D	D	L	E	D
I	D	L	E	S		O	I	L		R	O	S	A	N	N	E		I	V	Y
S	E	E	M		A	F	T		A	B	A		I	C	A	N	S	E	E	
	Y	O	U	V	E	H	A	D	Y	O	U	R	F	I	L	E	T			
S	P	O	N	G	E	S		B	R	O		E	T	A		W	I	N	K	
O	H	O		L	E	S	B	I	A	N		W	I	I		E	M	C	E	E
P	I	P	P	I	N		L	E	T	S	M	A	K	E	A	D	E	L	A	Y
		E	N	O	K	I			O	S	I	R	I	S		E	L	S		
	M	O	R	E		O	N	B	A	S	E			R	E	F			
B	A	C	K	S	T	A	G	E	P	A	S	S	E		B	L	A	R	E	D
L	A	T	I	S	H		C	P	R		W	A	Z	E		M	O	J	O	
A	L	O	E		U	N	S	O	L	I	C	I	T	E	D	B	I	D	E	T
M	O	P	S		G	R	I	M	E		O	N	E	S		O	N	I	C	E
E	X	I	T		S	A	T	E	S		B	E	N	T		G	E	N	T	S

4

	R	A	I	D		I	D	T	A	G		G	R	A	D	I	E	N	T
	Z	E	L	D	A		N	E	A	L	E		R	O	L	E	P	L	A	Y
J	O	L	L	Y	R	A	N	C	H	E	R		O	U	T	C	A	S	T	S
A	R	I	E	L		C	I	A	O		T	U	G	S	O	N			
I	B	E	G			T	E	L	E	S	C	O	P	E		D	E	V	I	L
L	A	S	E	R	S			T	O	N			G	E	M	I	N	I	
		B	L	I	S	S	F	U	L	I	G	N	O	R	A	N	C	E	
A	S	K		G	A	N	Y	M	E	D	E		U	F	O	S			
U	T	E	P		Y	E	L	L	S		W	I	L	D		B	I	F	F
G	R	E	A	S	E			T	A	M	A	L	E		T	E	T	R	A
H	A	P	P	Y	D	A	Y	S	A	R	E	H	E	R	E	A	G	A	I	N
T	I	T	A	N		M	O	U	L	I	N			R	O	I	L	E	D
S	N	O	W		J	O	S	E		T	A	M	P	A		N	I	N	O
		P	O	O	H		S	T	O	N	E	A	G	E		A	D	M	
C	H	E	E	R	Y	D	I	S	P	O	S	I	T	I	O	N			
D	E	I	M	O	S		H	E	M			N	O	S	I	E	R	
C	Y	N	I	C		C	H	E	W	B	A	C	C	A		A	M	B	I
	T	E	A	R	E	D		T	A	L	L		A	R	S	O	N	
S	T	A	T	E	L	A	W		M	E	R	R	Y	G	O	R	O	U	N	D
L	O	V	E	D	O	N	E		N	A	I	A	D		H	E	N	R	Y
R	O	A	D	S	T	E	R		O	R	A	T	E		M	A	G	E	

5

```
S N A R F   J U S T S O   M A N N E R E D
W A L D O   U N P A C K   I T S A L I V E
I D E A L B R E A K E R   N E W H A V E N
F I X   K E Y     E N A M E L     P A R S
T R A U M A   B U N T S E R I O U S L Y
    L U S H E S       A V E R S E
L A W N S T U D E N T S   A R L O   S A W
S I N A I   M E R L O T   S Y S T O L E
A M B   C O B   S C R U B S   H A S T E
T E A S   B E D   S O F A I R S O G O O D
    P E O R I A     O N E T W O
L I N E D E T E C T O R   E T A   N C O S
T H E C W     S E A D O G   I R E   A L A
D O R S A L S     L E B R O N   G O M A D
S P F   R O O S   L A B O R O F G L O V E
    A D U L T S     A S L O P E
  I N V I S I B L E S I N K   G L O B A L
C H O O     D A R W I N     S I A   E R A
H O T W A T E R   E X T R A I N N I N G S
A P I A R I S T   R A R I N G   T R I O S
S E T L I S T S   S M O O T H   S A N T O
```

6

```
C I R C E   A B R A M   O B J E C T O R S
U B E R X   H U E V O   B E A V E R H A T
L I F E C O A C H E S   I N B A L A N C E
  D E T E R   S Y R U P   T O N E P O E M
  R E L A Y   D Y L A N   U S S
U K E   T E A R   N O O K   T I B I A
S I N G L E S B A R S   D R I V E N U T S
U N D E A D   A T E A M   B E E   L I S T
A D U L T   S C E P T E R S   S T E L M O
L A M   E M M A   I S O   S P U T T E R
  T R O U B L E S H O O T E R S
M I G R A N T   O A F   P A R M   T S P
A Q U I L A   D O C I L I T Y   O P I N E
S U I T   C H E   H E I D I   M I A M O R
T I D E P O O L S   S P A M F I L T E R S
S T O R E   T I E D   B A I L   C E E
    A L E   A R R O W   B L A I R
B A R E S A L L   S I Z E D   E N N U I
A N I M A T I O N   P O L O G R O U N D S
G E T I N H E R E   U N L I T   D I C E S
S W E L T E R E D   P E S T O   E T H A N
```

7

```
LOCAL     THOU   JAKE
PARTI  AFC HENNA  ATON
STARE  MOA ELTON  WARD
   MISSIONIMPOSSIBLE
ITSALOSTCAUSE  ENOLA
MRI  ISLETS    LIN
PENPAL OLEELO  NEMEA
   HIS NOISEROCK ANT
GMAIL  GUT GASH  IDS
RIDS PSST OILSUP NET
ANAHEIM  RATBITE MAR
SIM SCISSOR FERRERA
POW CATHAY BAYS ANEW
IRE SHAY RON  STUDS
NES SASHAYING TIE
GOTTO SHAYNE RASPED
  OUI HAYLEY  BRA
ICONS NEEDLESSTOSAY
NEEDLEINAHAYSTACK
SELA ALGER SEE LAILA
URLS MMHMM SSN OLDEN
ETSY  STYE   NASTY
```

8

```
POEM PHIL TRIP INFECT
ENTOURAGE HURL SOOTHE
PECORINOCHEESE SCOTIA
PECLASS HUH AQUADUCK
   ALTO ELITESQUAD
ARI SILK ALEX EEL BIG
HAND NOOB LACED SODA
ENCODE RASSLED HIYALL
ABIDE SELL GLUTENFREE
ABSOFREAKINGLUTELY
DYE TUX PAR RAI SIR
  BESTRAPPERFORMANCE
THIRSTTRAP EASY BREED
VANITY IMEANIT SOYEAH
AIDE COEDS DOME ARGO
DRY RAH BUTT PUTS YET
  LATEPAPERS SCAM
ROLLATWO RAW TRUESUP
ORIENT BENICIODELTORO
DAMAGE OPUS MODELTANK
ELOPED YANK SHOW APSE
```

```
L E G U P   ■   A W A R D   ■   R A N S A C K
O P I N E D   ■   B A B O O N   ■   E P I C U R E
C O V E R E D B R I D G E   ■   G E T I T O N
A D E   ■   G A I A   ■   L I N E A R   ■   S O W   ■
L E S S O N S   ■   G I N A   ■   R E L I S T   ■
■   A I L   ■   M O E T   ■   P O T T Y M O U T H
G E R M A N A R M Y   ■   P A Y   ■   N A R N I A
A R I   ■   A Y E S   ■   P E R F I D Y   ■   E N D
D A D B O D S   ■   T E R R   ■   A M A   ■   A R G O
S T E E L E   ■   N O T E   ■   B R A   ■   O L S E N
■   G A R D E N A P A R T M E N T   ■
S P R A Y   ■   O W E   ■   P L A Y   ■   D E E P E R
T E E N   ■   B U D   ■   S E E D   ■   M I S R U L E
A R M   ■   S U R E D I D   ■   P O O F   ■   T E E
V I E F O R   ■   A R R   ■   D I R T Y T R I C K
E L M E R S G L U E   ■   O T O H   ■   R U N   ■
■   B E E T L E   ■   N T W T   ■   E D I T O R S
■   B E D   ■   A R I S E N   ■   A R E S   ■   R O C
C A R L S J R   ■   C O M P A S S N E E D L E
O R E O P I E   ■   U N P A C K   ■   S C R E E N
L S D T A B S   ■   G O T H S   ■   T A R O T
```

```
D O C   ■   S C A B   ■   A C H E S   ■   T E R M S   ■
O P A   ■   L O R I   ■   C H I L L   ■   A S I A N S
R E M   ■   I G E T A K I C K O U T O F Y O U
I R E   ■   M I T E R   ■   ■   S T A P L E R S
C A R R Y T H A T W E I G H T   ■   H E R E S
■   H A I   ■   O A T   ■   A X L E   ■   E R A   ■
C O C O   ■   ■   T C E L L   ■   R E G A T T A
H U R T S S O G O O D   ■   ■   P U S H I T
U S E   ■   P U P A E   ■   T O M S   ■   S K E E T
M E W   ■   E V E R T   ■   F I N A L   ■   E A S Y
■   I W A N N A B E S E D A T E D   ■
U S P S   ■   T E P I D   ■   E E L E D   ■   Z A P
R E A L M   ■   O R S O   ■   A D O R E   ■   O D E
S C R E A M   ■   I M C O M I N G O U T
A T A T R O T   ■   D E N C H   ■   M A L E
■   G N U   ■   A L T A   ■   A N A   ■   A N T   ■
A M E B A   ■   B A B Y O N E M O R E T I M E
C A N A R I E S   ■   A B U T S   ■   M O T
T H E K I D S A R E A L R I G H T   ■   A V A
S E R E N E   ■   M A R R Y   ■   T A R O   ■   L I P
■   R O S E S   ■   I T S M E   ■   S T O P   ■   S E E
```

11

```
BRAH  EGGO  MERLE  APSO
LAME  TRON  PAEAN  CRUMP
UNEDUCATEDGUESS  TAPER
RUNGS  NOLO  VEE  SIEGE
PSEUDO  BETTERMOU  RAP
TRALA  RBI  BIPOD
HAI  PLANT  APPALL  GUMP
ATOMS  THE  TONE  BOPIT
MITE  GOODSORT  SEDERS
STAR  GENUIN  TICLE  RED
SPAN  SAO  BURN
ISM  SILIC  RUBBER  IBAR
MAILIN  CAFENOIR  NONO
AURAS  COIF  DOE  TEXTS
CLAP  PANNED  PRIVA  YES
COOED  CUE  STERN
SEL  BRICATING  STIFFS
ALEXA  LOT  ZONA  FILTH
ALBUM  LASTDITCHEFFORT
BERRA  ATEAM  MAIM  TRAM
NAYS  CIAOS  EATS  YAWL
```

12

```
DISCS  CATS  ASKS  VAMPS
ICARE  ACHY  UNIT  INOIL
MERYL  IRAN  TIME  GATOR
DIFFERENCEOFOPINIONS
OSLO  HALFNOTES
CLAROS  OWETO  OUST  IMP
HIGHWAYMEDIAN  TATTLER
ALIEN  OAT  TNUT  EVITE
TALL  CURIO  BOOT  MARS
SCEPTER  NERD  AVOCADOS
STOCKDIVIDEND
HOTSAUCE  SODA  RATTRAP
OPAL  SKOR  SMELL  RELO
ORNOT  SNOW  SEA  HADIT
DAGWOOD  ANIMALPRODUCT
SHO  ALIA  ENEMY  AMEXES
SPAREROOM  AFEW
MODEOFTRANSPORTATION
ATARI  IAGO  HAIL  ENDOW
GOTIN  ETON  IKEA  ADELE
SHAFT  RENE  SSNS  MSDOS
```

13

R	A	D	N	E	R	░	S	O	T	S	░	S	E	A	M	S	░	B	F	A
A	S	I	A	G	O	░	N	C	A	A	░	C	L	I	O	A	W	A	R	D
P	H	A	R	O	S	░	I	T	L	L	░	H	I	M	A	L	A	Y	A	S
C	O	L	E	░	A	D	V	O	C	A	T	E	D	░	B	E	T	A	S	░
D	R	I	P	░	S	E	E	M	░	D	O	M	E	S	░	S	C	R	I	M
S	E	N	T	░	S	L	O	G	░	P	E	S	O	S	░	H	E	E	D	░
░	I	M	A	M	░	M	A	C	J	R	░	D	A	B	E	A	R	S	░	░
H	O	T	C	O	C	O	A	░	R	H	O	░	D	A	V	I	D	░	░	░
A	N	A	░	W	E	N	T	B	Y	E	B	Y	E	░	O	N	E	I	D	A
R	A	M	░	D	O	R	I	C	░	A	N	T	I	D	O	T	E	S	░	░
A	R	E	░	T	U	T	░	I	N	K	E	R	░	I	R	S	░	A	B	C
S	U	R	F	I	N	U	S	A	░	M	I	D	A	S	░	░	L	T	E	░
S	N	A	I	L	S	░	I	N	B	A	D	S	H	A	P	E	░	I	O	N
░	D	E	T	E	R	░	R	T	E	░	A	M	E	X	C	A	R	D	░	░
E	G	G	D	R	O	P	░	M	Y	E	R	S	░	O	A	T	H	░	░	░
L	E	A	R	░	W	E	I	R	D	░	S	O	T	U	░	A	L	L	Y	░
I	T	S	O	K	░	E	N	J	O	Y	░	J	E	S	U	░	L	I	E	U
░	F	L	U	E	S	░	D	O	N	O	T	O	P	E	N	░	K	O	N	G
B	R	I	N	G	I	T	I	N	░	S	H	U	E	░	C	U	A	N	D	O
T	E	N	D	E	R	A	G	E	░	H	I	R	E	░	U	N	R	E	E	L
W	E	E	░	L	E	G	O	S	░	I	N	N	S	░	T	I	T	L	E	D

14

A	C	T	O	R	S	░	A	D	R	E	P	░	S	C	A	M	P	E	R	S
F	R	O	M	E	A	R	T	O	E	A	R	░	P	O	W	E	R	N	A	P
L	I	N	E	I	T	E	M	V	E	T	O	░	A	M	A	R	E	T	T	O
A	M	E	N	D	░	T	O	E	D	░	P	A	R	E	R	░	P	I	E	T
T	E	S	S	░	B	A	S	S	░	F	E	R	R	I	E	D	░	C	A	L
░	░	░	░	B	R	I	T	░	H	O	L	D	O	N	░	U	N	I	T	E
S	P	A	T	I	A	L	░	M	E	L	L	O	W	░	C	R	A	N	E	S
H	I	G	H	E	S	T	B	I	D	D	E	R	░	C	O	S	I	G	N	S
R	E	H	A	B	░	H	O	G	G	E	D	░	M	O	O	L	A	░	░	░
I	P	A	D	░	R	E	N	N	E	R	░	S	A	I	L	E	D	O	F	F
N	A	S	░	P	E	R	N	O	D	░	B	A	R	N	E	Y	░	N	I	L
E	N	T	E	R	T	A	I	N	░	W	I	N	K	E	D	░	H	A	L	O
░	░	C	O	U	P	E	░	B	O	N	D	E	D	░	D	O	U	L	A	░
B	I	G	O	T	R	Y	░	F	O	R	G	E	T	A	B	O	U	T	I	T
A	L	A	N	O	N	░	B	R	O	K	E	R	░	P	A	T	R	O	N	S
L	O	G	O	N	░	T	E	E	M	E	D	░	R	H	Y	S	░	░	░	░
D	V	R	░	S	P	E	A	R	E	D	░	H	E	R	S	░	L	O	R	E
N	E	E	T	░	A	L	T	E	R	░	P	E	P	A	░	M	A	N	I	A
E	Y	E	R	O	L	L	S	░	A	S	I	W	A	S	S	A	Y	I	N	G
S	O	L	A	R	I	U	M	░	N	O	T	E	V	E	N	C	L	O	S	E
S	U	S	P	E	N	S	E	░	G	L	A	D	E	░	L	E	A	N	E	R

15

BAUM · NATCH · TWAS
ORWORSE · EMILE · ARCHFOE
HOISTED · SPEAR · BYTURNS
SYNCS · INTURMOIL · STEEP
NATS · SCRIP · SIDEB · SETI
ALE · APIAN · SOHOT · HOE
PER · LEN · GETEM · OBO · ENS
INDEED · LAC · RCCOLA
MUCHACHO · ETH · UKULELES
OPEL · HAH · COO · NET · ATRA
USHER · TAUTOLOGY · ASHEN
STORES · PRIOR · FATCAT
SAT · MEHDEINCANADA · ADA
ETES · QUINCEANERA · WREN
SELLS · EDDA · TGIF · CIERA
AIG · ISL · EEL · MUG
OLDPROS · EARSHOT
GORDIEHOWE · LESLIEHOPE
LEIA · SATAY · ILHAN · OLIN
EWES · BLIGE · FLITS · PLUS
SESH · YESES · TENET · SAME

16

TAROT · OGRE · BARRE · HTML
ALARM · OREL · FLEAS · AHOY
CONCONFUSESFUSES · VICE
OHBABY · BEATSME · LARKS
SAY · ILK · ANO · NATIONS
ELONELONGATESGATES
LEAVENED · REO · ELANTRA
ARIA · ANS · ACUMEN · RAT
MANMANDATESDATES · CASE
ESTATE · ATE · MED · MOPED
ROT · CYCLOPS · ION
CUMIN · AHS · MMA · DOGMAS
OPIE · ANAANAGRAMSGRAMS
BTS · ADSITE · IRA · ANON
ROSSSEA · BYU · ELECTORS
APPAPPRAISESRAISES
ELITISM · SEE · ATV · FAA
AFLAC · SOANDSO · EIDERS
LOLA · PROPROCURESCURES
POEM · GOREY · AMEX · HENNA
ODDS · AETNA · REST · ESSAY

17

S	C	A	M	S		E	V	E	R	G	T	R	E	E		A	K	I	T	A
H	A	N	O	I		P	A	P	E	R	H	A	T	S		W	A	G	E	D
A	N	N	U	L		E	S	O	T	E	R	I	C	A		A	Z	U	R	E
S	T	A	N	L	E	E		C	R	E	E	D		U	P	R	O	A	R	S
T	O	L	D	Y	A			H	O	N	E	S			I	D	O	N	O	T
A	S	S		M	R	T					R	T	E		A	R	E			
		M	E	L	L	O	W	Y		O	L	B	E	Y	E	S				
A	B	B	A		C	R	I	E	D	W	O	L	F		R	A	F	A		
B	L	O	O	D	O		S	I	L	E	N	T	U		I	G	I	R	L	S
E	A	R		A	R	L	O		L	A	A		E	R	N	O		C	U	P
T	H	E	P	L	A	Y		C	O	N	G	O		O	D	D	J	O	B	S
			H	A	N	D	S	A	W		E	N	Q	U	I	R	E			
P	R	O	D	I	G	I	E	S			B	U	G	G	Y	W	H	I	P	
F	I	N	S		E	A	R	T	H		J	A	I	H	O		S	A	M	E
F	C	C			E	L	O		O	I	L					S	A	T		
T	H	E	R	P	L	A	N	E	T		U	L	T	R	A	V	R	A	Y	S
		D	E	L	I	M	E		S	L	R		E	E	L	I	E	R		
G	R	A	D	A	T	E	S		T	O	N		R	A	W	O	N	I	O	N
O	U	I		C	O	N	T	R	O	V	E	R	S	I	A	L		G	P	A
A	T	L		I	U	D		A	N	E	Y	E		R	Y	E		H	E	S
T	H	Y		D	T	S		M	E	S	S	Y		S	S	T		T	N	T

18

	R	A	T	E	D	R		T	U	B	M	A	N			R	A	B	I	D
B	O	B	A	T	E	A		A	P	R	I	C	O	T		E	L	O	P	E
G	U	A	R	D	E	D	O	P	T	I	M	I	S	M		L	O	T	S	A
A	S	T	O		P	I	U		O	M	E	N		C	L	A	P	T	O	N
M	E	E	T		C	A	T	E		L	O	C	H		A	X	E	L		
E	D	S		C	U	L	T	U	R	E	S	H	O	C	K		C	E	C	E
			P	A	T		O	L	A	Y			T	E	E	N	I	D	O	L
B	B	G	U	N		T	W	O	S		G	O	O	D		S	A	U	N	A
Y	U	R	T	S		H	I	G	H	A	N	X	I	E	T	Y		P	A	N
E	G	O	T		Z	A	N	Y		W	A	I	L		A	N	W	A	R	
	S	W	E	D	E	N			T	O	W		D	O	C	E	N	T		
	B	I	D	E	N		N	O	O	K		A	M	E	S		T	G	I	F
D	U	N		C	O	M	I	C	R	E	L	I	E	F		O	B	E	S	E
A	N	G	L	O		I	N	T	O		O	R	G	Y		B	A	R	T	Y
U	N	C	A	R	I	N	G			A	L	B	A		H	E	R			
B	Y	O	B		U	N	B	R	I	D	L	E	D	J	O	Y		V	A	T
		N	E	R	D		O	E	N	O		D	O	U	R		D	I	V	A
N	O	C	L	A	S	S		S	F	P	D		S	I	M		A	G	E	S
O	B	E	L	I		C	R	E	A	T	U	R	E	C	O	M	F	O	R	T
M	I	R	E	D		I	P	A	N	E	M	A		E	N	R	O	U	T	E
S	E	N	D	S		I	T	T	E	A	M		D	E	T	E	R	S		

```
D R E S S A G E   M Y B A D   N A P L E S
R E S T A T E D   C O U L D   O M E A R A
U N P O I S E D   B U R D E N O F P O O F
G O O P D Y N A M I C S   E N M A S S E
      S M A   E T A   P E T E R
O D D J O B   B R E N D A N   R A M P E D
T E R I   O D E   S T I L T S   D R A C O
I A M M A L A L A   H E A R T   I M R A N
S L O M O   M I L W A U K E E B O O E R S
    S M O K E   E V E N   E E L   J E D
      R I C K   A D D E R   P O P O
    S S R   I T O   L O A F   T O R S O
T A M I N G O F T H E S H O O   L I T H E
A R I S E   W Y A T T   M I N U S S I G N
R A Z O R   N O R T H S   L O N   I C E R
T H E N F L   R E P E A L S   D O N K E Y
      B A R E S   T M I   S E N
I M I T A T E   B O O T S T R E N G T H
P E N E L O P E C O O S   E U P H O R I A
S A G E L Y   S O R T A   E M A I L I N G
O D E S S A   O P A H S   N P R T O T E S
```

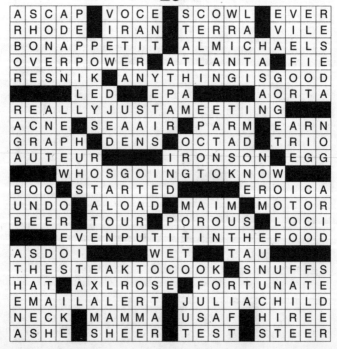

```
A S C A P   V O C E   S C O W L   E V E R
R H O D E   I R A N   T E R R A   V I L E
B O N A P P E T I T   A L M I C H A E L S
O V E R P O W E R   A T L A N T A   F I E
R E S N I K   A N Y T H I N G I S G O O D
      L E D   E P A     A O R T A
R E A L L Y J U S T A M E E T I N G
A C N E   S E A A I R   P A R M   E A R N
G R A P H   D E N S   O C T A D   T R I O
A U T E U R     I R O N S O N   E G G
    W H O S G O I N G T O K N O W
B O O   S T A R T E D   E R O I C A
U N D O   A L O A D   M A I M   M O T O R
B E E R   T O U R   P O R O U S   L O C I
    E V E N P U T I T I N T H E F O O D
A S D O I     W E T   T A U
T H E S T E A K T O C O O K   S N U F F S
H A T   A X L R O S E   F O R T U N A T E
E M A I L A L E R T   J U L I A C H I L D
N E C K   M A M M A   U S A F   H I R E E
A S H E   S H E E R   T E S T   S T E E R
```

21

Puzzle 21 grid (letters with circled asterisks):

```
A S P   S A T   O A S E S   T O M   R D A
(*)P A D P R O   A L E V E   A N T W E R P
L I B R A R Y   K E V I N   (*)N F A V O R
E L L I C E   Y (*)E L D   E U G E N E
S T O N E A G E   A N D   F R (*)J O L E S
  K (*)R I N   N O E   L A T I N
N O R I   S A N D (*)E G A N   O A T S
B R O N T E   T I R E D L Y   I F F (*)E R
C A T G U T   I C A N S E E   D A H L (*)A
  G R E E C E   A D S I T E
M A J O R (*)S   R A M E N   P O L A R (*)S
A L O U E T T E   S I R   N A T I V E T O
C O U R T   (*)S S A R A E   P E R I L
A U L D   G N A T   L A N E   N A N O
O D E   C U O M O S   A T T I L A   N A S
  B A S E   I L A N A   (*)M D B
O D I U M   (*)N C O G N I T O   J O Y C E
P R O S E C C O   W E E   O N E U P P E D
R A W   D O U B L E D (*)P P E R S   R E I
A K A   U P S E T S   E S P R I T   E L F
H E N   E Y E L E T   S U S A N S   S O Y
```

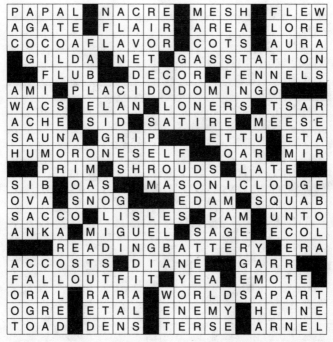

22

Puzzle 22 grid:

```
P A P A L   N A C R E   M E S H   F L E W
A G A T E   F L A I R   A R E A   L O R E
C O C O A F L A V O R   C O T S   A U R A
  G I L D A   N E T   G A S S T A T I O N
  F L U B   D E C O R   F E N N E L S
A M I   P L A C I D O D O M I N G O
W A C S   E L A N   L O N E R S   T S A R
A C H E   S I D   S A T I R E   M E E S E
S A U N A   G R I P   E T T U   E T A
H U M O R O N E S E L F   O A R   M I R
  P R I M   S H R O U D S   L A T E
S I B   O A S   M A S O N I C L O D G E
O V A   S N O G   E D A M   S Q U A B
S A C C O   L I S L E S   P A M   U N T O
A N K A   M I G U E L   S A G E   E C O L
  R E A D I N G B A T T E R Y   E R A
A C C O S T S   D I A N E   G A R R
F A L L O U T F I T   Y E A   E M O T E
O R A L   R A R A   W O R L D S A P A R T
O G R E   E T A L   E N E M Y   H E I N E
T O A D   D E N S   T E R S E   A R N E L
```

23

N	O	W	N	O	W		F	L	A	K		C	L	U		D	A	W	N	S
A	V	I	A	T	E		L	I	M	A		O	O	P		A	L	E	U	T
T	U	F	T	E	D		O	V	E	R	S	H	O	T		N	I	F	T	Y
O	M	E	A	R	A		W	E	S	T	W	E	F	O	R	G	E	T		
	G	L	I	S	T	E	N	S		I	R	A	N	I		N	B	C		
O	B	O	E		T	H	R	U		A	P	E		O	T	B		E	O	E
C	E	E		D	R	E		P	A	T	E	N	T	W	E	A	T	H	E	R
A	L	S	O	R	A	N	S		L	E	D	T	O			W	H	I	R	R
L	O	O	N	E	Y		E	M	I			O	P	U	L	E	N	C	E	
A	W	N	E	D		P	E	A	S	E		E	K	E	S		O	D	E	D
			G	I	A	N	T	W	I	Z	A	R	D							
O	C	T	S		P	E	S	O		E	R	E	C	T		G	O	M	A	D
F	O	O	T	P	A	T	H			E	R	A		S	E	C	E	D	E	
F	R	E	E	H		O	L	S	E	N		B	A	I	L	S	M	A	N	
A	R	T	W	I	N	K	W	E	T	T	E	R		R	C	S		O	Z	S
L	A	H		Z	E	N		G	I	S		E	W	O	K		C	R	E	E
	L	E	T		N	A	S	A	L		A	R	R	O	W	K	E	Y		
	W	A	K	E	V	I	C	T	O	R	I	A			E	A	R	W	I	G
A	M	I	S	H		E	X	I	S	T	E	N	T		A	R	I	A	N	A
F	A	N	T	A		R	E	E		T	E	S	H		V	A	U	N	T	S
T	W	E	E	N		Y	R	S		O	L	E	S		E	N	M	E	S	H

24

M	A	D		M	I	S	C		A	M	B	O		D	I	S	COS	T	U
A	R	A	B		A	S	A	D		R	O	A	N		A	S	A	M	A	N
M	I	N	E		C	A	TAN	D	M	O	U	S	E		S	U	D	O	K	U
E	S	T	A	T	E	S		R	E	D	E	E	M	S		P	I	K	E	S
T	E	E	T	H		G	I	L		D	I	D	I		E	R	A		
	SIN	N	E	R		A	V	I		L	I	N	I	N	G		A	R	E	
I	M	F	I	N	E		D	E	S	M	O	N	D		B	L	A	M	E	S
S	E	E	K	E	R	S		S	Y	N			S	O	O	N	E	S	T	
I	S	R		T	U	T		B	A	D	G	E		A	L	B	E	R	T	A
T	O	N		N	A	T	E		A	T	M	I	D	D	A	Y				
I	N	O	N	E		R	E	S	T	R	O	O	M	S		L	E	T	C	H
		O	L	I	V	E	O	Y	L		N	A	A	N			W	E	E	
R	I	B	C	A	G	E		T	R	I	G	O		C	I	T		O	D	E
I	D	E	A	T	E	D		O	N	A		K	N	E	E	P	A	D		
C	O	L	L	E	T		H	A	N	G	M	A	N		T	A	X	E	R	S
E	N	L		S	I	M	O	N	E		B	M	I		H	A	H	A		
	T	I	A		T	R	O	T		L	O	X		C	A	SIN	O	S		
A	C	COS	T	S		S	P	I	T	Z	E	R		S	I	T	U	A	T	E
M	A	I	T	A	I		E	Q	U	I	D	I	S	TAN	T		S	P	E	X
O	R	T	E	G	A		R	U	N	T		S	I	Z	E		T	O	R	E
K	E	Y	N	E	S		S	E	A	S		T	R	A	M			D	O	S

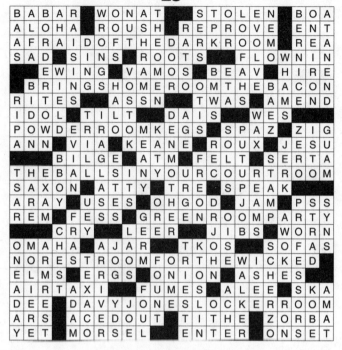

```
B A B A R ■ W O N A T ■ ■ S T O L E N ■ B O A
A L O H A ■ R O U S H ■ R E P R O V E ■ E N T
A F R A I D O F T H E D A R K R O O M ■ R E A
S A D ■ S I N S ■ R O O T S ■ ■ F L O W N I N
■ ■ E W I N G ■ V A M O S ■ B E A V ■ H I R E
■ B R I N G S H O M E R O O M T H E B A C O N
R I T E S ■ ■ A S S N ■ T W A S ■ A M E N D
I D O L ■ T I L T ■ D A I S ■ ■ W E S ■ ■
P O W D E R R O O M K E G S ■ S P A Z ■ Z I G
A N N ■ V I A ■ K E A N E ■ R O U X ■ J E S U
■ ■ B I L G E ■ A T M ■ F E L T ■ S E R T A
T H E B A L L S I N Y O U R C O U R T R O O M
S A X O N ■ A T T Y ■ T R E ■ S P E A K ■ ■
A R A Y ■ U S E S ■ O H G O D ■ J A M ■ P S S
R E M ■ F E S S ■ G R E E N R O O M P A R T Y
■ ■ C R Y ■ L E E R ■ J I B S ■ W O R N
O M A H A ■ A J A R ■ T K O S ■ ■ S O F A S
N O R E S T R O O M F O R T H E W I C K E D
E L M S ■ E R G S ■ O N I O N ■ A S H E S ■
A I R T A X I ■ F U M E S ■ A L E E ■ S K A
D E E ■ D A V Y J O N E S L O C K E R R O O M
A R S ■ A C E D O U T ■ T I T H E ■ Z O R B A
Y E T ■ M O R S E L ■ ■ E N T E R ■ O N S E T
```

```
■ L O F T ■ D E A D O N ■ ■ U P S I D E C
H E L L O ■ E R N E S T ■ E L E O N O R A
T O M E I ■ E R E S T U ■ H A R D L O O K
T I E C L I P S ■ P O P G U N ■ A A N D E
P I C K E D S ■ M I S L E D ■ P A Y E E S
■ ■ ■ S T E ■ R O S I E R ■ T I S ■ ■ ■
A C C ■ S A L I N E S ■ T W O H E A D S
L O O S ■ S L A T ■ S W O O N ■ X M E N
L O U T S ■ O L E O ■ T E E F ■ S T A L E
A L R E A D Y ■ S U P R A S ■ C A R R I E
■ T R I A D ■ S T E A K ■ A I L E Y ■
S M E L L Y ■ J O I N I N ■ G R E M L I N
O A S I S ■ F E R N ■ N E M O ■ S E L M A
C L A N ■ D L E I F ■ S A G E ■ W I N G
K I N G L E A R ■ E A S E O N T ■ S O S
■ ■ A U K ■ S P A T E S ■ O H M ■ ■
S P A W N S ■ P E A R L S ■ C L E A N S E
P A L E O ■ M O E S H A ■ L I A R L I A R
O N E F L E S H ■ H A N S O M ■ O A S T S
S E T T I N G S ■ A R T U R O ■ A W A I T
E D A S N E R ■ S T A N D C ■ D I N E
```

27

T	H	I	R	D	R	A	T	E		R	E	B	U	S		E	C	U	A
O	R	A	T	O	R	I	C	A	L		U	T	O	P	I	A	N	I	S	M
T	O	P	S	B	O	T	T	O	M		F	A	T	S	S	K	I	N	N	Y
T	D	S		B	O	A	S			P	U	S	H	Y		I	D	E	A	L
		R	E	P			S	K	I	S			D	D	S			
M	A	J	O	R	S	M	I	N	O	R		B	E	A	R	S	B	U	L	L
A	V	O	W			A	M	A	N	A		A	L	I	E		E	S	A	U
L	I	N	D	A		S	A	R	A	N		H	E	S	S		D	A	T	S
P	L	A	Y	S	W	O	R	K		H	E	A	V	Y	S	L	I	G	H	T
H	A	S		H	O	N	E		B	A	R	I			A	M	E	S	S
			C	O	S	T	C	O		A	S	S	E	N	T	
A	S	P	C	A			R	I	G	S		M	A	N	E		F	W	D
S	P	R	I	N	G	S	F	A	L	L		H	I	R	E	S	F	I	R	E
B	I	O	G		O	T	A	Y		A	B	O	R	T		T	O	X	I	N
I	R	M	A		T	R	I	O		N	O	T	C	H		R	E	N	T
G	O	S	R	E	T	U	R	N		C	A	S	H	S	C	H	A	R	G	E
			R	A	M		V	E	R	Y			H	E	Y	
A	G	A	I	N		M	I	S	E	R		W	E	A	L		Z	A	G
L	E	F	T	S	R	I	G	H	T		P	A	R	K	S	D	R	I	V	E
F	L	A	T	T	E	N	O	U	T		S	W	E	E	T	I	E	P	I	E
A	T	R	Y		A	G	R	E	E		T	E	N	S	E	N	E	S	S

28

E	A	T	M	E		E	R	A		C	I	T	E		A	R	A	R	A	T
S	C	R	A	M	B	L	E	D		O	N	E	M	O	R	E	T	I	M	E
S	A	Y	H	E	Y	K	I	D		H	U	S	B	A	N	D	T	O	B	E
E	S	T	E	R	S		N	E	V	E	R	S		T	A	H	I	T	I
S	T	O	R	Y		V	E	N	I	R	E		B	E	Z	E	L
			B	A	D	D	I	E		K	O	S		N	A	B	O	B
R	A	D		S	E	M	I	S			P	E	U				R	O	I
I	R	E		C	A	P	N		R	E	T	I	N	A	E		S	I	Z	E
D	U	M	D	U	M	S		D	A	M	A	S	C	U	S	S	T	E	E	L
O	B	I	E	S		H	E	L	P		T	E	E	T	E	R
F	A	T	T	E	D	C	A	L	F		T	E	R	R	A	C	O	T	T	A
		E	M	I	L	I	A		A	I	R	S			U	K	I	A	H
P	R	I	C	E	E	A	R	N	I	N	G	S		F	O	R	E	S	E	E
L	U	N	T		U	P	C	C	O	D	E		M	A	M	E		N	B	A
U	S	C			E	E	N			E	A	V	E	S		T	O	D
S	T	A	B	S		F	L	Y		B	O	U	T	O	N	
		R	A	H	A	L		T	A	R	T	A	R		C	O	I	G	N
	C	L	O	V	E	N		F	O	R	K	E	D		G	A	U	C	H	E
S	L	O	W	I	N	G	D	O	W	N		R	O	Y	A	L	T	I	E	S
R	A	I	N	O	R	S	H	I	N	E		P	R	E	S	I	D	E	N	T
O	R	N	E	R	Y		L	E	S	S		E	S	T		F	O	R	T	S

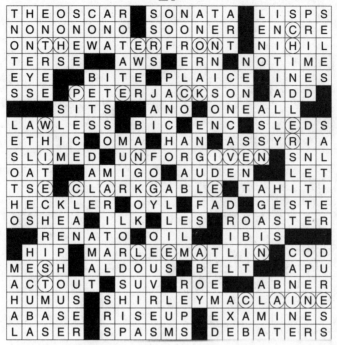

```
T H E O S C A R ■ S O N A T A ■ L I S P S
N O N O N O N O ■ S O O N E R ■ E N C R E
O N T H E W A T E R F R O N T ■ N I H I L
T E R S E ■ A W S ■ E R N ■ N O T I M E
E Y E ■ B I T E ■ P L A I C E ■ I N E S
S S E ■ P E T E R J A C K S O N ■ A D D
■ S I T S ■ A N O ■ O N E A L L ■
L A W L E S S ■ B I C ■ E N C ■ S L E D S
E T H I C ■ O M A ■ H A N ■ A S S Y R I A
S L I M E D ■ U N F O R G I V E N ■ S N L
O A T ■ A M I G O ■ A U D E N ■ L E T
T S E ■ C L A R K G A B L E ■ T A H I T I
H E C K L E R ■ O Y L ■ F A D ■ G E S T E
O S H E A ■ I L K ■ L E S ■ R O A S T E R
■ R E N A T O ■ O I L ■ I B I S ■
H I P ■ M A R L E E M A T L I N ■ C O D
M E S H ■ A L D O U S ■ B E L T ■ A P U
A C T O U T ■ S U V ■ R O E ■ A B N E R
H U M U S ■ S H I R L E Y M A C L A I N E
A B A S E ■ R I S E U P ■ E X A M I N E S
L A S E R ■ S P A S M S ■ D E B A T E R S
```

```
K O O L B I D ■ R E G S ■ C E C I L I A
O N L E A V E ■ A R O O M ■ U N I T I N G
I C E T R A Y ■ I N T R A ■ P R U S S I A
■ E S S E N ■ E L E C T S ■ S I D E A ■
■ D A D D Y S H A C K ■ C A L M S
I O C ■ M I A T A ■ G O O D F A T S
S T A R H A Z E R ■ W E B B ■ R I A
O H D E A R ■ D E N I M ■ J V D R I P S
L E G P A R T Y ■ S E G E R ■ E S T E E S
D R E S S ■ H A S T E ■ R E S E T S ■
E S S ■ N I X E D D R I N K S ■ A D O
■ S E E S I N ■ S O L T I ■ A S L A N
S N A T C H ■ S A U T E ■ S P Y B E A N S
P O P R U I Z ■ T H O S E ■ O M E N I I
A L P ■ E Y E S ■ S W I S S M I S T
M I L K D V D S ■ O P T I C ■ S H E
■ E E N I E ■ L O X P R O F I L E ■
■ G O N N A ■ S H R I N E ■ A S W A N
G O A T E E S ■ S O A M I ■ P U T I T O N
N U T T R E E ■ O S H E A ■ I R O N A G E
P R E S O R T ■ A S S N ■ C O P Y B O Z
```

```
H I G H C   B I O   F O R   D I O C E S E
O N E A L   A S C R I B E   E N R O L L S
I N N I E   N O T I F I C A N H E L P I T
  T R A N S L A T E   T I A   T A P E
U K E   I H A V E   S I M B A   S I R
T I E D   M E T E   I M P O S I T I O N S
E L L E R B E E   A M A I N   T O V
  B O Y S   S T A R K   N E S T S
T A B O O   B O O G I E   H O E   T I P
E V E N T H O R I Z O N   D I A S P O R A
M A L E   A U E L   M O T T   E G A D
P L U S S I G N   D I S A C C H A R I D E
T O G   U G H   B O R E R S   F L E E S
S N A R E   O N I C E   S P A M
  I D A   F E A S T   C A R R A D I O
D R Y V E R M O U T H   L O N I   N I N A
E A U   S M U R F   J I N G O   N E T
O M N I   R T E   H U N G A R I A N
D O N T B E A S T R A N G E R   G R E T A
A N A L Y S T   I N H O U S E   H E R O N
R A N L A T E   M A N   A T E   T A S T Y
```

```
M E A D O W   S M A S H   G O O D T I M E
O P T I M A   L E C H E   A C C R E D I T
P O R K E R F A R C E S   L A T I N A T E
E S A   L C D T V   A S E A   O P A R T
  A E R I E   A T I T   S P I N E S
P R E T T Y C R A S H A C C O U N T
L E W I S   L I E N   C O S T   S A S
O N E L   O G L E S   A S T E R O I D S
T O R T E B R A G   C O B   S O F T O N
  N O A H   B A A B A A   N A P S
  I G A V E I T M Y B R E S T S H O R T
T N U T   L I B E L S   T H A I
A T C A M P   A S E   C R O W C H I R P
P E C T O R A L S   G L O S S   O T O E
E L I   R O B T   T R U E   C H E L A
  H O M E R A W A Y F R O M H O M E R
A L A N I S   T E N S   A L O E S
  R O M P S   S E L F   O N A I R   C U T
M O T L I E S T   F R I S T F R I G H T S
E S T E E M E D   T E R S E   E S P A N A
T E A T R E E S   H E R O D   S H A P E R
```

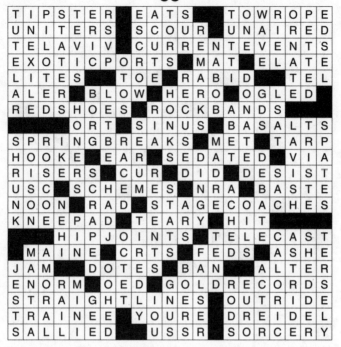

33

Puzzle 33 grid answers:

TIPSTER · EATS · TOWROPE
UNITERS · SCOUR · UNAIRED
TELAVIV · CURRENTEVENTS
EXOTICPORTS · MAT · ELATE
LITES · TOE · RABID · TEL
ALER · BLOW · HERO · OGLED
REDSHOES · ROCKBANDS
ORT · SINUS · BASALTS
SPRINGBREAKS · MET · TARP
HOOKE · EAR · SEDATED · VIA
RISERS · CUR · DID · DESIST
USC · SCHEMES · NRA · BASTE
NOON · RAD · STAGECOACHES
KNEEPAD · TEARY · HIT
HIPJOINTS · TELECAST
MAINE · CRTS · FEDS · ASHE
JAM · DOTES · BAN · ALTER
ENORM · OED · GOLDRECORDS
STRAIGHTLINES · OUTRIDE
TRAINEE · YOURE · DREIDEL
SALLIED · USSR · SORCERY

Puzzle 34 grid answers:

ANIM · BASIC · NEMO · BIPED
TONI · ALIAS · ADAM · ELAND
TOENAILCLIPPERS · DIDOS
INSULTS · HONK · FRED
CASEYSTENGEL · STRODEIN
NETS · AVIONIC · RIO · DOO
STRETTO · AKEEM · END
ATPLAY · TELEPHONE · NIA
ARIA · PURIM · RIA · DYEVAT
BONA · ESE · PITY · SERE
AISLE · SLUTSKAYA · SALAD
TAMA · ENRY · ART · SOLO
ENRAPT · AAA · GAMMA · EPIC
MII · THIRDGEAR · BERETS
MVP · YESNO · AMADEUS
YEE · HIE · NATURAL · HIST
SADCASES · POTATOMASHER
SENT · OGPU · COROLLA
SQUAD · SPORTSEQUIPMENT
GUISE · EURO · POTTS · EPEE
TOTED · APEX · ASSET · RPTS

Grid 35:

R	I	C	S	■	S	L	A	V	S	■	S	E	P	A	L	■	R	D	S	■
E	L	L	A	■	P	E	R	O	T	■	U	S	O	N	E	■	E	R	I	S
C	L	A	Y	M	A	N	E	X	E	M	P	T	I	O	N	■	J	A	M	A
A	S	S	H	E	■	T	A	P	P	E	T	S	■	D	I	S	O	W	N	S
P	E	S	E	T	A	■	■	O	U	I	■	■	P	A	N	P	I	P	E	S
S	E	A	L	O	V	E	A	P	P	R	O	V	A	L	■	I	C	I	L	Y
■	■	■	L	O	A	T	H	■	■	A	I	L	■	W	R	E	N	■	■	■
L	I	M	O	■	T	H	E	B	E	A	S	T	■	A	A	A	■	C	B	S
E	L	Y	■	M	A	Y	D	O	U	B	T	A	W	I	L	L	■	E	A	T
A	L	L	G	I	R	L	■	S	R	S	■	■	O	R	T	■	E	N	T	R
K	E	A	T	S	■	■	C	H	O	C	T	A	W	■	■	L	A	T	H	E
A	G	U	E	■	H	O	O	■	■	O	O	P	■	S	P	A	R	E	M	E
G	I	G	■	K	E	Y	P	A	W	N	M	O	V	I	N	G	■	R	A	T
E	T	H	■	U	R	L	■	N	O	D	E	S	I	R	E	■	L	S	T	S
■	■	■	T	A	W	S	■	G	O	V	■	■	■	S	O	U	S	A	■	■
A	D	E	L	A	■	M	I	N	E	D	O	V	E	R	M	A	T	T	E	R
B	U	R	L	I	V	E	S	■	■	O	N	E	■	■	O	L	E	O	L	E
A	M	M	E	T	E	R	■	D	E	S	T	I	J	L	■	I	S	L	E	D
S	P	I	N	■	G	R	A	Y	T	O	I	L	E	O	F	C	H	I	N	A
H	O	L	D	■	A	I	D	E	D	■	M	E	T	A	L	■	O	F	A	N
■	N	E	E	■	N	E	E	D	S	■	E	D	E	M	A	■	W	E	S	T

36

Grid 36:

W	A	L	E	S	A	■	A	R	C	■	■	G	E	R	■	S	K	I	T	S
A	B	O	R	T	S	■	L	O	O	■	R	E	N	O	■	T	E	N	E	T
D	I	S	G	U	S	T	I	N	G	W	I	N	D	S	■	J	E	A	N	E
S	E	E	■	A	A	H	E	D	■	E	G	R	E	T	■	A	P	R	O	N
■	■	S	E	R	M	O	N	O	N	T	H	E	D	I	S	M	O	U	N	T
I	C	A	N	T	■	■	■	O	T	T	■	■	G	E	N	T	S	■	■	■
G	O	D	I	S	F	I	G	U	R	E	■	A	B	E	T	S	■	■	■	■
G	L	A	D	■	A	R	M	S	■	R	I	G	O	R	S	■	D	O	D	O
Y	A	Y	S	■	B	E	A	D	S	■	N	E	H	I	■	S	U	P	E	R
■	■	■	D	I	S	C	O	U	N	T	E	R	C	U	L	T	U	R	E
A	N	G	O	R	A	■	■	S	I	R	■	■	S	A	Y	S	N	O	■
F	O	O	D	A	N	D	D	I	S	L	O	D	G	I	N	G	■	■	■
R	E	A	D	Y	■	R	O	D	E	■	S	O	U	S	A	■	M	S	E	C
O	L	D	S	■	P	A	G	O	D	A	■	C	M	L	V	■	O	T	R	O
■	■	N	I	G	E	L	■	D	I	S	M	A	Y	Q	U	E	E	N	■
■	P	A	T	E	N	■	■	O	O	N	■	■	■	U	N	P	I	N	■
C	A	B	B	A	G	E	D	I	S	P	A	T	C	H	K	I	D	S	■
A	L	L	O	R	■	D	O	N	A	T	■	A	M	A	I	N	■	A	L	E
P	L	A	N	E	■	D	U	C	K	A	N	D	D	I	S	C	O	V	E	R
R	I	T	E	S	■	A	G	U	A	■	E	A	R	■	S	E	R	E	N	A
I	D	E	S	T	■	S	S	R	■	E	S	S	■	A	S	T	R	O	S

37

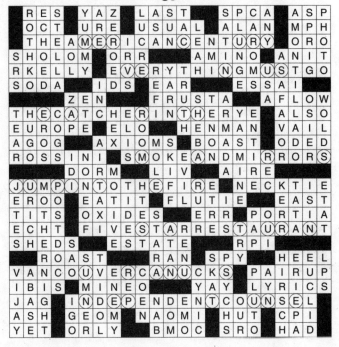

38

39

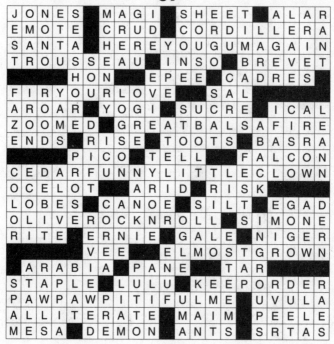

```
JONES ▮ MAGI ▮ SHEET ▮ ALAR
EMOTE ▮ CRUD ▮ CORDILLERA
SANTA ▮ HEREYOUGUMAGAIN
TROUSSEAU ▮ INSO ▮ BREVET
▮ HON ▮ EPEE ▮ CADRES ▮
FIRYOURLOVE ▮ SAL ▮
AROAR ▮ YOGI ▮ SUCRE ▮ ICAL
ZOOMED ▮ GREATBALSAFIRE
ENDS ▮ RISE ▮ TOOTS ▮ BASRA
▮ PICO ▮ TELL ▮ FALCON
CEDARFUNNYLITTLECLOWN
OCELOT ▮ ARID ▮ RISK ▮
LOBES ▮ CANOE ▮ SILT ▮ EGAD
OLIVEROCKNROLL ▮ SIMONE
RITE ▮ ERNIE ▮ GALE ▮ NIGER
▮ VEE ▮ ELMOSTGROWN
ARABIA ▮ PANE ▮ TAR ▮
STAPLE ▮ LULU ▮ KEEPORDER
PAWPAWPITIFULME ▮ UVULA
ALLITERATE ▮ MAIM ▮ PEELE
MESA ▮ DEMON ▮ ANTS ▮ SRTAS
```

40

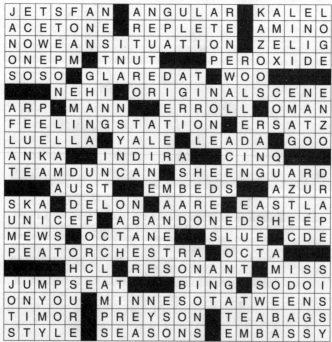

```
JETSFAN ▮ ANGULAR ▮ KALEL
ACETONE ▮ REPLETE ▮ AMINO
NOWEANSITUATION ▮ ZELIG
ONEPM ▮ TNUT ▮ PEROXIDE
SOSO ▮ GLAREDAT ▮ WOO ▮
▮ NEHI ▮ ORIGINALSCENE
ARP ▮ MANN ▮ ERROLL ▮ OMAN
FEELINGSTATION ▮ ERSATZ
LUELLA ▮ YALE ▮ LEADA ▮ GOO
ANKA ▮ INDIRA ▮ CINQ ▮
TEAMDUNCAN ▮ SHEENGUARD
▮ AUST ▮ EMBEDS ▮ AZUR
SKA ▮ DELON ▮ AARE ▮ EASTLA
UNICEF ▮ ABANDONEDSHEEP
MEWS ▮ OCTANE ▮ SLUE ▮ CDE
PEATORCHESTRA ▮ OCTA ▮
▮ HCL ▮ RESONANT ▮ MISS
JUMPSEAT ▮ BING ▮ SODOI
ONYOU ▮ MINNESOTATWEENS
TIMOR ▮ PREYSON ▮ TEABAGS
STYLE ▮ SEASONS ▮ EMBASSY
```

```
P C L A B   A N A S A Z I   A B R A M
E R A T O   I N U N I S O N   A R R O W S
W Y M A N   T I L T A T W I N D M I L L S
  R U S S O   B N A I   A R I E L
I N S I S T E N C E   E R N I E F O R D
T O P   Q U A   R A D S   A C E S   V E E
A M E N U   S B A R R O   M E N   F E D S
L A C I E   Y U K   A P O P   J A R R E
  D I P S Y   M E D I   R U T   A R B O R
  A S T O O P   I N C A P S   C R E S T
E S L   I S L E   A B O   S A C K   E E S
N A R C O   I R O N O N   A R M P I T
C L E A N   O C T   A N I L   D O N H O
L A L A S   R O A R   W E D   T R O V E
A Z A N   S F O   A D V I S E   J I V E S
S A T   E A R P   A S I S   S O U   E R S
P R I C E L I S T   C H E C K S I N T O
  V O L T A   E A V E   B E S T S
F L I P P E R A N D E R S O N   I L L G O
L E T S O N   G O A R O U N D   C A V E R
A S Y E T   A R R A Y E D   E M I L Y
```

```
T O S C A L E   M A M B O   A G H A S
A R E A R U G   A D A P T E R   D R A F T
S (C) A R I N G   G E O R G E L A Z E N (B) Y
S A N G   A S S I S I   B O B   C A S E
  S C O W   I T I S S O   N O H O
  O P E C   M A R T I N I   A O R T A L
S O N A R S   I T E   R O G E R M O O R E
T U N N E L S   E S L   O N D E M A N D
A S E T   E W E S   (A) P A R T   S A D E
M E R S   W I G   (A) D A M   I T I N
P L Y   T I M O T H Y D A L T O N   D J S
  G U S T   B O D S   S L Y   B A A L
H M O S   E A S Y A   D U E L   I N M E
F E E L S B A D   Y A O   S A L L I E D
I A N F L E M I N G   U M S   N O L E S S
E D U C E S   A S P I R I N   D A H L
  O S S O   C O R O N A   M U C H
O A H U   I M (F)   (E) R A G O N   D R E I
P I E R C E B R O S N A N   P A S S A I C
E R A S E   R A S H E S T   A N T O I N E
R E P E L   E T T A S   L O U N G E S
```

43

L	A	D	D		A	L	B	U	M			J	A	I			S	A	W	S
A	G	R	I		L	E	O	N	E	S		O	W	N		R	A	B	A	T
B	U	Y	A	B	L	E	B	E	L	T		H	O	T	P	O	T	A	T	O
S	E	C	R	E	T	S			M	O	R	A	L	L	Y	S	A	F	E	R
		L	I	T	E		C	O	L	O	N			G	E	N	T	R	Y	
T	H	E	S	A	L	I	V	A	T	I	O	N	A	R	M	Y				
H	E	A	T	S		N	A	S	H			D	E	Y		A	D	A	M	
U	R	N	S		A	I	L	S		H	A	Z	E		O	C	A	L	A	
D	O	S		M	E	G	A		G	R	A	S		S	A	R	O	N	G	S
	C	O	R	O	N	E	R	O	N	T	H	E	M	A	R	K	E	T	
	P	A	O	L	O		C	L	A	U	D	I	A		I	N	N	E	R	
H	U	M	M	A	B	L	E	B	E	G	I	N	N	I	N	G	S		
E	R	I	T	R	E	A		O	M	E	N		S	M	E	E		B	M	W
A	S	S	E	S		R	O	W	E		G	A	P	S		B	R	I	O	
L	E	S	S		P	G	A		M	A	R	E		E	L	I	T	E	
	R	I	O	T	I	N	G	I	M	P	L	E	M	E	N	T	S	
C	H	O	S	E	N		M	E	E	S	E		L	A	N	G	
R	E	N	T	A	S	E	N	A	T	O	R		S	L	I	D	I	N	G
A	T	T	A	C	K	D	O	G		R	E	D	S	K	E	L	E	T	O	N
S	T	A	R	T		I	R	E		G	A	I	T	E	R		R	O	N	A
H	Y	P	E		T	A	D		D	O	P	E	Y		S	N	O	W	

44

U	R	S	A		D	E	A	D	C	A	L	M		I	P	A	N	E	M	A
N	O	E	S		U	N	L	O	A	D	E	D		R	A	V	A	G	E	D
Q	U	A	K	I	N	G	A	S	P	E	N	S		A	L	A	M	O	D	E
U	N	R	O	B	E		B	A	R	N	S		S	T	E			Y	I	P
O	D	I	U	M		S	A	G	A			Q	U	E	B	E	C	A	C	T
T	E	N	T		A	P	S	E		S	O	U	P		L	L	A	N	O	S
E	R	G		B	L	O	T		S	K	U	A		O	U	S	T			
			Q	U	A	T	E	R	N	A	R	Y	A	G	E		C	H	A	S
	S	T	U	R	M		R	I	O	T		S	I	R		S	H	O	R	T
S	T	O	O	G	E	S		G	O	E	S		R	I	S	E		S	R	A
Q	U	A	I	L	I	N	G	A	T		Q	U	E	S	T	A	F	T	E	R
U	P	S		E	N	O	L		S	L	U	G		H	E	W	L	E	T	T
I	O	T	A	S		C	E	E		Y	E	L	P		W	A	U	L	S	
B	R	Y	N		Q	A	N	T	A	S	A	I	R	W	A	Y	S	
			G	L	U	T		A	M	O	K		O	A	R	S		F	O	E
S	T	R	I	P	E		O	P	A	L		E	X	I	T		M	A	N	X
Q	U	E	E	N	A	N	N	E			T	A	I	L		H	A	S	A	T
U	R	N			S	E	E		S	W	A	R	M		G	E	N	T	L	E
A	N	T	O	N	I	A		Q	U	I	E	T	A	M	E	R	I	C	A	N
S	T	A	I	N	E	R		V	E	R	B	A	T	I	M		L	A	R	D
H	O	L	L	E	R	S		C	R	Y	O	G	E	N	S		A	R	K	S

45

T	O	P	S	O	F	F	■	C	A	N	D	I	D	■	■	G	R	O	P	E
E	V	E	N	P	A	R	■	A	D	O	R	N	E	D	■	H	O	H	O	S
R	E	P	O	S	S	E	S	S	E	D	A	U	T	O	■	I	S	H	O	T
S	N	U	B	■	■	E	A	T	■	■	C	R	A	N	E	■	S	E	L	A
E	S	P	■	R	E	L	Y	I	N	G	O	N	I	N	S	T	I	N	C	T
■	■	B	O	X	Y	■	R	A	I	■	S	L	A	S	H	■	R	U	E	■
T	R	U	A	N	T	■	C	O	N	G	A	■	■	■	A	H	Y	E	S	■
R	E	P	A	I	R	M	A	N	U	A	L	■	M	E	T	R	O	■	■	■
I	F	S	■	■	A	O	L	■	■	M	E	A	L	S	■	T	E	S	T	■
N	U	T	C	A	S	E	■	R	E	P	O	R	T	F	O	R	D	U	T	Y
A	T	A	L	L	■	J	E	E	R	S	A	T	■	■	C	O	R	E	R	■
R	E	T	A	I	L	O	U	T	L	E	T	S	■	N	I	A	G	A	R	A
Y	S	E	R	■	B	L	A	D	E	■	■	T	A	D	■	■	S	E	N	■
■	■	■	E	S	S	E	N	■	R	E	C	O	N	M	I	S	S	I	O	N
P	I	N	T	A	■	■	S	L	A	N	T	■	G	O	E	A	S	Y	■	■
G	N	U	■	L	L	A	M	A	■	H	R	S	■	M	I	N	X	■	■	■
R	E	M	O	T	E	P	O	S	S	I	B	I	L	I	T	Y	■	S	R	O
A	X	E	D	■	B	E	D	E	W	■	■	L	E	G	■	■	A	M	E	N
T	I	R	E	D	■	R	E	V	E	R	S	E	E	N	G	I	N	E	E	R
E	L	I	T	E	■	S	L	E	E	P	I	N	■	O	L	D	N	A	V	Y
D	E	C	O	Y	■	■	A	R	T	I	S	T	■	N	O	S	I	R	E	E

46

A	C	R	E	■	P	L	E	B	E	■	S	A	M	O	A	■	A	C	T	S
R	O	O	M	■	O	A	R	E	D	■	A	F	O	U	L	■	C	O	H	O
C	A	S	E	C	L	O	S	E	D	■	F	O	O	T	L	O	C	K	E	R
S	T	E	R	E	O	■	T	R	A	D	E	R	■	S	U	P	R	E	M	E
■	■	■	G	A	S	■	■	■	A	R	E	■	C	R	E	A	S	E	S	■
T	I	M	E	S	■	A	P	R	E	S	■	■	C	O	E	D	■	■	■	■
I	N	A	N	E	■	R	O	A	D	H	A	Z	A	R	D	■	■	D	O	T
P	S	S	T	■	S	A	R	G	E	■	M	O	R	E	■	S	N	O	R	E
O	U	T	■	S	C	R	E	E	N	D	O	O	R	■	O	C	E	L	O	T
F	R	E	E	L	O	A	D	■	■	E	L	M	■	C	U	R	L	■	■	■
F	E	R	V	E	N	T	■	S	A	L	E	S	■	S	E	L	V	A	G	E
■	■	C	E	D	E	■	■	E	F	T	■	■	C	H	A	P	E	R	O	N
O	R	A	N	G	S	■	S	P	R	A	Y	P	A	I	N	T	■	S	A	T
P	U	R	S	E	■	C	I	A	O	■	A	E	G	I	S	■	M	I	T	E
T	E	D	■	■	W	A	L	L	S	T	R	E	E	T	■	S	A	G	E	R
■	■	■	T	H	R	O	■	■	E	N	T	R	E	■	L	I	N	E	S	■
C	A	L	I	B	E	R	■	C	C	X	■	■	■	J	U	N	■	■	■	■
O	D	Y	S	S	E	Y	■	L	A	T	H	E	D	■	O	R	M	O	N	D
P	O	O	L	P	L	A	Y	E	R	■	G	R	A	P	H	P	A	P	E	R
A	R	N	E	■	I	L	E	F	T	■	T	I	T	A	N	■	S	E	M	I
Y	E	S	T	■	E	L	A	T	E	■	V	E	E	P	S	■	T	R	O	P

47

```
L A P L A T A ■ A P E S U I T ■ ■ P E N S
E C L A I R S ■ R O M A N C E ■ P E R O T
S H O W M E T H E M O N K E Y ■ E D I N A
T E T R ■ E R A S E ■ G N U ■ N E A T E R
■ ■ E P S O N ■ ■ T R I P L E K L U T Z
P O R N O ■ S T R A I T ■ O W I E ■ ■ ■
D R A C U L A ■ R I C A ■ U G A N D A N S
A F T E R A S K O R T ■ A M O R ■ R E O
S E E ■ S N I D E ■ P L A N K A H E A D
■ ■ M A I E R ■ M O I ■ ■ V O I L A ■
■ W I N K W I N K S I T U A T I O N ■
E N O L A ■ ■ Y I N ■ ■ S H O A T ■ ■
B A R K T E N D E R ■ E S S E N ■ C T R
A T M ■ D I R T ■ A V E R A G E J O K E
N O S E D I V E ■ B R E R ■ P A L M T O P
■ ■ L E S E ■ C O I N E D ■ A B Y S S
G U N K C O N T R O L ■ U V U L A ■ ■
U T A H A N ■ E A T ■ A C M E S ■ R B I S
I T M A Y ■ I N F L A T A B L E K R A F T
L E E R S ■ D E T E N T E ■ M I N I B A R
E R S T ■ S T Y G I A N ■ A T T E S T S
```

48

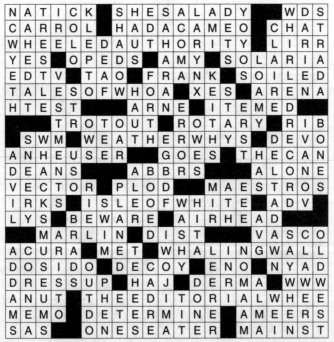

```
N A T I C K ■ S H E S A L A D Y ■ W D S
C A R R O L ■ H A D A C A M E O ■ C H A T
W H E E L E D A U T H O R I T Y ■ L I R R
Y E S ■ O P E D S ■ A M Y ■ S O L A R I A
E D T V ■ T A O ■ F R A N K ■ S O I L E D
T A L E S O F W H O A ■ X E S ■ A R E N A
H T E S T ■ ■ A R N E ■ I T E M E D ■
■ ■ T R O T O U T ■ R O T A R Y ■ R I B
■ S W M ■ W E A T H E R W H Y S ■ D E V O
A N H E U S E R ■ G O E S ■ T H E C A N
D E A N S ■ ■ A B B R S ■ A L O N E
V E C T O R ■ P L O D ■ M A E S T R O S
I R K S ■ I S L E O F W H I T E ■ A D V
L Y S ■ B E W A R E ■ A I R H E A D ■
■ M A R L I N ■ D I S T ■ V A S C O
A C U R A ■ M E T ■ W H A L I N G W A L L
D O S I D O ■ D E C O Y ■ E N O ■ N Y A D
D R E S S U P ■ H A J ■ D E R M A ■ W W W
A N U T ■ T H E E D I T O R I A L W H E E
M E M O ■ D E T E R M I N E ■ A M E E R S
S A S ■ O N E S E A T E R ■ M A I N S T
```

51

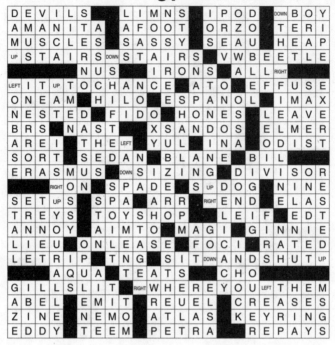

```
D E V I L S ■ L I M N S ■ I P O D ■[DOWN]B O Y
A M A N I T A ■ A F O O T ■ O R Z O ■ T E R I
M U S C L E S ■ S A S S Y ■ S E A U ■ H E A P
[UP]S T A I R S[DOWN]S T A I R S ■ V W B E E T L E
■ ■ ■ N U S ■ ■ I R O N S ■ A L L[RIGHT]■ ■
[LEFT]I T[UP]T O C H A N C E ■ A T O ■ E F F U S E
O N E A M ■ H I L O ■ E S P A N O L ■ I M A X
N E S T E D ■ F I D O ■ H O N E S ■ L E A V E
B R S ■ N A S T ■ ■ X S A N D O S ■ E L M E R
A R E I ■ T H E[LEFT]■ Y U L ■ I N A ■ O D I S T
S O R T ■ S E D A N ■ B L A N E ■ B I L ■ ■
E R A S M U S ■[DOWN]S I Z I N G ■ D I V I S O R
■ ■[RIGHT]O N ■ S P A D E ■ S[UP]D O G ■ N I N E
S E T[UP]S ■ S P A ■ A R R ■[RIGHT]E N D ■ E L A S
T R E Y S ■ T O Y S H O P ■ L E I F ■ E D T
A N N O Y ■ A I M T O ■ M A G I ■ G I N N I E
L I E U ■ O N L E A S E ■ F O C I ■ R A T E D
L E T R I P ■ T N G ■ S I T[DOWN]A N D S H U T[UP]
■ ■ A Q U A ■ T E A T S ■ ■ C H O ■ ■ ■
G I L L S L I T ■[RIGHT]W H E R E Y O U[LEFT]T H E M
A B E L ■ E M I T ■ R E U E L ■ C R E A S E S
Z I N E ■ N E M O ■ A T L A S ■ K E Y R I N G
E D D Y ■ T E E M ■ P E T R A ■ R E P A Y S
```

52

```
T E E M ■ A L O A D ■ M L I X ■ A G A S P
A X L E ■ V A L L I ■ E I N E ■ S H I N E
R E V E R E N D E V E R E N D ■ S O R E N
P R E T E N D S ■ E L I T E ■ L I S T E N
S T S ■ Y U M ■ H I S T O R Y I S T O R Y
■ ■ ■ U N E A T E N ■ ■ E M I T ■ ■ ■
S A W T O ■ S E A T A C ■ A W E ■ O L A V
S P O T L E S S P O T L E S S ■ S W O R E
R E W E D S ■ ■ W O N T ■ G E N O M E
■ ■ R S T U ■ P I T S T O P I T S T O P
I S A ■ A S K I N ■ E R R E D ■ S R S
M A N D A T E A N D A T E ■ G E T S ■ ■
E N G I N E ■ T O I L ■ ■ O R E L S E
A T E S T ■ F I N A L I S T I N A L I S T
N A R C ■ E E E ■ N Y M P H S ■ V I D E O
■ ■ J I V E ■ ■ P E D A G O G ■ ■ ■
L A B O R E D A B O R E D ■ O I L ■ S H E
U N O C A L ■ G O F O R ■ M A N T O M A N
E N O K I ■ S O N A T I N A O N A T I N A
G E N E S ■ O R E G ■ L A T K E ■ T R O T
O X E Y E ■ B A S E ■ S T A I D ■ O K I E
```

53

V	A	N	C	A	M	P	■	■	A	L	A	M	E	D	A	■	G	E	T	Z
O	V	E	R	L	O	U	D	■	S	E	N	A	T	O	R	■	A	Q	U	A
L	E	G	A	L	D	R	I	N	K	I	N	G	A	G	E	■	T	U	R	K
G	R	E	W	■	■	I	D	O	S	■	■	■	L	E	T	M	E	I	N	■
A	T	V	■	T	I	T	U	S	■	H	Q	S	■	S	H	E	M	P	■	■
■	■	■	E	S	C	A	P	E	R	O	U	T	E	■	A	L	A	M	O	S
■	P	A	Q	U	I	N	■	S	I	M	I	A	N	S	■	I	N	E	P	T
N	A	T	U	R	E	S	■	B	E	N	■	Y	O	W	S	■	N	A	Y	■
E	C	L	A	I	R	■	M	U	S	I	C	R	A	C	K	S	■	T	H	X
H	E	A	L	S	■	F	O	P	■	N	E	A	■	C	R	A	W	L	■	■
I	S	N	T	■	E	R	G	O	T	■	S	T	E	E	P	■	H	O	J	O
■	T	O	S	C	A	■	N	A	S	■	O	R	R	■	B	I	C	E	P	■
F	R	I	■	T	O	P	R	A	N	K	I	N	G	■	M	U	S	K	E	T
L	A	C	■	A	L	P	O	■	T	I	T	■	F	O	R	K	E	R	S	■
O	C	C	A	M	■	E	S	T	R	E	E	T	■	R	I	S	E	R	S	■
G	E	H	R	I	G	■	Y	O	U	R	M	A	J	E	S	T	Y	■	■	■
■	A	R	N	A	Z	■	E	M	S	■	P	O	E	T	S	■	A	P	B	■
C	R	E	A	T	O	R	■	■	K	E	R	F	■	■	P	E	R	I	■	■
J	U	T	S	■	S	W	E	E	P	U	N	D	E	R	T	H	E	R	U	G
A	B	E	T	■	B	I	Z	A	R	R	E	■	L	O	W	E	R	I	N	G
W	A	R	S	■	Y	E	A	R	O	N	E	■	■	M	O	N	K	E	E	S

54

T	I	P	S	■	A	C	E	S	I	T	■	G	A	I	A	■	I	C	S
U	V	E	A	■	S	O	L	U	T	E	■	U	N	C	L	E	S	A	M
P	A	N	T	S	■	T	H	E	M	A	L	T	E	S	E	F	A	L	C	O
A	N	A	T	O	L	I	A	N	■	■	A	S	A	■	R	U	E	H	L
C	A	L	I	F	O	R	N	I	A	S	U	I	T	■	S	E	X	T	E	T
■	■	G	A	P	■	■	M	O	N	■	S	A	W	S	■	■	■	■
■	T	H	R	E	E	D	A	Y	S	O	F	T	H	E	C	O	N	D	O
E	D	I	T	■	■	D	R	T	■	■	I	A	M	■	O	D	E	O	N
V	O	N	■	E	N	A	M	I	■	A	S	R	E	D	■	D	R	E	I
A	H	A	R	D	D	A	Y	S	N	I	G	H	■	■	I	N	M	O	S	T
■	■	I	O	U	S	■	■	T	N	N	■	U	S	I	A	■	■	■
I	N	S	Y	N	C	■	T	H	E	E	L	E	P	H	A	N	T	M	A
S	A	L	A	■	E	D	D	I	E	■	S	I	X	T	Y	■	A	R	P
I	Z	O	D	S	■	A	A	S	■	E	G	O	■	■	F	R	E	E	■
N	I	G	H	T	O	F	T	H	E	L	I	V	I	N	G	D	E	A	■
■	■	R	A	T	E	■	N	E	O	■	■	R	E	L	■	■	■	■
S	H	M	E	A	R	■	B	E	V	E	R	L	Y	H	I	L	L	S	C	O
N	O	I	S	Y	■	E	O	E	■	■	S	A	I	N	T	O	L	A	F
A	C	L	O	C	K	W	O	R	K	O	R	A	N	G	■	A	V	A	N	T
R	U	N	S	A	M	O	K	■	S	W	A	T	C	H	■	E	T	T	E
E	S	E	■	T	S	K	S	■	U	N	I	S	Y	S	■	R	E	I	N

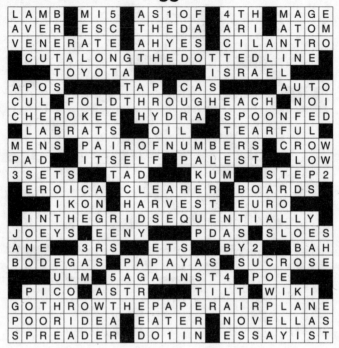

```
L A M B ■ M I 5 ■ A S 1 O F ■ 4 T H ■ M A G E
A V E R ■ E S C ■ T H E D A ■ A R I ■ A T O M
V E N E R A T E ■ A H Y E S ■ C I L A N T R O
■ C U T A L O N G T H E D O T T E D L I N E ■
■ T O Y O T A ■ ■ ■ I S R A E L ■ ■ ■
A P O S ■ ■ T A P ■ C A S ■ ■ A U T O
C U L ■ F O L D T H R O U G H E A C H ■ N O I
C H E R O K E E ■ H Y D R A ■ S P O O N F E D
■ L A B R A T S ■ O I L ■ T E A R F U L ■
M E N S ■ P A I R O F N U M B E R S ■ C R O W
P A D ■ I T S E L F ■ P A L E S T ■ L O W
3 S E T S ■ T A D ■ K U M ■ S T E P 2
■ E R O I C A ■ C L E A R E R ■ B O A R D S ■
■ I K O N ■ H A R V E S T ■ E U R O ■
■ I N T H E G R I D S E Q U E N T I A L L Y ■
J O E Y S ■ E E N Y ■ P D A S ■ S L O E S
A N E ■ 3 R S ■ E T S ■ B Y 2 ■ B A H
B O D E G A S ■ P A P A Y A S ■ S U C R O S E
■ U L M ■ 5 A G A I N S T 4 ■ P O E ■
■ P I C O ■ A S T R ■ T I L T ■ W I K I
G O T H R O W T H E P A P E R A I R P L A N E
P O O R I D E A ■ E A T E R ■ N O V E L L A S
S P R E A D E R ■ D O 1 I N ■ E S S A Y I S T
```

```
G O T E A M ■ L E T S A T ■ S U R E B E T
A P O L L O ■ I S I N T O ■ O N E B A S E
S A Y I T A I N T S O O T ■ N O W O R S E
■ S T A N C E ■ C I S C O ■ A L D E N
A S T I R ■ E A T S A ■ O R A T I O N S
I P O S ■ A L L O T T H E S A M E ■ T E Y
W A R M T H ■ B E S A M E ■ A R L O ■
A M Y ■ H O A G I E ■ H I L T ■ S O F T Y
■ C R Y S T A L B A L L O T ■ C A R O
A T A R I ■ K O S ■ A H S ■ U N S A V E D
L U N A C I E S ■ R N A ■ A C T A L O N E
A T A N E N D ■ T I D ■ U M A ■ Y E N T L
M U C K ■ B I G O T B U S I N E S S ■
O S T E R ■ N A N U ■ N T E S T S ■ S S N
■ O D O M ■ L I A I S E ■ A O R T A E
J I F ■ S C H O O L M A R M O T ■ A E R O
E N G R A V E R ■ B Y R O N ■ F I T I N
S H O E R ■ A E S I R ■ L E A R N S ■
S U D S I E R ■ L O O T A N D B E H O L D
E M O T E R S ■ A N K A R A ■ U R A N I A
L E T S S E E ■ B E E P E R ■ G E T S B Y
```

57

```
A I R S   ■   M O N G O L S ■ O L I V E S
T R U C K S ■ S K I L L E T ■ D E S I L U
I M M U N E   R E L I A B L E S A U C E S
T A P S I N ■ P E L T ■ ■ K O D ■ T V A
■   S I G H S   F A Z E T H E N A T I O N
P A T ■ H O U S E ■ A M E S ■ O M N ■
A L E ■ T R E E ■ A S T E R ■ I S T ■
S M A L L A R M ■ T H E N O O S E H O U R
T A K E I ■ I B S E N ■ L A T E N E D
■ A N Y ■ P E E L ■ R A G A ■ O Y S
■ T H E O H R E A L L Y F A C T O R ■
A P U ■ H O O P ■ F O U R ■ S W F ■
M O N S O O N ■ S I E N A ■ O M N I S
B E A T T H E P R E S S ■ M I S D E A L T
■ A T O ■ O A T H S ■ E L E A ■ V I E
■ H E N ■ E L M O ■ A S S A Y ■ Y E W
S U N D A Y M O A N I N G ■ A S S E S ■
A M I ■ R E A ■ O I L S ■ O H D E A R
W A S H I N G T O N W E A K ■ N O S A L E
E N L I S T ■ O N E A C R E ■ S W E L L S
D E E D E E ■ N O T N E E D ■ L S A T
```

58

```
■ S T U A R T ■ R O S I E ■   O M E G A
■ P A S T O R ■ E R A S E ■ C A R O L E R
Y O K O O N O ■ L I [FEB] A N ■ A U G M E N T
E T E ■ B A [JAN] O B E Y ■ S [MAR] T Y ■ C O B
A T T S ■ A W A I T ■ P O O R ■ A T M O
S E E I N G R E D ■ G U T S Y ■ T R I O
T R A [DEC] O M M I S S I O N S ■ R [APR] O C K
■ A D A Y ■ T O I T ■ G A T O ■
C A D R E ■ S W A N N ■ B E N E F I T S
O T O ■ A U S T I N ■ G I A N T ■ I T O O
M A [NOV] E R B O A R D ■ A N C I E N T [MAY] A N
B R A Y ■ O A T E S ■ L I K E S O ■ B I G
S I N E W A V E ■ F E L T S ■ B A E R S
■ D A T E ■ N I K I ■ M O L D ■
D E C [OCT] S ■ A D R E N A L I N E [JUN] K I E
I M H O ■ A B R A M ■ B O N E S C A N S
S U E R ■ H A C K ■ D W E L T ■ T R O T
C L E ■ J O [SEP] H ■ A R A T ■ [JUL] E S ■ A R E
M A S C A R A ■ F R [AUG] H T ■ E P I S O D E
A T E A W A Y ■ A C H O O ■ P E R U K E
N E S T S ■ M O T O R ■ S E E D E R
```

59

Grid 59:

C	H	I	N	T	Z	■	W	O	O	D	L	O	T	■	C	H	E	Q	U	E
M	A	D	E	R	A	■	O	N	A	T	E	A	R	■	A	U	B	U	R	N
D	R	E	W	U	N	I	V	E	R	S	I	T	Y	■	S	T	R	E	S	S
■	■	H	E	I	N	E	■	■	■	G	E	S	T	E	■	O	E	I	L	■
C	D	R	A	T	E	S	■	F	I	S	H	S	T	O	R	Y	■	N	N	E
H	U	E	V	O	S	■	S	A	N	E	■	■	S	T	E	A	M	E	R	■
O	B	I	E	■	■	D	E	B	U	T	S	■	R	I	A	L	T	O	■	■
M	A	G	N	U	M	O	P	U	S	■	P	A	A	R	■	L	I	T	R	E
P	I	N	■	P	A	R	T	■	E	Z	I	N	E	■	C	A	S	H	I	N
■	■	M	I	S	S	U	S	■	E	L	K	■	H	O	T	S	E	A	T	■
P	O	S	E	■	H	A	M	M	E	R	T	H	R	O	W	■	U	R	L	S
A	P	P	A	R	E	L	■	E	N	O	■	S	A	M	P	L	E	■	■	■
L	E	A	N	E	D	■	B	A	L	S	A	■	G	E	E	D	■	M	S	S
E	N	D	I	T	■	R	A	R	A	■	F	E	L	L	A	S	L	E	E	P
■	■	E	E	R	I	E	R	■	I	N	T	R	A	Y	■	E	D	E	R	■
A	R	C	S	I	N	E	■	■	B	E	A	N	■	S	A	F	I	R	E	■
R	E	A	■	M	A	S	O	N	J	A	R	S	■	L	A	C	T	A	S	E
M	U	S	E	■	H	E	L	I	O	■	■	■	A	G	N	E	W	■	■	■
O	B	I	S	P	O	■	L	E	A	D	D	E	T	E	C	T	I	V	E	S
R	E	N	T	A	L	■	A	C	D	E	L	C	O	■	T	E	N	S	E	S
S	N	O	O	Z	E	■	S	E	S	S	I	O	N	■	A	N	G	O	L	A

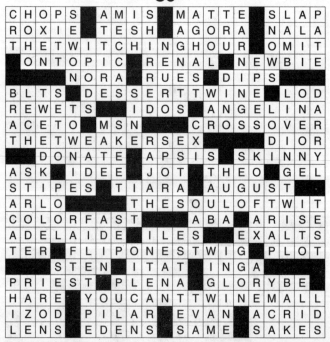

60

Grid 60:

C	H	O	P	S	■	A	M	I	S	■	M	A	T	T	E	■	S	L	A	P
R	O	X	I	E	■	T	E	S	H	■	A	G	O	R	A	■	N	A	L	A
T	H	E	T	W	I	T	C	H	I	N	G	H	O	U	R	■	O	M	I	T
■	O	N	T	O	P	I	C	■	■	R	E	N	A	L	■	N	E	W	B	I	E
■	■	■	N	O	R	A	■	R	U	E	S	■	D	I	P	S	■	■
B	L	T	S	■	D	E	S	S	E	R	T	T	W	I	N	E	■	L	O	D
R	E	W	E	T	S	■	I	D	O	S	■	A	N	G	E	L	I	N	A
A	C	E	T	O	■	M	S	N	■	■	C	R	O	S	S	O	V	E	R
T	H	E	T	W	E	A	K	E	R	S	E	X	■	■	■	D	I	O	R
■	D	O	N	A	T	E	■	A	P	S	I	S	■	S	K	I	N	N	Y
A	S	K	■	I	D	E	E	■	J	O	T	■	T	H	E	O	■	G	E	L
S	T	I	P	E	S	■	T	I	A	R	A	■	A	U	G	U	S	T	■	■
A	R	L	O	■	■	T	H	E	S	O	U	L	O	F	T	W	I	T
C	O	L	O	R	F	A	S	T	■	A	B	A	■	A	R	I	S	E
A	D	E	L	A	I	D	E	■	I	L	E	S	■	E	X	A	L	T	S
T	E	R	■	F	L	I	P	O	N	E	S	T	W	I	G	■	P	L	O	T
■	■	S	T	E	N	■	I	T	A	T	■	I	N	G	A	■	■	■
P	R	I	E	S	T	■	P	L	E	N	A	■	G	L	O	R	Y	B	E
H	A	R	E	■	Y	O	U	C	A	N	T	T	W	I	N	E	M	A	L	L
I	Z	O	D	■	P	I	L	A	R	■	E	V	A	N	■	A	C	R	I	D
L	E	N	S	■	E	D	E	N	S	■	S	A	M	E	■	S	A	K	E	S

```
P A E L L A S ■ A C R O S S ■ A T T E S T E D
A N C I E N T ■ C H E W U P ■ P R O F O R M A
S E C O N D O ■ C I N E M A ■ P O R T R A I T
T W E N T Y P O U N D N O T E ■ P I S T I L S
■ ■ ■ Y P R E S ■ ■ L A S H ■ ■ ■ L I U
I V E S ■ B E T A S ■ P R E T T Y P O I S O N
C I T Y P O L I C E ■ E A S E L ■ I N N ■ ■
I R O N A L L O Y ■ I N N E R ■ K E T C H U P
E I N S T E I N ■ S N A G ■ V I T A L I T Y
R D S ■ E R N S ■ C E L E B R I T Y P O K E R
■ ■ S N O G ■ P A R T ■ L E A S ■ ■ V E R O
B E R E T S ■ D I R T Y P O O L ■ T H E S I S
L E E R ■ ■ I O N E ■ P E A S ■ B O E R ■ ■
U N I V E R S I T Y P O S T ■ D U M A ■ B S A
R I C E B E L T ■ R I O S ■ U S T R O O P S
B E H O O V E ■ S P I N S ■ P E T I T G R I S
■ ■ U N U ■ C O R O T ■ T R E A T Y P O R T
P A R T Y P O O P E R S ■ H E A R S ■ U N O S
A N O ■ ■ C P U S ■ H E R S H ■ ■ ■ ■ ■
R I T C H I E ■ P U B L I C I T Y P O S T E R
A M A R I L L O ■ M A I D E N ■ M E R C Y M E
D A T A F L O W ■ E D S E L S ■ E S C A P E D
E L E G I S T S ■ S E A R L E ■ S T A T O R S
```

```
S P I K E ■ G A M E ■ D R U B ■ S P A T S
A L O F T ■ A W O L ■ R A T E ■ P E R E C
D U T C H S T E W I N D I E S ■ A T O N E
E S A ■ O P E D ■ ■ O R S ■ O A R S M E N
■ ■ ■ L I L ■ L O N E A R T S S T A T E
I A M ■ O N E M O R E ■ O S T E O ■ ■
S H A G G Y G O D S T O R Y ■ A R R O W S
I M P L Y ■ ■ T I E ■ R A K E ■ ■ E Z I O
T A L I ■ A C H ■ R I B R O A S T ■ Z S A
I D E D ■ B A R B ■ L I E ■ R O O M I E S
■ ■ G E N E R A L P O T S O F F I C E ■
B A R S O A P ■ O A S ■ T N U T ■ L S A T
E G O ■ P R E O W N E D ■ T L C ■ E M E R
E N V S ■ T R O I ■ R I A ■ D A I R Y
P I E C E S ■ I N C O O L P A R E N T I S
■ ■ O P T I N ■ S W E E T E N ■ H E T
O N E T H I N G S T A N D ■ A C T ■ ■
G O L F E R S ■ C I G ■ A N T I ■ C A B
H O A R D ■ T H R E E L I M E I S L A N D
A S N E R ■ E M A G ■ O W E N ■ T Y P E A
M E D E A ■ P O P S ■ B O N D ■ S N O W Y
```

```
D O M S █ P U P █ █ O B O E █ C R E A T E
O B I E █ E S O █ I M O U T █ L E C T I N
G E T T A K E N █ C A N T D O A T H I N G
M Y T H R O A T H U R T S █ L I E O V E R
A S S █ B E L I E █ █ O T T E R S █ E D S
█ █ R O T O █ Y A W N E R █ E T C █ █ █
C A B A R E T █ M G R █ P I T █ A F A R
A L I C I A █ N O R A D █ B I G S M I L E
S E R I O █ S E M I P R O A T H L E T E S
K E D S █ H E W █ P U R L I E U █ T S P
█ █ S T O I C █ I M A G E █ A N G I O █
S O N █ D R E S S E R █ I N T █ D A B S
T H E R O A D T O A T H E N S █ H I T I T
O N S I M M E R █ L I E N S █ B O D E G A
P O T S █ D I P █ E A T █ S O W S E A R
█ █ E N S █ P R E S T O █ O L I O █ █
P J S █ U N I S E X █ M S D O S █ A D A
O A T H A Y S █ S H O W B O A T H O T E L
L I E U N D E R O A T H █ F L I E D O U T
A M E R C E █ A L L O Y █ A Y E █ I N C A
R E N T E R █ I D E S █ R E S █ N E E R
```

```
I T A L █ B E L L E █ A T O N A L █ P A Z
C E C E █ O N I O N █ S A T I N Y █ U M A
E X C H A N G E O F S T R I N G S █ T I P
S T E A M █ U T A H █ S O L O M O N S █
█ █ D R A M A █ N A M E █ E L O N █ █
N A E █ H O L Y S T R O L L E R █ U S M A
C U D D L E D U P █ I D E A L █ D E T E R
O N T O █ O M E █ A R O S E █ A T M
S T O N E A R M E D B A N D I T S █ I R A
█ █ A P L A Y █ E L R O Y █ R E A R E D
N A S T I L Y █ B R I E R █ L A R U S S A
E N T I C E █ G R I N S █ H E W E D █
P T A █ U L T R A V I O L E T S T R A Y S
A R R █ R E O I L █ A L I █ E L E E
L U C R E █ J P E G S █ C O N V E Y I N G
I M H O █ G O E S A L L S T O U T █ C S A
█ █ E R N O █ S L O E █ N E A L E █
K E N Y A T T A █ T V A D █ T O P A Z
E X E █ W H E R E T H E B O Y S S T A R E
D I M █ A I R A C E █ L E V E E █ T U N E
S T Y █ B M I N O R █ S L E P T █ O L E S
```

65

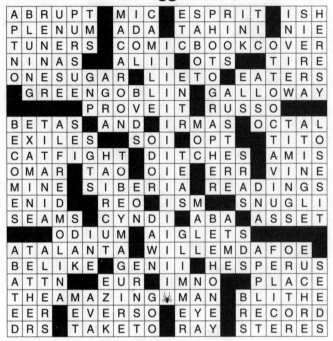

A	B	R	U	P	T	■	M	I	C	■	E	S	P	R	I	T	■	I	S	H
P	L	E	N	U	M	■	A	D	A	■	T	A	H	I	N	I	■	N	I	E
T	U	N	E	R	S	■	C	O	M	I	C	B	O	O	K	C	O	V	E	R
N	I	N	A	S	■	■	A	L	I	I	■	O	T	S	■	■	T	I	R	E
O	N	E	S	U	G	A	R	■	L	I	E	T	O	■	E	A	T	E	R	S
■	G	R	E	E	N	G	O	B	L	I	N	■	G	A	L	L	O	W	A	Y
■	■	■	P	R	O	V	E	I	T	■	■	R	U	S	S	O	■	■	■	■
B	E	T	A	S	■	A	N	D	■	I	R	M	A	S	■	O	C	T	A	L
E	X	I	L	E	S	■	S	O	I	■	O	P	T	■	■	T	I	T	O	■
C	A	T	F	I	G	H	T	■	D	I	T	C	H	E	S	■	A	M	I	S
O	M	A	R	■	T	A	O	■	O	I	E	■	E	R	R	■	V	I	N	E
M	I	N	E	■	S	I	B	E	R	I	A	■	R	E	A	D	I	N	G	S
E	N	I	D	■	R	E	O	■	I	S	M	■	■	S	N	U	G	L	I	■
S	E	A	M	S	■	C	Y	N	D	I	■	A	B	A	■	A	S	S	E	T
■	■	■	O	D	I	U	M	■	A	I	G	L	E	T	S	■	■	■	■	■
A	T	A	L	A	N	T	A	■	W	I	L	L	E	M	D	A	F	O	E	■
B	E	L	I	K	E	■	G	E	N	I	I	■	H	E	S	P	E	R	U	S
A	T	T	N	■	■	E	U	R	■	I	M	N	O	■	■	P	L	A	C	E
T	H	E	A	M	A	Z	I	N	G	✳	M	A	N	■	B	L	I	T	H	E
E	E	R	■	E	V	E	R	S	O	■	E	Y	E	■	R	E	C	O	R	D
D	R	S	■	T	A	K	E	T	O	■	■	R	A	Y	■	S	T	E	R	E	S

66

T	I	E	P	O	L	O	■	A	D	A	P	T	S	■	B	B	G	U	N	S
A	M	M	O	N	I	A	■	N	I	C	A	E	A	■	Y	O	U	S	E	E
W	H	E	R	E	S	T	H	E	B	R	I	E	F	■	T	A	S	M	A	N
S	O	R	T	■	T	H	U	G	S	■	S	M	A	S	H	■	H	I	R	T
■	■	S	P	O	S	E	■	■	F	A	E	R	I	E	■	E	N	T	O	■
A	L	B	I	O	N	■	■	B	R	A	N	D	I	N	B	O	S	T	O	N
F	A	L	D	O	■	P	S	E	U	D	O	■	■	E	Y	E	■	■	■	■
B	R	I	E	R	B	E	W	A	R	E	■	T	E	X	■	I	N	B	A	D
S	A	P	■	B	E	G	E	T	■	■	A	U	S	■	S	L	O	A	N	E
■	■	C	O	C	O	A	■	B	E	T	R	O	T	H	■	I	D	E	A	■
K	E	E	P	Y	O	U	R	E	Y	E	O	N	T	H	E	B	R	A	W	L
A	X	I	L	■	O	T	O	L	O	G	Y	■	E	R	N	I	E	■	■	■
M	A	N	U	A	L	■	F	I	B	■	■	C	R	A	Z	E	■	A	A	S
A	M	E	S	S	■	M	F	A	■	M	E	D	I	C	I	N	E	B	R	O
■	■	■	P	E	I	■	■	P	I	E	R	C	E	■	N	U	B	I	A	■
B	R	E	A	S	T	S	E	L	L	E	R	S	■	■	B	I	P	E	D	S
E	E	N	Y	■	A	D	I	E	U	S	■	■	I	S	I	A	H	■	■	■
E	D	G	E	■	G	O	F	E	R	■	O	A	T	E	R	■	O	D	O	R
T	H	I	S	B	E	■	F	L	A	T	B	R	E	A	D	T	R	U	C	K
L	A	N	I	E	R	■	E	E	L	P	O	T	■	T	I	E	I	N	T	O
E	T	E	R	N	E	■	L	E	S	S	E	E	■	S	E	M	A	N	A	S

69

Grid 69:

G	R	A	D	E	D	■	H	T	M	L	■	D	A	M	P	S	■	S	A	X
N	O	J	I	V	E	■	A	R	E	A	■	E	L	I	O	T	■	P	R	Y
A	T	O	N	I	C	■	W	O	N	T	■	V	I	S	O	R	■	Y	U	L
R	E	B	A	T	E	S	■	T	H	E	R	E	S	T	H	E	R	O	B	E
■	■	■	R	A	M	I	S	■	A	D	U	L	T	■	■	■	T	E	N	A	M
U	S	S	■	■	D	E	O	D	A	T	O	■	P	A	C	E	■	■	■
C	L	A	I	M	■	E	G	R	E	T	■	P	E	A	C	H	F	O	E	S
L	O	A	M	A	N	D	A	B	N	E	R	■	A	R	T	Y	■	P	L	Y
A	B	B	A	C	Y	■	■	■	A	R	R	A	S	■	L	I	E	N
■	■	R	A	S	S	L	E	■	K	N	I	T	S	■	L	A	N	C	E
■	A	R	E	W	E	H	A	V	I	N	G	P	H	O	N	E	Y	E	T
G	N	A	T	S	■	A	N	E	N	T	■	S	A	L	O	N	S	■
O	D	D	S	■	E	V	A	N	S	■	■	■	O	O	L	O	N	G
L	O	I	■	T	A	U	R	■	P	E	R	S	I	A	N	R	O	G	U	E
F	R	I	A	R	T	O	K	E	■	C	O	A	T	I	■	E	W	O	K	S
■	■	L	O	S	T	■	S	C	O	L	D	E	D	■	■	D	E	T
S	C	R	A	P	■	■	S	T	A	L	L	■	M	E	D	I	C	■
P	A	I	N	I	N	T	H	E	B	O	A	T	■	D	E	C	O	D	E	S
I	T	T	■	C	O	R	A	L	■	G	W	E	N	■	C	A	V	O	R	T
F	E	Z	■	A	T	O	L	L	■	I	A	N	A	■	A	M	E	L	I	A
F	R	Y	■	L	I	N	E	A	■	C	Y	T	E	■	L	E	T	T	E	R

70

Grid 70:

A	C	E	D	■	V	E	N	N	■	E	S	T	■	I	R	E	F	U	S	E
S	U	M	O	■	I	M	A	C	■	D	C	I	■	T	E	A	R	S	A	T
K	E	E	P	S	S	T	R	A	I	G	H	T	■	S	A	T	I	D	L	E
M	I	N	I	M	I	■	C	A	P	E	L	L	A	■	D	I	C	O	T	■
E	N	D	N	O	T	E	S	■	S	W	E	E	P	S	S	T	A	L	L	S
■	■	G	L	O	M	■	S	O	A	P	■	O	P	T	■	S	L	A	P
A	R	I	■	T	R	I	T	E	■	Y	S	I	D	R	O	■	S	A	K	I
D	U	M	P	S	S	T	O	C	K	S	■	N	A	Y	■	D	E	R	E	K
E	T	T	E	■	■	L	Y	E	■	S	T	L	■	D	R	E	S	S	Y
S	T	O	R	A	B	L	E	■	N	C	A	R	■	U	E	Y	■
■	Y	O	U	R	A	T	T	E	N	T	I	O	N	P	L	E	A	S	E
■	■	■	R	I	D	■	Y	A	R	D	■	I	N	E	R	R	A	N	T
J	A	N	S	E	N	■	R	E	N	■	O	O	P	■	■	L	U	T	E
E	L	E	C	T	■	T	A	U	■	S	K	I	P	S	S	T	O	N	E	S
S	L	U	R	■	P	O	M	P	E	O	■	L	Y	N	C	H	■	A	R	T
T	O	R	A	■	O	U	R	■	X	M	A	S	■	I	R	E	S	■
S	W	A	P	S	S	T	O	R	I	E	S	■	A	T	A	L	A	N	T	A
■	A	L	I	C	E	■	D	I	T	M	A	R	S	■	P	O	N	I	E	S
I	N	G	R	O	U	P	■	D	R	O	P	S	S	T	I	T	C	H	E	S
S	C	I	O	R	R	A	■	G	O	R	■	V	A	I	N	■	T	I	N	E
M	E	A	N	E	S	T	■	E	W	E	■	P	I	N	G	■	A	L	A	S

71

```
W A T T ■ D E B A T E ■ T O N G S ■ D A R E
A S H E ■ D R E A M O N ■ E F I L E ■ I T E M
G A E A ■ R O L L I N G I N T H E A I S L E S
■ P E T R E L ■ S C I ■ N O H ■ A L L M A N ■
■ V A N I L L A I C E C R E A M ■ S A N T A
■ B I B S ■ E O S ■ B A S E S ■ S A L T E D
S I L L ■ U R L ■ S S E ■ I S A K ■ A R E ■
W A D E I N ■ L O W E R E A S T S I D E ■ ■
I N E ■ S R I ■ N E E ■ A L I ■ I R E P E A T
S C A T H E D ■ M A K E S A N E N T R A N C E
S A D R ■ S L I E R ■ V E R G E ■ M U S T Y
■ ■ A P T E R ■ C E L ■ R E G A L ■ ■
M A R C O ■ A L T A R ■ S O O T Y ■ E N D E
T H E H O U S E O F M I R T H ■ C R A T E R S
S A L E R N O ■ V A R ■ I O N ■ H A D ■ C I T
■ A S L I K E L Y A S N O T ■ T A C K L E
A P P ■ E L O I ■ V E E ■ O P E ■ H A L E
V A R L E T ■ O N E T O ■ I D A ■ D I N S ■
G R E E T ■ P L A C I N G E N D T O E N D ■
■ O N S A L E ■ M H O ■ U R E ■ S A V A N T
C L A S S A C T I O N L A W S U I T ■ S E E P
D E M O ■ R A I S E ■ E N I S L E S ■ E C R U
S E E N ■ K N O T S ■ D O N E E S ■ A K I N
```

72

```
B I K E R S ■ N A C HO ■ S O R E L O S E R
A O R T I C ■ I D A HO ■ O R I G I N A T E
S U I S S E ■ P A T HO ■ D E P O N E N T S
S S S ■ E N D A T ■ H O R A S ■ E A T A T
O A K T R E E ■ E C H O E S ■ S H U L A ■
■ R E S O L D ■ C H O P ■ S H A P A B L E
A P I N ■ N O R ■ S H O O A W A Y ■ R A I L
B U N D L E S U P ■ H O S E A ■ R U M B L E
A G G R O ■ M U C H O ■ S T E I N ■ Y A M
C E L I C A ■ C O H O S ■ H A D U P ■ ■
K T E L ■ L O O K W H O S H E R E ■ A J A M
■ S E T A L ■ S H O R E ■ S E T O N S
A B C ■ L A R D S ■ H O S N I ■ T I L E D
M O H A I R ■ M A C HO ■ S A I D H E L L O
C O R P ■ B O A T S H O E ■ M D I ■ N Y E S
S K I P T O W N ■ P H O N ■ B L A S T S ■
■ S L A Y S ■ C O H O S T ■ E L A S T I C
L E T I N ■ O R T HO ■ O N S E T ■ N S A
I M M E D I A T E ■ H O A R Y ■ C U B I S T
A M A R E T T O S ■ H O B O S ■ T R O C H E
M E S S M A T E S ■ H O U S E ■ S N A K E S
```

73

```
RON   SAW  ORBITS    DOWEL
INARUSH  BARNETT   IRENE
PULASKI  EVILEYE  ORING
ASAGIFT  SEDAN  APR  LUG
     GEO  BELLY   ISRAELIS
GATE  RAE   ESPN  EMT
ROAD  TREATS  SUNYATSEN
ARK   HATCH  BANE  SUPRA
STEPHEN  NEGATIVE   YIP
PASSIM  MESON  SELLECCA
    ASHORE  SUN  OREIDA
TATTOOER  ADORN  VENTED
EDU   NECKLACE  MANACLE
MIRED  FURY  KAPUT   HEM
PANDERSTO  ESPOSO  RENO
    GSA  ICBM  PER  ERIN
IMPETIGO  ROAMS  MAT
NYU  ILL  JETTA  JUPITUS
ELTON  OPINION  ASARULE
POOLE  WILDONE  WIREMEN
TUNED   PLANET  ACT  SET
```

74

```
BIRDS  SMITHS  ADE  NEMO
ATEUP  TOWARD  URN  ADIP
RISKY  ONETHINKATATIME
ASIAN  ATRA  ASTHMATIC
KINKOFTHEROAD  RILE
    IVES  XSANDOS  DID
GUSSET  MIMEO  EAN  CODE
UNA  LADYSINKSTHEBLUES
SLRS  OWEN  ASL  EATME
HIAWATHA  UFOS  HEN
 THISMAYSTINKALITTLE
    NTS  EENY  DISSOLVE
RANDR  ALL  XMAN  NOES
THELORDOFTHERINKS  YRS
EAVE  AIN  EASER  NEEDTO
STE  LINEARA  SONY
    REEL  BIGBANKTHEORY
PAMDAWBER  OHIO  OHGEE
AWINKANDAPRAYER  RODAN
GENA  YAO  DETECT  ALERT
ODDS  SIM  TOSSES  SENSE
```

```
B E A T   A R C H   T S A R   S P O T O N
A T L E I S U R E   R A R A   H A D A G O
S A L T W A T E R T A F F Y   O P I N E D
A P N E A   G E N E V A   S Y R I N G E S
L E I   N E E D   N E R F   I T S
    G O N E R   R E L I E F P I T C H E R
I S H T A R   C O T   N A P E   L A N E
B A T H   P R O   O L D I E   R A S T A
E M E E R   R I M I N I   R E P E N T E D
T E R R A   E M I N E N T   E D G E R S
    P U P P E T S T R I N G S
S H A R P S   R E L E A S E   E A G E R
C A R E E N E D   R E L I N E   A B U S E
A T O L L   D O I N G   P O T   A N N A
R E M I   L I N T   S S T   H I T T E R
P R A C T I C A L J O K E   T O N E R
    O T T   L O R I   F O O L   I F S
S O U R P U S S   T A L L E R   A N G L E
I M P A I R   L I T T L E R E D W A G O N
B I T I N G   U L E E   M A R E S N E S T
S T O D G Y   R E D D   S L O W   U R S A
```

```
W A I L S   C A A N   A M I G O   A M F M
A S S E T   A S T O   W A T E R   R A R A
S H U T U P S H O P   A M E N C O R N E R
P E Z   F R E E Z E F R A M E   C O D E S
S N U F F E D   A D S   S E W A R D
    A S P   F U R   A S T A   L E E
M O S T   L O O K O U T M O U N T A I N
U S H E R   O G L E   S H O D   A Y N
S I T D O W N R E S T A U R A N T S
E R E   B O G E Y   R I D E   E W E R S
S I T C O M S   B U R   A M E R I C A
  S L A T E   S C A T   E M C E E   S O W
    D O N T L E A V E M E H A N G I N G
  N P R   E Y R E   A B L E   S I N C E
F A R E W E L L A D D R E S S   A G E E
E V E   O I L Y   E N D   C A N
M A S S O N   P E N   G A U T A M A
O R A T E   C A R R Y O N B A G S   N A N
R O G E R B A C O N   S O R R Y S I G H T
A N E W   T R I N I   L A I T   I S L E S
L E S S   W E D G E   O H O H   E M E R Y
```

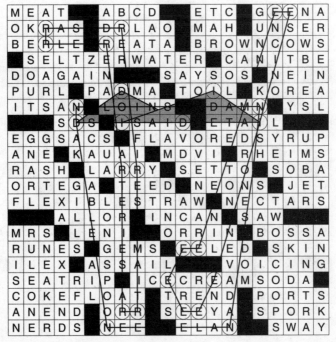

77

79

```
H O L L O W   ▮   C L O D   ▮   A T T A I N E D
E R O I C A   ▮   F R O D O   ▮   M O I S T U R E
C O U N T S N O(I)S E S   ▮   A N T I E T A M
▮   S E A H O R S E   ▮   U T I L S   ▮   C S I
C O I N   ▮   L I(M)P S E R V I C E   ▮   F R E T
R U N S T O   ▮   I S E E   ▮   D O R A
E N G   ▮   R A B B I T(P)E A R S   ▮   P A C E S
E C U   ▮   I D E A S   ▮   E A S E   ▮   K E A
P E P S   ▮   C H I C K E N F(L)I N G E R S
▮   W O R K S   ▮   H O N E S   ▮   D E A R I E
S O M E D A Y   ▮   D I V O T   ▮   G E N U S E S
E V A D E D   ▮   S A L I C   ▮   L E A D S
T A K E S O N T H E C H(A)I N   ▮   S F P D
A T E   ▮   S N E E   ▮   G R E T A   ▮   R O E
T E S L A   ▮   B R O W(N)B E A T E N   ▮   E R I
▮   G I N A   ▮   B E A U   ▮   A S S E T S
I D O L   ▮   F A C E(T)P O W D E R   ▮   E A S T
R O O   ▮   A L L O Y   ▮   Y E A R L O N G
I N D I C A T E   ▮   P(S)A L M R E A D E R S
S H O W E R E D   ▮   A U N T S   ▮   S H I N E S
H O N O R E R S   ▮   L E T S   ▮   S U N T A N
```

80

```
J A B   ▮   O P A L S   ▮   O L D A G E   ▮   A D D L E
U S E   ▮   N O R A H   ▮   C O O L I T   ▮   L A U E R
N I L   ▮   P L A(C)E S T O G O P E O P L E T O
G A L P A L   ▮   S P E A K S U P   ▮   G H E T T O
▮   P O T O K   ▮   H U D   ▮   C L A Y
T H E(P)R I N C E S S A N D T H E   ▮   F L U
H I P P O   ▮   O A R S   ▮   K A U A I   ▮   M A R A T
A R P E L   ▮   W M D   ▮   W I T H R(E)L A T I V(E)
W E E D   ▮   T H A   ▮   Z E N   ▮   F A D E S I N
S S R   ▮   S H O C K E R   ▮   M A E   ▮   K R A K E N
▮   T H E W H(I)T E S O F T H E(I)R
J A G U A R   ▮   O D A   ▮   H A R V A R D   ▮   T A N
I N A T R E E   ▮   I O N   ▮   O S S   ▮   S A G O
B E S T O F L(U)C K T O   ▮   P I K   ▮   A T P A R
E S S E N   ▮   I S A A C   ▮   T E L E   ▮   N A D I A
S T Y   ▮   H E A L T H(Y)W E A L T H(Y)A N D
▮   B O I L   ▮   S E P   ▮   L I E I N
M O T O W N   ▮   D I T S I E S T   ▮   N U N C I O
W H E(R)E T H E W I L D T H I N G S   ▮   E R R
A N N A N   ▮   A M I N O R   ▮   O D I L E   ▮   R A Y
H O S T S   ▮   G I N K G O   ▮   W E B E R   ▮   S E X
```

81

A	C	E	■	A	S	C	A	P	■	C	O	R	A	L	■	N	O	A	H	S
M	R	X	■	S	M	A	R	T	■	A	R	E	T	E	■	O	P	R	A	H
B	O	X	S	C	O	R	E	S	■	N	I	S	E	I	■	T	E	T	R	A
L	O	O	P	H	O	L	E	■	R	A	S	C	A	L	■	O	N	E	A	L
E	N	N	E	■	C	A	L	L	E	D	O	U	T	A	T	F	I	R	S	T
■	■	W	A	H	■	I	N	A	N	E	■	■	A	T	T	Y	S	■	■
■	S	T	E	P	■	C	A	P	E	■	■	R	O	P	E	■	■	■
F	A	I	R	B	A	L	L	■	W	A	L	K	E	D	I	N	A	R	U	N
E	L	M	S	■	M	A	O	■	S	L	E	N	D	E	R	■	L	U	K	E
Z	E	E	■	P	I	N	O	N	■	I	C	E	■	■	C	O	B	R	A
■	S	W	I	N	G	F	O	R	T	H	E	F	E	N	C	E	S	■
S	P	L	A	T	■	■	S	E	T	■	L	I	L	A	C	■	I	N	K
O	D	O	R	■	E	N	F	I	E	L	D	■	E	I	N	■	S	T	A	G
B	A	T	T	I	N	G	O	R	D	E	R	■	F	O	U	L	T	I	P	S
■	■	D	O	O	R	■	■	Y	E	S	T	■	I	O	N	A	■	■
■	N	O	S	E	R	■	A	S	T	O	R	■	■	C	E	O	■	■
B	O	T	T	O	M	O	F	T	H	E	F	I	F	T	H	■	P	L	E	A
R	E	O	R	G	■	B	E	L	I	E	F	■	R	E	A	L	T	O	R	S
A	V	O	I	R	■	A	D	A	R	N	■	F	U	L	L	C	O	U	N	T
G	I	L	D	A	■	M	I	S	T	S	■	A	I	L	E	D	■	T	I	E
G	L	E	E	M	■	A	N	T	S	Y	■	S	T	A	T	S	■	S	E	R

82

W	I	N	■	D	O	W	N	S	■	A	D	A	P	T	■	C	S	I	S
A	N	A	S	■	A	W	A	I	T	■	V	O	T	R	E	■	R	A	N	K
R	U	I	N	■	T	E	S	S	A	■	O	R	T	O	N	■	A	L	O	U
D	I	V	I	D	E	D	H	I	G	H	W	A	Y	■	P	A	C	E	R
S	T	E	V	E	■	■	G	E	E	■	S	M	I	R	K	S	■	■
■	E	V	I	L	■	B	E	A	D	S	■	I	N	P	E	R	I	L
F	A	L	L	E	N	A	P	A	R	T	■	L	A	S	S	■	D	O	L	L
L	I	E	■	L	A	T	I	N	S	■	R	O	M	E	■	S	W	O	R	D
A	R	M	B	O	N	E	S	■	■	S	E	V	E	R	■	L	I	M	E	S
B	E	A	R	P	I	T	■	A	C	U	M	E	N	■	I	O	N	■
■	S	N	O	■	T	O	R	N	A	S	U	N	D	E	R	■	D	S	T
■	K	E	Y	■	H	A	R	A	S	S	■	R	E	T	O	T	A	L
H	I	D	E	R	■	G	O	T	O	N	■	E	M	P	O	W	E	R	S
I	S	I	N	G	■	I	D	O	L	■	T	O	R	I	E	S	■	A	S	A
G	A	R	P	■	E	G	A	L	■	B	A	N	A	N	A	S	P	L	I	T
H	O	T	R	O	L	L	■	E	B	O	L	A	■	E	T	U	I	■
■	B	O	R	G	I	A	■	O	A	K	■	■	P	C	L	A	B	■
■	T	I	M	E	R	■	F	R	A	C	T	U	R	E	D	S	K	U	L	L
W	I	K	I	■	E	A	T	A	T	■	O	D	E	T	O	■	E	N	D	E
A	V	E	S	■	C	U	R	I	E	■	M	O	T	T	O	■	R	N	A	S
Y	O	R	E	■	O	F	A	L	L	■	E	N	D	E	R	■	S	S	S

83

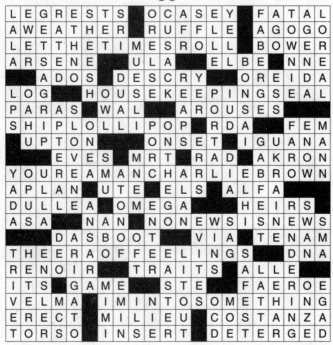

```
L E G R E S T S ■ O C A S E Y ■ F A T A L
A W E A T H E R ■ R U F F L E ■ A G O G O
L E T T H E T I M E S R O L L ■ B O W E R
A R S E N E ■ ■ U L A ■ ■ E L B E ■ N N E
■ ■ A D O S ■ D E S C R Y ■ ■ O R E I D A
L O G ■ H O U S E K E E P I N G S E A L ■
P A R A S ■ W A L ■ ■ A R O U S E S ■ ■
S H I P L O L L I P O P ■ R D A ■ ■ F E M
■ U P T O N ■ ■ O N S E T ■ I G U A N A
■ ■ E V E S ■ M R T ■ R A D ■ A K R O N
Y O U R E A M A N C H A R L I E B R O W N
A P L A N ■ U T E ■ E L S ■ A L F A ■ ■
D U L L E A ■ O M E G A ■ ■ H E I R S ■
A S A ■ N A N ■ N O N E W S I S N E W S
■ ■ D A S B O O T ■ V I A ■ T E N A M
T H E E R A O F F E E L I N G S ■ D N A
R E N O I R ■ ■ T R A I T S ■ A L L E ■
I T S ■ G A M E ■ ■ S T E ■ F A E R O E
V E L M A ■ I M I N T O S O M E T H I N G
E R E C T ■ M I L I E U ■ C O S T A N Z A
T O R S O ■ I N S E R T ■ D E T E R G E D
```

84

```
H I P P O ■ S T E M ■ A T T A R ■ D A L I
A L A I N ■ T I T O ■ B A H A I ■ E L A N
S L I C E S I N T O ■ E B E R T ■ G I G A
■ N O T E N O U G H T O R E T I R E O N
A S K ■ O A K ■ ■ E T U I ■ ■ D E N S E
G O I N G T O B E A R E L A T I V E ■ ■
E L L I O T ■ A F L ■ D I L A T E ■ F A X
G A L L ■ L C D T V S ■ ■ T I L ■ S A T E
A C E ■ S E A L ■ A I R P O L L U T I O N
P E R O T ■ L O W ■ R A E ■ ■ D H A R M A
■ ■ L E T I T A L L H A N G O U T ■ ■
A Z A L E A ■ C I O ■ T A O ■ R E E K S
F I N A L L Y G O T I T ■ D U M A ■ A I T
A N T S ■ C I R ■ N O L I T A ■ I S M E
R E E ■ R E P U T E ■ R A N ■ F A C T O R
■ ■ R E D E F I N E T H E M I S S I O N
S A L E S ■ F L A W ■ ■ O O P ■ N N E
T H A T H A S N T B E E N W A S H E D ■
Y E T I ■ L I E S L ■ A M I N O A C I D S
L A I N ■ A N S A E ■ S E R E ■ L H A S A
E D N A ■ N E S T S ■ E X E D ■ T O N T O
```

85

P	R	O	N	G		R	O	N	D	O		L	A	P	D		R	P	M	S
R	U	M	O	R		O	C	E	A	N		I	N	R	I		I	R	M	A
O	N	E	M	O	R	E	T	I	M	E		M	N	E	M	O	N	I	C	S
	E	N	E		E	G	O	M	A	N	I	A		S	M	U	G	G	L	E
		N	E	U			A	G	A	S		S	E	E	I	T				
J	I	F		E	N	G	I	N	E	M	O	U	N	T	S		O	U	L	U
A	M	I	L	L	I	O	N		D	E	L	L	A		T	E	N	N	I	S
P	A	N	A	S	O	N	I	C		D	A	P	S		R	E	E	V	E	
E	D	D	Y		N	O	T	T	O	M	E	N	T	I	O	N		M	E	M
D	E	I	S	T		S	R	T	A		O	M	N	I	V	O	R	E		
	N	O	O	I	L		L	E	X	U	S		A	T	E	A	T			
M	A	G	N	E	T	I	C		I	S	I	S			S	M	I	L	E	
A	R	N		D	I	V	I	N	E	M	O	T	H	E	R		P	O	O	L
D	I	E	C	I		E	N	O	L		E	A	S	E	M	E	N	T	S	
R	A	M	O	N	A		E	N	I	A	C		L	A	T	E	D	A	T	E
E	L	O	N		N	O	M	E	N	C	L	A	T	U	R	E		L	O	S
			T	R	A	L	A		O	C	A	S			I	T	T			
V	I	D	E	O	E	D		I	R	O	N	M	I	K	E		O	I	D	
O	N	E	M	O	M	E	N	T		S	T	A	T	E	S	W	O	M	E	N
C	O	E	N		I	S	I	T		T	O	R	I	C		A	T	S	E	A
E	N	D	S		A	T	T	Y		S	N	A	C	K		S	H	O	R	N

86

A	R	R	O	W		R	C	V	R			T	B	S	P		C	P	A	S
B	O	I	S	E		O	H	I	O		K	O	R	E	A		L	O	L	L
C	A	P	R	I		B	E	E	R	B	U	R	I	A	L	P	O	L	K	A
	R	E	I	G	N	O	F	T	E	R	R	I	E	R		I	S	L	E	T
		C	H	E	T			M	O	T	I	F			L	E	O	N	E	
A	B	S		H	I	D	E					E	N	M	I	T	I	E	S	
B	O	T	A	N	I	C	A	L	G	U	A	R	D	I	A	N	S			
U	S	A	G	E		S	I	E	N	N	A		C	I	G		D	O	T	
T	H	R	A	S	H		K	O	D	I	A	K	M	O	M	E	N	T		
	C	I	T	I	B	A	N	K		D	U	E		N	A	S	T	Y		
C	O	H	N		M	A	G	O	O		G	E	R	R	Y		I	D	O	L
A	M	A	S	S		R	O	O		E	R	A	S	A	B	L	E			
P	A	R	T	Y	I	N	G	G	I	F	T			M	A	M	M	A	L	
T	N	T		R	O	E		I	L	D	U	C	E		M	A	O	R	I	
		L	I	T	T	L	E	O	R	P	H	E	A	N	A	N	N	I	E	
R	E	S	O	N	A	T	E			E	L	S	E			A	D	D		
O	R	I	N	G		C	U	O	M	O		C	A	L	F					
D	O	D	G	E		P	A	R	K	I	N	G	M	E	T	E	O	R	S	
M	I	L	E	S	P	E	R	G	A	L	L	E	O	N		G	R	O	H	L
A	C	E	S		C	A	R	E	Y		A	R	O	D		I	G	L	O	O
N	A	S	T		S	L	E	D			Y	E	N	S		T	E	L	E	X

```
A R T S   L E A F L I K E     T S G A R P
N E H I   L E N A O L I N   S H E L T E R
G A E L I C W A R N I N G   H A V A R T I
E L I O T     E G A D   A R T E S I A N
R A S   C L A S S I C A C T I O N S U I T
E L L   H U G O       L I E N     M L S
D E E D   R U S T I C B U C K E T S
    O S A K A   A B O M B     A L C A N
U P F O R   U N S E T   L A I L A A L I
S U M   S C A N N E D   K I N G L Y R I C
E R A T   R O D I N   C N O T E   S P E E
F I N E T U N I C   P R O N E T O   E N T
U T I L I Z E D   B E E T S   P A N S Y
L Y C E E     I R E S T   Z I P I T
    O R I G I N A L C Y N I C   L E V I
S O O   W I S C     O T O E   R A M
T O P I C O F T H E M O R N I N G   A R P
A L I M E N T S   C E R A   G O N N A
M A N M A D E   G R E A T L Y M Y S T I C
P L E A S E D   P U T T O S E A   L I S T
S A D D E R   A S S E N T T O   O C H S
```

```
B R A S S   S T R A W   S O P   G R A S S
R A B A T   T R O T H   T W A   T O V A H
A C E L A   R O S E A G A I N   O T E R O
S K E T C H O U T   T H I N G S   C R A P
    S K I P P E D   I N G R A M   A L P
P A P   S P H E R I C   S T A V E   G E E
O N A T   S E R E N E R   O V E R S E E R
P A R E N T   D A T E D   Y A L L
S T A M B E R G   H U N C H   S O A R E D
T O D   C R O O K   S I T O N   T W I N E
A L I T   S T I E S   N E V I L   S P E W
R I G H T   S N I T S   N E N E S   P R Y
S A M E A S   G R A T E   R E T R I E V E
    U N T O   A L E P H   S A D D A Y
J O H N G A L T   E A S E F U L   S I T E
U N E   L Y D I A   M O R O N I C   T E D
M E W   E E L E R S   M E R I D I A
P H E W   R A G T O P   W A T E R D R O P
I O D I C   T A L L A D E G A   C A I R O
N U T S O   I M A   S A G E R   U P P E R
G R O P E   N E B   S W O R D   S T E N T
```

89

```
C A B A L ■ P A R C ■ I D I D ■ C O M E T
A L E R O ■ A B E L ■ N A V Y ■ E L O P E
P L A Y W I T H M A T C H E S ■ D I V A N
■ ■ C A S S I O ■ S E A L ■ L E A V E ■
J O H N ■ L O R I S E S ■ G E T R E A L ■
A L B ■ M E S S W I T H T E X A S ■ M A G
C L A W A T ■ ■ I C H ■ R O I L ■ S U C H
O I L E D ■ C I S ■ S O D A ■ P A S T E
B E L I E V E T H E H Y P E ■ T O M C A T
■ ■ R A I S E ■ L O R E ■ F I R E L I T
D O H ■ D R A M ■ P I U ■ P A R T ■ E D O
A M A T E U R ■ R A S P ■ O V E R T ■ ■
G I V E N S ■ Q U I T Y O U R D A Y J O B
A G E N T ■ D U B S ■ R T E ■ I R E N E
M O A T ■ S O I L ■ N B A ■ S T A L I N
A S C ■ Q U O T E M E O N T H I S ■ L C D
■ H O T W I R E ■ O W N G O A L ■ A Y E S
■ ■ W H E T S ■ S C A M ■ A D V E R B ■
H U M O R ■ T A L K T O S T R A N G E R S
A P A R T ■ E S A U ■ T H E O ■ D U A N E
G I N N Y ■ P I M P ■ S E E N ■ S E N A T
```

90

```
M A W R ■ W A D I ■ S C A M ■ I R A N
E U R O ■ E G A D ■ D I A N A ■ S T O L E
G R E A T D A Z E ■ E M P T Y Z E S T E R
A A N D W ■ S A W B I T ■ S O L A C E D
■ H I K E ■ S H A L O M ■ N F L ■
A L P A C I N O ■ A S A R U L E ■ L A H R
M A I Z E L O B S T E R ■ D I S A G R E E
A T T A ■ T R E A T S ■ M C M ■ T O E I N
S T O R K ■ M Y T H ■ R E A P ■ T O N N E
S E N D E R ■ S E E J U S T I C E D O Z E
■ ■ I O U ■ H A M ■ D I M ■ ■
H I G H L I G H T E R P E Z ■ A P P E A R
E N R O L ■ L E V Y ■ R E E L ■ T O N G A
A L A M O ■ I A S ■ C O L L E T ■ O L A V
R E V E R S E R ■ F R A S I E R C R A Z E
S T E M ■ A S S U R E S ■ G R O U P I E S
■ ■ A M Y ■ T R E A T Y ■ Y U L E ■ ■
M A S K I N G ■ G E T S I N ■ P O S S E
E M P E R O R Z E R O ■ K I D Z A P P E R
S M O R E ■ A S O U R ■ E T U I ■ L A V A
H O T S ■ M A N N ■ S E E P ■ E Y E S
```

91

```
I S L A   E L M S T   A F O U L   E A S Y
S T A R   T E A M O   N E R V E   A L T O
R A N C H A X L E S   G R E E N O R G A N
  R O T O T I L L   V E R S A T I L E  
M C L I I   C A L L A   E T S   L I B R A
C H I C   F O R   I C A R E   U S E R I D
S Y N   B O N D P L A N   I N N E R A C E
    S U N   S O T T O   A U B E      
A P P L E T S   L I E N S   T E D D I E S
S A R A N   E V E N S   A T T N   I N L A
S L I M A W N I N G   A L E R T R E B E L
A M M O   R A P T   O V U L E   U S O N E
M E A N T I T   A S S E T   E Y E E X A M
    O N O R   O M N E S   U R L      
J O L T O G R E   L O U D O W L S   H O G
A L A R M S   M A S S E   M A E   P O P E
M A C A U   G I N   E S S E N   M R M O M
    U N C O U N T E D   P O T A T O E S  
C O N C H L A D L E   F I N A L G U I S E
I R A E   A R E E L   F R E D O   S C U M
A B E S   F E R R Y   F O S S E   T E M P
```

92

```
T R I P   W A L E S A   C I G A R   J A Y
Y E T I   A N O D E S   C L A R O   A X E
R A Z Z   D E F E N S I V E P A X   C I A
A M A Z E D A T   T I P   S P A R K S  
    A V E R Y   T S A R S   A N A P  
S P I R E D     P O I S O N T H E H O O D
A L T E R   G M A   S P I R O   A W R Y
B A H T S   P A P E R   E T O   P L E N A
E Z E R   N A T U R A L   S O L I   R O D
  A L E X I   Z A N T A C   P U L P  
  P A S T E O N A T R U E S T O R Y
    T O R N   S N I V E L   S T A V E
K O S   U O F A   I N A W I N K   W E R E
E R U P T   O V A   G E O D E   I N T R A
M A G I   F L O C K   R E D   O S T E R
P L A Q U E D I A M O N D   O N M E D S
  R U N E   D I A N A   A E R I E  
  S P E E D S   R E N   S A L A D B A R
R H O   S E C R E T P A L A T E   A R L O
A O L   C R A B S   I N C H E S   L U L U
G E L   O S R I C   N A D I R S   S T Y X
```

93

94

```
S A M E H E R E    O P A Q U E    P A I L S
T R A V E L E D    M E D U S A    E L L I E
A N G E L M A N A G E M E N T    N I T T I
G O I N    S P A R    R I B    S E N O R A S
      T E T E    M A S T E R    G A T O
S H A U N    D O R M    S C A L Y M O V I E
S A L A D A    N E A P    P I P E    A M A
T H E L I G H T S T U F F    M T S    T E S
S A X    C A W    T I N L I K E    J O L T
      D O T Y    C O S I    H A I R D O
P I L A T E S O F T H E C A R I B B E A N
A G E N T S    V I A L    E N D S
Y U N G    P I E D I S H    C G I    M S G
C A N    T W O    F A N T A S T I C F O U L
U N O    V O L E    E Y R E    S A L O M E
T A X I D R I V E L    E M A J    T E R S E
      L O I S    A R I O S I    A B E T
F I E N N E S    O E R    N A C L    C H A P
E D W I N    W E D D I N G C L A S H E R S
S E I Z E    A R E T O O    H Y S T E R I A
T A S E R    M A S O N S    S N E E R S A T
```

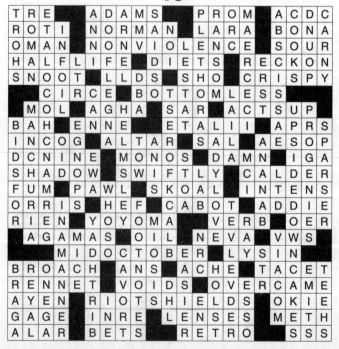

```
T R E    A D A M S    P R O M    A C D C
R O T I    N O R M A N    L A R A    B O N A
O M A N    N O N V I O L E N C E    S O U R
H A L F L I F E    D I E T S    R E C K O N
S N O O T    L L D S    S H O    C R I S P Y
    C I R C E    B O T T O M L E S S
  M O L    A G H A    S A R    A C T S U P
B A H    E N N E    E T A L I I    A P R S
I N C O G    A L T A R    S A L    A E S O P
D C N I N E    M O N O S    D A M N    I G A
S H A D O W    S W I F T L Y    C A L D E R
F U M    P A W L    S K O A L    I N T E N S
O R R I S    H E F    C A B O T    A D D I E
R I E N    Y O Y O M A    V E R B    O E R
  A G A M A S    O I L    N E V A    V W S
    M I D O C T O B E R    L Y S I N
B R O A C H    A N S    A C H E    T A C E T
R E N N E T    V O I D S    O V E R C A M E
A Y E N    R I O T S H I E L D S    O K I E
G A G E    I N R E    L E N S E S    M E T H
A L A R    B E T S    R E T R O    S S S
```

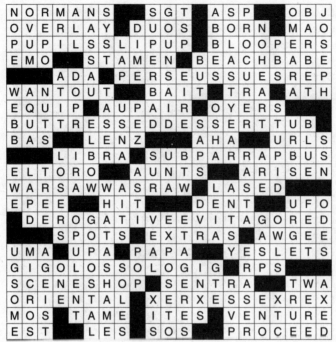

```
N O R M A N S   S G T   A S P     O B J
O V E R L A Y   D U O S   B O R N   M A O
P U P I L S S L I P U P   B L O O P E R S
E M O     S T A M E N   B E A C H B A B E
      A D A   P E R S E U S S U E S R E P
W A N T O U T   B A I T   T R A   A T H
E Q U I P   A U P A I R   O Y E R S
B U T T R E S S E D D E S S E R T T U B
B A S   L E N Z     A H A   U R L S
      L I B R A   S U B P A R R A P B U S
E L T O R O   A U N T S   A R I S E N
W A R S A W W A S R A W   L A S E D
E P E E   H I T   D E N T   U F O
  D E R O G A T I V E E V I T A G O R E D
  S P O T S   E X T R A S   A W G E E
U M A   U P A   P A P A   Y E S L E T S
G I G O L O S S O L O G I G   R P S
S C E N E S H O P   S E N T R A   T W A
O R I E N T A L   X E R X E S S E X R E X
M O S   T A M E   I T E S   V E N T U R E
E S T   L E S   S O S   P R O C E E D
```

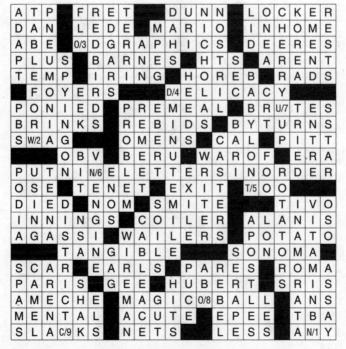

```
A T P   F R E T   D U N N   L O C K E R
D A N   L E D E   M A R I O   I N H O M E
A B E   0/3 D G R A P H I C S   D E E R E S
P L U S   B A R N E S   H T S   A R E N T
T E M P   I R I N G   H O R E B   R A D S
  F O Y E R S   D/4 E L I C A C Y
P O N I E D   P R E M E A L   B R U/7 T E S
B R I N K S   R E B I D S   B Y T U R N S
S W/2 A G   O M E N S   C A L   P I T T
    O B V   B E R U   W A R O F   E R A
P U T N I N/6 E L E T T E R S I N O R D E R
O S E   T E N E T   E X I T   T/5 O O
D I E D   N O M   S M I T E   T I V O
I N N I N G S   C O I L E R   A L A N I S
A G A S S I   W A I L E R S   P O T A T O
    T A N G I B L E   S O N O M A
S C A R   E A R L S   P A R E S   R O M A
P A R I S   G E E   H U B E R T   S R I S
A M E C H E   M A G I C 0/8 B A L L   A N S
M E N T A L   A C U T E   E P E E   T B A
S L A C/9 K S   N E T S   L E S S   A N/1 Y
```

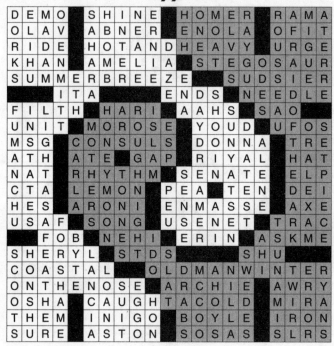

D	E	M	O		S	H	I	N	E		H	O	M	E	R		R	A	M	A
O	L	A	V		A	B	N	E	R		E	N	O	L	A		O	F	I	T
R	I	D	E		H	O	T	A	N	D	H	E	A	V	Y		U	R	G	E
K	H	A	N		A	M	E	L	I	A		S	T	E	G	O	S	A	U	R
S	U	M	M	E	R	B	R	E	E	Z	E			S	U	D	S	I	E	R
			I	T	A			E	N	D	S		N	E	E	D	L	E		
F	I	L	T	H		H	A	R	I		A	A	H	S		S	A	O		
U	N	I	T		M	O	R	O	S	E		Y	O	U	D		U	F	O	S
M	S	G		C	O	N	S	U	L	S		D	O	N	N	A		T	R	E
A	T	H		A	T	E		G	A	P		R	I	Y	A	L		H	A	T
N	A	T		R	H	Y	T	H	M		S	E	N	A	T	E		E	L	P
C	T	A		L	E	M	O	N		P	E	A		T	E	N		D	E	I
H	E	S		A	R	O	N	I		E	N	M	A	S	S	E		A	X	E
U	S	A	F		S	O	N	G		U	S	E	N	E	T		T	R	A	C
		F	O	B		N	E	H	I		E	R	I	N		A	S	K	M	E
S	H	E	R	Y	L		S	T	D	S				S	H	U				
C	O	A	S	T	A	L			O	L	D	M	A	N	W	I	N	T	E	R
O	N	T	H	E	N	O	S	E		A	R	C	H	I	E		A	W	R	Y
O	S	H	A		C	A	U	G	H	T	A	C	O	L	D		M	I	R	A
T	H	E	M		I	N	I	G	O		B	O	Y	L	E		I	R	O	N
S	U	R	E		A	S	T	O	N		S	O	S	A	S		S	L	R	S

D	E	S	K	S		I	P	O	D		C	L	A	M	S		A	N	A	P
A	L	C	O	A		N	I	L	E		A	A	R	O	N		N	O	L	O
D	I	A	R	Y	Q	U	E	E	N		P	R	I	S	O	N	G	R	A	B
S	A	R	A		U	N	D	O		S	A	S	S			U	R	A	N	O
			E	N	I	A	C			A	P	B		E	A	R	L	Y	D	A	Y
B	E	D		I	N	T	E	R	N	A	L	A	N	G	E	L				
E	U	C	L	I	D		D	O	O	M	E	D		L	A	S	H	O	U	T
E	R	O	O		A	M	I	S	S			O	W	E	D		E	S	T	E
B	O	W	S	P	R	I	T	S		M	A	R	I	T	A	L	A	R	T	S
			T	R	Y	T	O		G	I	B	E	D			E	D	I	E	S
M	O	S	H	E		T	R	E	A	S	U	R	E	D		A	C	C	R	A
I	N	T	E	L			I	N	L	E	T		B	O	F	F	O			
T	R	I	A	L	B	L	A	Z	E	R		L	E	G	I	S	L	A	T	E
E	Y	E	R		O	I	L	Y		M	O	R	E	L		D	R	E	A	
R	E	S	T	O	R	E		M	Y	F	O	O	T		M	E	S	M	E	R
			R	O	U	G	E	E	L	E	P	H	A	N	T		Y	S	L	
D	I	G	S	I	N	T	O		S	O	N		C	O	S	E	C			
I	R	A	T	E		F	R	O	G		A	N	T	I		F	R	A	U	
D	E	V	I	L	S	L	I	A	R		T	R	O	T	R	E	F	O	R	M
O	N	E	L		E	O	S	I	N		S	L	O	W		R	I	P	U	P
K	A	L	E		E	T	H	N	O		K	O	K	O		R	E	S	T	S

The New York Times

SMART PUZZLES

Presented with Style

Available at your local bookstore or online at
us.macmillan.com/author/thenewyorktimes

 ST. MARTIN'S GRIFFIN